Design Patterns for Cloud Native Applications

Patterns in Practice Using APIs, Data, Events, and Streams

Kasun Indrasiri and Sriskandarajah Suhothayan

Beijing · Boston · Farnham · Sebastopol · Tokyo

Design Patterns for Cloud Native Applications

by Kasun Indrasiri and Sriskandarajah Suhothayan

Published by O'Reilly Media, Inc., 1005 Gravenstein Highway North, Sebastopol, CA 95472.

O'Reilly books may be purchased for educational, business, or sales promotional use. Online editions are also available for most titles (*http://oreilly.com*). For more information, contact our corporate/institutional sales department: 800-998-9938 or *corporate@oreilly.com*.

Acquisitions Editor: Jennifer Pollock
Development Editor: Nicole Taché
Production Editor: Deborah Baker
Copyeditor: Sharon Wilkey
Proofreader: Penelope Perkins

Indexer: Potomac Indexing, LLC
Interior Designer: David Futato
Cover Designer: Karen Montgomery
Illustrator: Kate Dullea

June 2021:   First Edition

Revision History for the First Edition
2021-05-14:   First Release

See *http://oreilly.com/catalog/errata.csp?isbn=9781492090717* for release details.

978-1-492-09071-7

[LSI]

Table of Contents

Preface

Cloud Native architecture is all about building software applications as a collection of independent, loosely coupled, business capability–oriented services (microservices) that can run on dynamic environments (public, private, hybrid, multicloud) in an automated, scalable, resilient, manageable, and observable way.

Writing applications to work natively on the cloud is increasingly common due to the agility, reliability, affordability, and scalability it provides. In current cloud native architecture, the focus is mostly on deployment and operational aspects of applications. However, when building cloud native applications, we can't apply conventional application development patterns and techniques. This book addresses this issue by defining proven solutions as patterns based on APIs, data, events, and streams. It aims to help architects and developers incrementally design, develop, and deploy cloud native applications that are optimal for their use cases, and that can be managed and maintained with minimal cost, time, and effort.

There is a wide range of design patterns that architects and developers can apply when building cloud native applications. In this book, we mainly focus on the development patterns that must be applied when building the business logic of cloud native applications, when connecting them, and when enabling external parties to consume them. Depending on the nature of your application, and the patterns you use to build it, the cross-cutting capabilities such as deployment, scaling, security, and observability may be implemented differently. For that reason, we spend some time discussing the trade-offs and ramifications of using the various patterns. We organize these patterns into seven key areas: communication, connectivity, composition, data, events, stream processing, and API management and consumption.

The chapters in the book are organized as follows:

Chapter 1, Introduction to Cloud Native
> This chapter helps you understand what cloud native is by exploring the key characteristics of cloud native applications. We focus on the importance of using design patterns for building cloud native applications.

Chapter 2, Communication Patterns

This gives you a broad understanding of the communication patterns and implementation technologies that you can use to build cloud native applications. We mainly focus here on foundational communication patterns for synchronous and asynchronous communication.

Chapter 3, Connectivity and Composition Patterns

Here we explore a wide range of patterns that build connectivity between microservices as well as with other existing systems in a cloud native application. We also look at creating business functionalities by integrating services using Service Composition patterns.

Chapter 4, Data Management Patterns

In this chapter we look at patterns for managing data in cloud native applications. We focus on the selection of data stores, and how data can be integrated with cloud native applications via data composition, while supporting scalability and reliability and optimizing for performance.

Chapter 5, Event-Driven Architecture Patterns

We cover the design patterns for building event-driven architectures using cloud native applications. Here, we focus on basic event delivery, event sourcing, and how events can be orchestrated among various asynchronous cloud native applications.

Chapter 6, Stream-Processing Patterns

This chapter explores patterns for processing event streams at scale by both stateful and stateless cloud native applications. We also look at patterns for building reliability into real-time applications, so that they can preserve their in-memory states across failures.

Chapter 7, API Management and Consumption Patterns

This chapter explores some of the most commonly used patterns in API management. We also cover a few API Consumption patterns, which are essential in building frontend applications such as a web application, mobile application, or desktop application on top of the managed APIs.

Chapter 8, Cloud Native Patterns in Practice

This final chapter shows you how to apply various cloud native patterns when building different aspects of a real-world cloud native application.

Conventions Used in This Book

The following typographical conventions are used in this book:

 This element signifies a tip or suggestion.

 This element signifies a general note.

 This element indicates a warning or caution.

O'Reilly Online Learning

 For more than 40 years, *O'Reilly Media* has provided technology and business training, knowledge, and insight to help companies succeed.

Our unique network of experts and innovators share their knowledge and expertise through books, articles, and our online learning platform. O'Reilly's online learning platform gives you on-demand access to live training courses, in-depth learning paths, interactive coding environments, and a vast collection of text and video from O'Reilly and 200+ other publishers. For more information, visit *http://oreilly.com*.

How to Contact Us

Please address comments and questions concerning this book to the publisher:

O'Reilly Media, Inc.
1005 Gravenstein Highway North
Sebastopol, CA 95472
800-998-9938 (in the United States or Canada)
707-829-0515 (international or local)

707-829-0104 (fax)

You can access the web page for this book, where we list errata and any additional information, at *https://oreil.ly/Design_Patterns_for_CloudNative_Apps*.

Email *bookquestions@oreilly.com* to comment or ask technical questions about this book.

For news and information about our books and courses, visit *http://oreilly.com*.

Find us on Facebook: *http://facebook.com/oreilly*

Follow us on Twitter: *http://twitter.com/oreillymedia*

Watch us on YouTube: *http://youtube.com/oreillymedia*

Acknowledgments

With gratitude, we thank the cloud native community in general, and special thanks to our present and previous employers, and the colleagues, customers, friends, and tech enthusiasts whom we have met at conferences and meetups, who gave us experience with and exposure to cloud native technologies.

Our grateful thanks go to the tech reviewers of the book, Josh Armitage, Hibri Marzook, and Shayon Mukherjee. We would also like to thank our Development Editor Nicole Taché for her guidance in bringing the book into its current shape, and our Acquisitions Editor Jennifer Pollock for all her support, which led to the acceptance our proposal. Last but not least, we thank the entire crew who worked on publishing this book.

Kasun would like to thank his wife Imesha and daughter Methuki for their support and patience during the time spent writing this book. He is also grateful for his parents, sister, and his relatives who have been behind him all the way.

Suho would like to thank his wife, Sinthuja, for seeding the idea of writing a book on design patterns, for reading the draft scripts, and for sharing her knowledge on data management patterns. Most importantly, he would like to thank Sinthuja for rearranging all her plans to accommodate his work on the book. Thank you so much!

CHAPTER 1

Introduction to Cloud Native

The software development landscape is constantly changing and evolving through modern architectural paradigms and technologies. From time to time, software architecture goes through a fundamental shift with the emergence of breakthrough technologies and approaches. One such breakthrough is *cloud native architecture*. It is such a major shift in the context of software application development, one that changes the way we build, ship, and manage software applications. Cloud native architecture has become an enabler of agility, speed, safety, and adaptability for software applications.

This chapter helps you understand what cloud native is by exploring the key characteristics of cloud native applications. We'll also introduce a development methodology that you can use throughout the life cycle of cloud native applications. Then we'll focus on the importance of using design patterns for developing cloud native applications. Let's begin our discussion by defining *cloud native*.

What Is Cloud Native?

So, what's the formal definition of *cloud native*? The sad news is, there's no such definition. Cloud native means different things to different people. The closest general definition is from the Cloud Native Computing Foundation (CNCF), an organization dedicated to building sustainable ecosystems and fostering communities to support the growth and health of open source, cloud native applications. CNCF serves as the vendor-neutral home for many of the fastest-growing open source projects that can be used in building cloud native applications.

Cloud Native Definition from CNCF

Cloud native technologies empower organizations to build and run scalable applications in modern, dynamic environments such as public, private, and hybrid clouds. Containers, service meshes, microservices, immutable infrastructure, and declarative APIs exemplify this approach. These techniques enable loosely coupled systems that are resilient, manageable, and observable. Combined with robust automation, they allow engineers to make high-impact changes frequently and predictably with minimal toil.

For the purposes of this book, we take a bottom-up approach to defining *cloud native*. We look at all the characteristics of cloud native applications, across the board, by going through every stage in the life cycle of a cloud native application—including design, development, packaging, deployment, and governance. Based on those characteristics, we've come up with the following definition:

> Cloud native is building software applications as a collection of independent, loosely coupled, business-capability-oriented services (microservices) that can run on dynamic environments (public, private, hybrid, multicloud) in an automated, scalable, resilient, manageable, and observable way.

Exploring these characteristics further helps us understand cloud native applications. Let's look more closely at the characteristics in our definition.

Designed as a Collection of Microservices

A cloud native application is designed as a collection of loosely coupled and independent services that are serving a well-defined business capability. These are known as *microservices*. Microservices are the foundational architectural principle that is essential to building cloud native applications. It's virtually impossible to build a proper cloud native application without knowing the basics of microservices architecture.

Microservices architecture is a style of building software applications. Before the advent of microservices architecture, we used to build software applications as monolithic applications catering to various complex business scenarios. These monolithic applications are inherently complex, hard to scale, expensive to maintain, and hinder the agility of development teams. Monolithic applications communicate with one another by using proprietary communication protocols and often share a single database.

Microservices architecture is about building a software application as a collection of independent, autonomous (developed, deployed, and scaled independently), business-capability-oriented and loosely coupled services.[1]

Service-oriented architecture (SOA) emerged as a better architectural style to address the limitations of the monolithic application architecture. SOA is built around the concept of modularity and building a software application as a collection of services to serve a specific business capability. The realizations of SOA, such as web services, were implemented using complex standards and message formats, and introduced centralized monolithic components into the architecture.

In a typical SOA-based design, software applications are built using a set of coarse-grained services, such as web services, that often leverage open standards and a central monolithic integration layer known as the *enterprise service bus (ESB)*. An API management layer can be used on top of this architecture so you can expose the capabilities as managed APIs.

Figure 1-1 shows a simple online retail application designed using SOA. All the business capabilities are created at the services layer as coarse-grained services that run on a monolithic application server runtime. Those services and the rest of the systems are integrated using an ESB. Then an API gateway is placed as the front door to the SOA implementation, where you control and manage your business capabilities.

This approach has worked for many enterprises, and a lot of enterprise software applications are still built using SOA. However, its inherent complexities and limitations hinder the agility of developing software applications. Most implementations of SOA result in a lack of independently scalable applications, inter-application dependencies that hinder independent application development and deployment, reliability issues of being a centralized application, and constraints on using diverse technologies for the application.

Microservices architecture, on the other hand, eliminates the limitations of SOA implementations by introducing more fine-grained and business-oriented services while eliminating centralized components such as ESB. In microservices architecture, a software application is designed as a collection of autonomous and business-capability-oriented services that are developed, deployed, and often managed independently by different teams. The granularity of the service is determined by the application of concepts such as the bounded context in the Driven Design paradigm.[2]

---

1 Source: *Microservices for the Enterprise* by Kasun Indrasiri and Prabath Siriwardena (Apress).

2 Source: Chapter 2 of *Microservices for the Enterprise*.

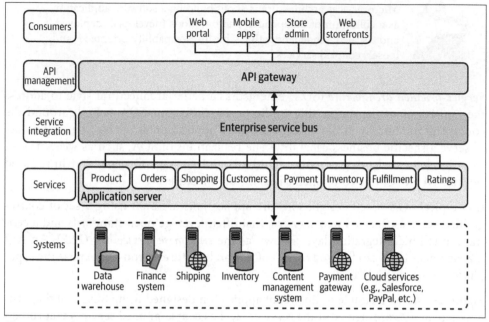

Figure 1-1. An online retail application scenario built using an SOA/ESB with API management

We can transform our earlier SOA/ESB-based online retail application to microservices, as shown in Figure 1-2. The main idea here is to introduce microservices for each business capability that we identify during the design phase, as we apply the concepts of domain-driven design (explained later in this chapter) and eliminate the centralized integration at the ESB layer.

Monolithic-to-microservice transformation techniques are discussed in detail in *Building Microservices* by Sam Newman (O'Reilly).

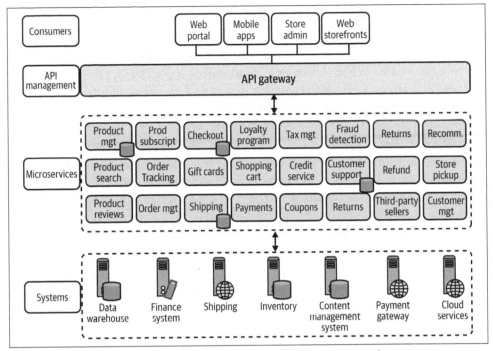

Figure 1-2. An online retail application built using microservices architecture

Rather than using an ESB layer to integrate the services, microservices themselves create the compositions through lightweight interservice communication that's required to build the business capability offered by the microservice. Therefore, these microservices are called *smart endpoints* that are connected via *dumb pipes*, which refers to the lightweight interservice communication techniques.[3] Microservices may connect to other existing systems and in some cases may expose a simplified interface (often known as a *facade*) for those systems as well.

The microservices don't share databases, and external parties can access the data only via the service interface. Each microservice needs to implement the business logic as well as the interservice communication features that include resiliency, security, and so on.

As cloud native applications are designed as a collection of microservices, almost every concept that you apply in microservices relates to the cloud native context as well. Therefore, we discuss most of the patterns and fundamentals of microservices architecture throughout the book.

---

3 You can find more information in "Smart Endpoints and Dumb Pipes" (*https://oreil.ly/3sY6G*) by Martin Fowler.

Use Containerization and Container Orchestration

Just as microservices are important in the phase of designing and developing cloud native applications, containers are important in the packaging and running of cloud native applications. When developing cloud native applications, the microservices that we build are packaged into container images and executed on top of a container host. Let's dig deeper to understand what this really means.

What are containers?

A *container* is a running process that is isolated from the host operating system and other processes in the system. A container interacts with its own private filesystem, which is provided by a container image. The container image is a binary that is formed by packaging everything that's needed to run an application: application code, its dependencies, and runtime. These container images are immutable and often stored in a repository known as a *container registry*.

To execute a container, you can create a running process out of the container image, which is known as a *container instance*. The container instance runs on top of the container runtime engine.

Figure 1-3 compares the execution of three microservice runtimes on virtual machines (VMs) versus on a container runtime engine. Running microservices as containers is drastically different from the conventional VM execution that runs a full-blown guest operating system with virtual access to host resources through a component known as a *hypervisor*. Since containers run on top of a container runtime, they share the kernel of the host machine, processor, and memory with other containers. Hence, running microservices on containers is a lightweight, discrete process compared to running them on top of a VM. For example, an application that runs on a VM and takes several minutes to load may take only a few seconds to load in containers.

The process of converting microservices or applications to run on top of containers is known as *containerization*. Docker has become the de facto platform for building, running, and sharing containerized applications.

Containerization makes your microservices portable and guarantees execution consistency across multiple environments. Containers are a key driving force to make microservices independent and autonomous as they are self-sufficient and encapsulated, allowing you to replace or upgrade one without disrupting others, while utilizing the resources better than VMs. They also eliminate additional runtime preconfiguration, and are much more lightweight compared to VMs.

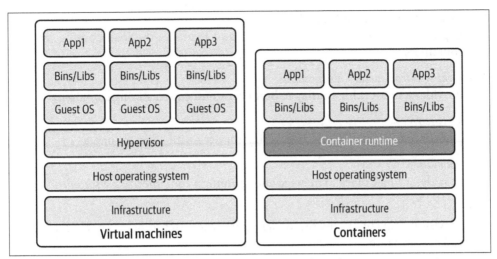

Figure 1-3. Comparing application execution on virtual machines versus containers

Containerization of your microservices and running them by leveraging a container engine is only one part in the development life cycle of your cloud native application. But how do you manage your containers' execution and the life cycle of the containers? That's where container orchestration comes into the picture.

Why container orchestration?

Container orchestration is the process of managing the containers' life cycle. When you operate real-world cloud native applications, it's nearly impossible to manually manage containers. Hence, a container orchestration system is an essential part of building a cloud native architecture.

Let's have a close look at some of the key features and capabilities of a container orchestration system:

Automatic provisioning
  Automatically provisions container instances and deployment of containers

High availability
  Automatically reprovisions containers when one container runtime fails

Scaling
  Based on the demand, automatically adds or removes container instances to scale up or scale down the application

Resource management
  Allocates resources among the containers

Service interfaces and load balancing
  Exposes containers to external systems and manages the load coming into the containers

Networking infrastructure abstractions
  Provides a networking overlay to build communication among containers

Service discovery
  Offers built-in capability of discovering services with a service name

Control plane
  Provides a single place to manage and monitor a containerized system

Affinity
  Provisions containers nearby or far apart from each other, helping availability and performance

Health monitoring
  Automatically detects failures and provides self-healing

Rolling upgrades
  Coordinates incremental upgrades with zero downtime

Componentization and isolation
  Introduces logical separation between various application domains by using concepts such as namespaces

In the cloud native landscape, Kubernetes has become the de facto container orchestration system.

Kubernetes

Kubernetes creates an abstraction layer on top of containers to simplify container orchestration by automating the deployment, scaling, fault tolerance, networking, and various other container management requirements that we discussed earlier.

Since Kubernetes is adopted across multiple platforms and cloud vendors, it's becoming the universal container management platform. All the major cloud providers offer Kubernetes as a managed service.

Applications designed to run on Kubernetes can be deployed on any cloud service or on-premises data center that supports Kubernetes, without making any changes to the application (as long as you don't use any platform-specific features such as load balancers). Kubernetes makes application workloads portable, easier to scale, and easier to extend. It is now the standardized platform that you can design your application to, so that it won't be coupled to any underlying infrastructure. Kubernetes brings in key abstractions that help standardize applications and simplify container orchestration (Figure 1-4).

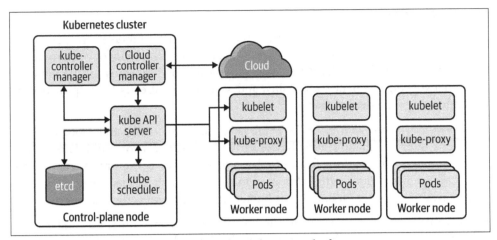

Figure 1-4. Fundamental components of a Kubernetes platform

A Kubernetes cluster comprises a set of nodes that run on virtual or physical machines. Among these nodes is at least one control-plane node and several worker nodes. The *control-plane node* is responsible for managing and scheduling application instances across the cluster. Therefore, the services that the Kubernetes control-plane node runs are known as the *Kubernetes control plane*.

The Kubernetes API server takes care of all the communication between the control-plane and worker nodes. When a certain workload needs to be assigned to a given node, the *kube-scheduler* assigns workloads to each worker node based on the available resources and policies. Each Kubernetes node runs an agent process known as a *kubelet*, which maintains the node states. This is the component that directly communicates with the Kubernetes API server, receiving instructions as well as reporting states of each node.

A *pod* is the basic deployment unit representing an application runtime that runs on a given node. One pod can have one or more containers running inside it. A pod is assigned a unique IP address within the Kubernetes cluster.

Kubernetes further simplifies application deployment and management by introducing abstractions such as Service, Deployment, and ReplicaSet. A *Service* provides a logical grouping for a set of pods as a network service, so that one service can have multiple load-balanced pods. A *ReplicaSet* defines the number of replicas the application should have. The *Deployment* handles how changes to the application are rolled out.

All these Kubernetes objects are specified by using either YAML or JavaScript Object Notation (JSON) and applied via the Kubernetes control plane by interacting with the Kubernetes API server. You can refer to the official Kubernetes documentation (*https://kubernetes.io*) for further information on Kubernetes.

Serverless functions

A given microservice of a cloud native application can be modeled as a *serverless function*. This programmatic function serves the business capability of a microservice that runs on a cloud infrastructure. With serverless functions, most of the management, networking, resiliency, scalability, and security are already being provided by the underlying serverless platform.

Serverless platforms such as AWS Lambda, Azure Functions, and Google Cloud Functions offer automatic scaling based on the load, support for multiple programming languages, and built-in features related to resilience communication, security, and observability. Microservices that need to support bursts of loads, batch jobs, and event-driven services are suitable to be implemented using serverless functions.

When you are using a serverless function, you may be using containers underneath, but that is transparent to the microservices developer. You can simply write a function with the business logic of your microservice and hand that over to the serverless platform to execute it. The details of how it is executed and deployed are also hidden away from the user.

Virtual machines

You may opt to run your microservices without using containers. While using containers to build cloud native applications is not mandatory, you need to manage the complexities and overhead of running applications on top of VMs. For this reason, in most real-world implementations of cloud native architecture, we often see the adoption of containers, container orchestrations, or higher-level abstractions such as serverless functions.

Automate the Development Life Cycle

When it comes to the delivery of cloud native applications, it's important to be agile, quick, and safe. To achieve this, we need to streamline the entire life cycle of cloud native application development and automate every possible step.

Automation in the context of cloud native applications is all about automating the manual tasks of the development life cycle. This includes tasks such as running integration tests, builds, releases, configuration management, infrastructure management, and continuous integration (CI) and continuous delivery/deployment (CD).

In the development life cycle shown in Figure 1-5, you can see all the stages of building a cloud native application.

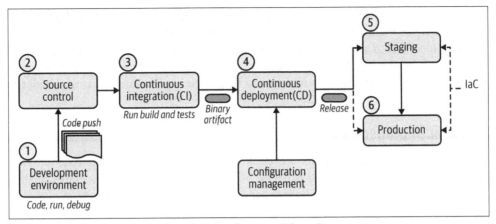

Figure 1-5. Cloud native application development life cycle

The development life cycle starts as the developers develop their code, and then run, debug, and push their changes into a central source-control repository such as Git. In the event of a code push, it automatically triggers the *continuous integration* process. This is where the code is built, the tests are executed, and the application gets packaged into a binary. A continuous integration tool automatically builds and runs unit tests on the new code changes to immediately surface any errors.

In deploying artifacts to different environments, the *continuous deployment* process kicks in. It picks the binary artifact that is built and applies an environment-specific configuration by using *configuration management* tools, and deploys the release to a specified environment. In this phase, we may run multiple parallel test stages before we push the changes to a production deployment. The final push to the production environment may be fully automated or may involve a manual approval step.

The difference between *continuous delivery* and *continuous deployment* is that in continuous delivery, manual approval is necessary to update to production. With continuous deployment, the update to production happens automatically, without explicit approval.

In automating the creation of the target environment (dev, staging, or production), the technique of *infrastructure as code (IaC)* is commonly used. With the IaC model, the management of infrastructure (networks, VMs, load balancers, and connection topology) is done using a declarative model that is similar to the source code of an application. With this model, we can continuously create the required environment by using the descriptor without any manual intervention. This improves the speed and efficiency of the development process while keeping the consistency and reduced management overhead. Therefore, IaC techniques are an integral part of the continuous delivery pipeline.

Once we define the designed state of the deployment, platforms such as Kubernetes can take care of maintaining that deployment state with the use of *reconciliation loops*. The key idea is to maintain the deployment state without any user intervention. For example, if we specify that a given application should run three replicas at a given time, Kubernetes reconciliation makes sure that three applications are running all the time.

Dynamic Management

When cloud native applications are deployed into a production environment, we need to manage and observe the behavior of the application. Here are some of the key capabilities needed to dynamically manage cloud native applications:

Autoscaling
    Scales the application instances up or down based on the traffic or load

High availability
    In the event of a failure, provides the ability to spawn new instances in the current data center or shift traffic to different data centers

Resource optimization
    Ensures optimum use of resources, with dynamic scaling and no up-front costs but with real-time automated response to scaling needs

Observability
    Enables logs, metrics, and tracing of the cloud native application with central control

Quality of service (QoS)
    Enables end-to-end security, throttling, compliancy, and versioning across applications

Central control plane
    Provides a central place to manage every aspect of the cloud native application

Resource provisioning
    Manages resource allocations (CPU, memory, storage, network) for each application

Multicloud support
    Provides the ability to manage and run the application across several cloud environments, including private, hybrid, and public clouds (as a given application may require components and services from multiple cloud providers)

Most capabilities of dynamic management are offered as part of popular cloud services such as Amazon Web Services (AWS), Microsoft Azure, and Google Cloud Platform (GCP). Containers and container orchestration systems such as Kubernetes play a major role in democratizing your applications across these cloud platforms so that your applications aren't coupled to a specific vendor.

Methodology for Building Cloud Native Apps

Building cloud native applications requires you to follow a new development methodology, one that is different from the conventional approach that many of us have practiced. Some people believe the way to build cloud native applications is to use the Twelve-Factor App (*https://12factor.net*) methodology. However, we've found that this methodology has several gaps; it doesn't cover every aspect of the cloud native application development life cycle.

Therefore, we have come up with a more complete and pragmatic methodology for building cloud native apps. We break this approach into phases and reuse some of the existing methodologies whenever necessary. Figure 1-6 illustrates the key phases of our methodology for building cloud native applications.

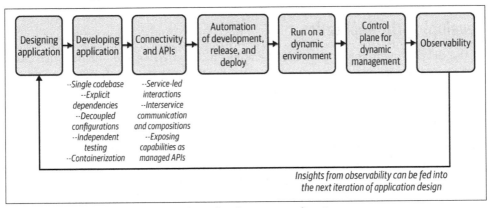

Figure 1-6. Methodology for building cloud native applications

Let's dive into the details of each phase.

Designing the Application

When you are building a cloud native application that comprises microservices, you cannot just jump into the application development right away. You need to design the application around the business capabilities that you want to cater to. This requires you to clearly identify the business capabilities that the application has to offer as well as the external dependencies (services or systems) that the application needs to consume.

Therefore, in the design phase, you should have a closer look at the business use case and identify the microservices that you want to build. The designing of a cloud native application can use the domain-driven design (DDD) methodology, which builds abstractions over complex business logic and represents them in the software components.[4]

The DDD process starts with analyzing the business domain (e.g., retail or healthcare) and defining boundaries within that domain where a particular domain model applies. These are known as *bounded contexts*. For example, an organization might have bounded contexts such as sales, human resources (HR), support, and so on. Each bounded context can be further broken into *aggregates*, clusters of domain objects that can be treated as a single unit.

These bounded contexts may or may not be directly mapped to a microservice. When we are designing a cloud native application, typically we can start with a service for each bounded context and break it into smaller services that are built around aggregates as we progress. Once the DDD for the cloud native application is completed, you can also finalize the service interfaces/definitions and the communication styles while identifying the microservices.

Developing the Application

In the development phase, we build the application based on the business use cases and service interfaces that we have identified in the design phase. In this section, we outline key aspects of the development process that enable cloud native applications.

Independent codebase

Each microservice of a cloud native application should have a *codebase* tracked on a version-control system (such as Git). Multiple instances of the service, known as *deploys*, will be running. So, as Figure 1-7 shows, you can deploy the service into different environments such as dev, staging, and production—all using the same codebase (but they may use different versions of the codebase).

Having an independent codebase means that the life cycle of the microservice can be completely independent from the rest of the system. And you can explicitly import external dependencies such as libraries.

---

4 For more information on domain-driven design, see *Domain-Driven Design* by Eric Evans (Addison-Wesley Professional).

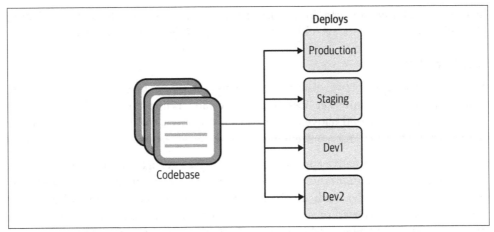

Figure 1-7. A single codebase with multiple deployments into different environments

Explicit dependencies

All the code-level dependencies of a microservice must be explicitly declared and isolated from one another. The dependencies should be declared in a manifest that is part of the microservice code, and the service shouldn't depend on any system-wide dependencies that are not declared explicitly.

Decoupled configurations

As we discussed earlier, cloud native applications contain a single codebase of a service that is deployed into multiple environments. This is possible only if the configuration of the microservice is fully decoupled from the microservice code. The codebase of a service is environment agnostic, and configuration varies among different deployments.

Independent testing

A microservice should have self-contained tests that independently verify its functionality. Usually, these tests are an integral part of the development cycle of the microservice, and verification of the microservice occurs during the build and deploy stages. We can consider these *unit tests* as they are localized to the scope of a given microservice.

However, because a cloud native application contains multiple microservices that work together to serve a certain business use case, unit tests alone can't test the application's overall functionality. We also need system-wide tests, known as *integration tests*. These tests collect microservices and other systems together and test them as a single unit in order to verify that they collaborate as intended, to achieve the larger business capability. You can find more details of microservice testing in "Testing Strategies in a Microservice Architecture" (*https://oreil.ly/rKa6u*), by Toby Clemson.

Containerization

Most of the concepts that we discussed in previous steps can be demonstrated by containerization of the microservices that you build. While containerization is not mandatory to build cloud native applications, it is quite useful in implementing most of their characteristics and requirements.

Encapsulating a cloud native application into a single package with all the dependencies, runtimes, and configurations is enabled through containerization. Containerization (using technologies such as Docker) makes microservices *immutable*, which means they can be started or stopped at a moment's notice and discard any faulty instances instead of being fixed or upgraded. This requires the microservices that we containerize to have a fast startup time and graceful shutdown times. Therefore, containerization works best when you leverage container native frameworks and technologies. (If fast startup time cannot be achieved because of an inherent limitation of the applications that we containerize, container orchestration systems such as Kubernetes provide readiness and liveness checks to ensure that the applications are ready to serve their consumers.)

When developing microservices, it is often required to connect with other microservices and/or expose business capabilities to external consumers as APIs. We cater to these requirements in the *next* phase, as we establish connectivity.

Connectivity, Compositions, and APIs

As we discussed at the beginning of this chapter, cloud native applications are distributed applications that are connected via network communication. As we design them as a collection of microservices, we often need to have interactions between those services and external systems. Therefore, having connectivity between the services and properly defining APIs and service interfaces is critical.

Service-led interactions

All microservices and applications should expose their capabilities as a *service*. Similarly, any external capabilities and resources that a microservice consumes should also be declared as a service (often known as a *backing service*).

The notion of a service is an abstraction that helps microservice interaction in many ways. A service is an enabler for dynamic service discovery, keeping a repository/registry of service metadata. It also allows you to implement concepts such as load balancing. That's why the service abstraction is built into container orchestration platforms such as Kubernetes as a first-class abstraction. Therefore, when you build a cloud native application with a set of microservices, its capabilities can be declared as services (for example, a Kubernetes service). Any external application/service or resource (such as a database or message broker) that we consume should also be declared as a service that we can consume over the network.

Interservice communication and compositions

The interaction between services and other systems is a key part of the development of cloud native applications. These interactions happen over the network, using various communication patterns and protocols. These interactions may involve consuming multiple services, creating compositions, creating event-based consumers or producers, and so on. We also have to build certain features—such as application-level security, resilient communication (circuit breakers, retry logic with backoff and time-outs), routing, publishing metrics, and traces to observability tools—as part of the interservice communication logic, though they are not really part of the business logic. (We discuss interservice communication and composition in detail in Chapters 2, and 3, and 5.)

Therefore, as the service developer, you need to have the required capabilities in the technology stack that you use to build the services. Some of the commodity features that are not directly related to the business logic of the services (for example, resilient communication) can be implemented outside the application layer (often using the underlying runtime platforms such as the cloud provider that runs our applications). We'll discuss all these patterns in detail in the upcoming chapters.

Exposing capabilities as managed APIs

For certain capabilities, the notion of a service may further extend into the concept of a *managed API*. Since most of the business capabilities of a cloud native application can be exposed to external and internal parties, we want to make it a managed service/API. This means you can use an API gateway and a management plane (API management/control plane) to implement capabilities (of the APIs that you expose to the consumers), such as security, throttling, caching, versioning, monetization (creating revenue from the APIs exposed), enabling a developer portal, and so on.

The *API gateway* acts as the front door to your capabilities, and a *developer portal* can nurture an ecosystem around your APIs. API management should be done for external as well as internal consumption of your services. However, API management is not built into container orchestration platforms such as Kubernetes. Therefore, you need to explicitly use API management technologies to expose your microservices as managed APIs.

Automating the Development, Release, and Deployment

As we noted previously in this chapter, automating as many steps as possible in the development, release, and delivery process is a vital part of building cloud native applications The various stages of building cloud native applications (such as testing, code push, build, integration tests, release, deployment, and running) should be automated by using continuous integration, continuous deployment, IaC, and continuous delivery techniques and frameworks.

 Continuous Delivery by Jez Humble and David Farley (Addison-Wesley Professional) is a great reference on how to implement a continuous delivery strategy for your software applications.

Running in a Dynamic Environment

In the running, or execution, phase of your cloud native application, you can set up the applications to be deployed and executed in an execution environment as part of the previous phase. The key idea here is to ensure that your application is independent from the execution environment and that it can be executed in various execution environments (dev, staging, production, etc.) without any changes to the application code. Since you use containers as the delivery model, the execution runtime often contains a container orchestration system. The execution environment can be a local environment; a public, hybrid, or private cloud; or even multiple cloud environments.

As Kubernetes is the most popular choice for container orchestration, we can use it as the universal runtime abstraction to deploy our applications so that their behavior will be similar across execution environments and multicloud scenarios. The dynamic nature of the environment—including container provisioning, resource management, immutability, and autoscaling—can be completely offloaded to Kubernetes. Also, as the container orchestration platform provides most of the dynamic-execution-related features, the application needs to worry only about capabilities that are within its scope (for example, scaling, concurrency requirements of a single runtime).

The orchestration platforms, such as Kubernetes, by default run your application as a stateless process (the state of the application is not maintained or persisted). However, if the application requires state, you have to explicitly use an external state store to keep the application state outside your application (such as in a data store) so that you can decouple the application state from the container life cycle. If you plan to run cloud native applications in a local data center or a private cloud, you can still benefit from Kubernetes, as it takes care of a lot of complexities of container orchestration.

Control Plane for Dynamic Management

In this phase, we use a central management and administration layer known as the *control plane* that allows you to control the behavior of the dynamic environments that your applications are running. This control plane is the main interaction point between the DevOps and developers who run their application in a runtime environment. Usually, such cloud control planes consist of a web interface as well as a representational state transfer (REST) or remote procedure call (RPC) API. Most cloud providers offer such control planes as part of their cloud service offerings.

Observability and Monitoring

Once you deploy and run your applications, the next phase of building cloud native applications is to observe their runtime behavior. *Observability*, in the context of a software application, refers to the ability to understand and explain a system's state without deploying any new code. This is essential for troubleshooting, recording business transactions, identifying anomalies, identifying business patterns, generating insights, and so on.

In the observability and monitoring phase, you need to enable key observability aspects in your cloud native application. These include logging, metrics, tracing, and service visualization. Tools are explicitly built for each of these aspects, and most cloud providers offer these capabilities out of the box as managed cloud services. From the application-code level, you may have to enable agents or client libraries without changing your application's code.

With that, we have discussed all the phases of the methodology for building cloud native applications.

Design Patterns for Building Cloud Native Apps

In the previous sections, we explored all the key characteristics of cloud native applications and the methodology for building them. As you have seen, cloud native architecture requires a significant change in the methodology, technology, and architecture for building software applications.

We cannot simply stick to the conventional design pattern of building software applications. Some patterns are becoming obsolete, others require certain changes or tweaks, and new patterns are emerging to serve the specific needs of cloud native architecture. These patterns can be applied at different stages of a cloud native application development life cycle. While the industry tends to focus on deployment and delivery of cloud native applications, the complexity of building the business logic, using various communication patterns, and connecting cloud native applications has often been overlooked.

In this book, we focus on the design patterns that you can use when building cloud native applications. These are the patterns that you have to apply when building the business logic of cloud native applications, connecting them, and enabling external parties to consume them. Depending on the nature of the cloud native application and the patterns you use to build it, the cross-cutting capabilities such as deployment, scaling, security, and observability may also be implemented differently. We discuss those capabilities from the perspective of cloud native application development and dive into them whenever required.

In the following chapters, we examine patterns in the context of six key areas: *communication, connectivity and composition, data management, event-driven architecture, stream processing*, and *API management and consumption*. Let's briefly summarize each one.

Communication Patterns

As you have learned, a cloud native application is composed of a collection of microservices, distributed across a network. The cloud native *communication patterns* are all about how these services can communicate both with each other and with external entities.

To build even a very simple business use case, your application needs to consume external services (which could be another service, a database, or a message broker, for example). Therefore, building the interaction between your application and these external services is becoming one of the most common and yet most complex tasks in building cloud native applications.

Most of the conventional interservice communication patterns and technologies of the distributed computing world are not directly applicable in the context of cloud native application development. We need to select communication patterns that are well suited for cloud native attributes of the application (for example, patterns that allow service autonomy and scalability) as well as the business use case (for example, some may require delivery guarantees, while others may require real-time responses).

The interservice communication among cloud native applications is implemented using either synchronous or asynchronous communication patterns. In *synchronous communication*, we use patterns such as request/response and RPC. In *asynchronous communication*, we use patterns such as queue-based and publisher-subscriber (pub-sub) messaging. In most real-world use cases, you need to use both categories together to build the service interactions. Service interface definitions and contracts also play a vital role when it comes to communication patterns, as they're the standard way of expressing how a given service can be consumed.

In addition to the service-to-service interactions, certain cloud native applications may have to communicate with external parties such as frontend clients or backing services. As an application developer, you need to work with a lot of moving parts and a lot of interactions with external services and systems.

In Chapter 2, we discuss all these communication patterns in detail, along with the related implementation technologies and protocols.

Connectivity and Composition Patterns

The more microservices you have, the more interservice communication will take place. Therefore, when you design cloud native applications, you need to bring in certain capabilities and abstractions that reduce the complexity of interservice communication. That's where the *connectivity and composition patterns* come into the picture.

Connectivity

In the context of interservice communication, *connectivity* refers to establishing a reliable, secure, discoverable, manageable, and observable communication channel among services. For example, when a given service calls another service, you need to apply certain reliability patterns such as retrying or establishing a secure communication channel. They are not part of the business logic of the application but are essential to building strong connectivity.

In Chapter 3, we discuss various patterns related to resilient communication, security, service discovery, traffic routing, and observability in interservice communication. We'll also explore how interservice connectivity infrastructures such as a service mesh and sidecar architecture facilitate these requirements.

Compositions

When building cloud native applications, it's quite common to create a service by plumbing, or integrating, one or more other services or systems. These are known as *compositions* (also known as *composite services* and *integration services*).

As we discussed at the beginning of the chapter, services and systems were often built using SOA before the cloud native era. In SOA, all the services, data, and systems are integrated using an ESB—so when creating compositions, ESB was the default choice. A plethora of composition patterns were used in this architecture, which were commonly known as *enterprise integration patterns* (*EIPs*).

However, in the cloud native era, we don't use a central composition layer. All such tasks need to be done as part of the services we develop. Therefore, in Chapter 3, we dive into all those composition patterns and identify which ones we should apply to building cloud native applications.

Data Management Patterns

Most cloud native applications that you develop need to take care of some data management. Your application is often backed by a database that acts as persistent storage to store the application state or the business data required to build the service. As you learned previously, cloud native applications are inherently distributed. Hence, data management is also done in a completely decentralized way.

In conventional monolithic applications, we used to have a central, shared data store, with which many applications interacted. With cloud native applications, we let a given microservice own its data store, and external parties can interact with it only via that service interface. With this segregated data management approach, accessing, sharing, and synchronizing data among microservices becomes challenging. That's why knowing the cloud native data management patterns is essential for cloud native application development.

In Chapter 4, we explore a wide range of cloud native data management patterns covering decentralized data management, data composition, data scaling, data store implementations, handling transactions, and caching.

Event-Driven Architecture Patterns

When we discussed cloud native communication patterns, we discussed asynchronous messaging as an interservice communication technique. That is the foundation of event-driven cloud native applications. *Event-driven architecture* (*EDA*) has been widely used in application development for decades. In the context of cloud native applications, EDA plays a vital role, as it's a great way to enable autonomous microservices. Unlike synchronous communication techniques such as querying or RPC, EDA enables more decoupled microservice interactions.

Therefore, we dedicate Chapter 5 to exploring most of the commonly used patterns in EDA and how to leverage them for building cloud native applications. We cover various aspects of cloud native EDA, including event delivery patterns (queue-based, pub-sub), delivery semantics and reliability, event schemas, and related implementation technologies and protocols.

Stream-Processing Patterns

In EDAs, we deal with a single event at a time. In other words, the microservice's business logic is written to deal with a single event at a time. There's no correlation between subsequent events. A *stream*, on the other hand, is a sequence of events or data elements made available over time. Those events are processed by the application in a stateful manner.

The implementation and deployment architecture of such a microservice changes drastically from an event-driven microservice because it has to handle state, do efficient data processing, manage various scaling and concurrency semantics, and so on. That's why we have dedicated Chapter 6 to stream-based cloud native patterns.

The notion of building application logic to process or produce such a stream is commonly known as *stream processing*. Building cloud native applications by using stream-based architecture is becoming common, as it enables the microservices to process massive continuous data streams statefully.

API Management and Consumption Patterns

In most medium or large-scale use cases of cloud native architecture, you have to expose certain business capabilities of your applications to the external or internal parties that are outside your application scope. You need to expose such capabilities as managed services or APIs. This allows you more control over how external parties consume those capabilities, and enables external parties to easily discover and provide feedback on those APIs.

Exposing these capabilities is often done by using a separate API gateway layer that acts as the front door to all the APIs that you expose. The API gateway also includes a management plane and developer portal that are built around the APIs exposed. Chapter 7 covers several patterns related to API management and consumption.

Now that you've learned the foundational concepts of cloud native application development, let's place those concepts into a reference model so you can understand how they are used in a real-world cloud native application architecture.

Reference Architecture for Cloud Native Apps

In most real-world cloud native applications, we commonly see a combination of development strategies. Figure 1-8 shows these various strategies in a generalized architecture. This reference architecture comprises multiple microservices that are communicating with different communication patterns. Each service may use its own data or persistent store, and there is a shared or private event broker infrastructure as well. The interaction among microservices represents all the communication patterns that we can implement. Each communication link can be implemented by using connectivity patterns related to reliability, security, routing, and so on.

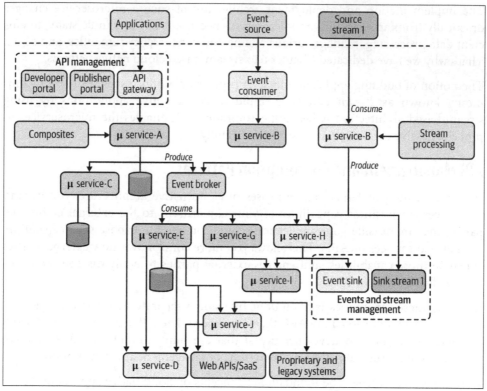

Figure 1-8. A generalized architecture for building cloud native applications with APIs, events, and streams

As you can see, microservices are creating composites out of one or more services, such as microservices A, E, and G. Such services are built using various composition patterns. When that application needs to be exposed as a managed business capability outside your application's realm, you can leverage API management. All the external applications can consume those capabilities via an API gateway, and you manage it via the other components of the API management layer. For the services that are based on EDA, often it is essential to have an event broker solution in place. Services may use a shared broker as the simple eventing infrastructure or can have their private event brokers as well.

Stream-processing services follow a similar approach, but the stream-processing logic may be implemented using a drastically different set of patterns and technologies. Both event- and stream-based services feature event/stream management for the producer (sink) side of the service.

This reference architecture may look complex at first glance, but in the upcoming chapters, we dive into every aspect and explore the patterns, implementation technologies, and protocols that you can use to realize it.

Summary

Cloud native is a modern architectural style that empowers organizations to build agile, reliable, safe, scalable, and manageable delivery of software applications. Cloud native is a way of building software applications as a collection of loosely coupled, business-capability-oriented services that can run in dynamic environments in an automated, scalable, resilient, manageable, and observable way.

Cloud native applications are designed as a collection of microservices, packaged into containers and managed with container orchestration systems such as Kubernetes, automated with CI/CD, and managed and observed in a dynamic environment. By considering all these characteristics, we can use a complete and pragmatic methodology for building cloud native apps that covers design, development, interconnectivity, API management, and execution and management in a dynamic environment.

We can apply a wide range of design patterns when building cloud native applications. In this book, we focus mainly on the development patterns that you have to apply when building the business logic of cloud native applications, connecting them, and enabling external parties to consume them. We discuss these patterns under six key areas: communication, connectivity and composition, data management, event-driven architecture, stream processing, and API management and consumption. In the next chapter, we dive into cloud native communication patterns.

CHAPTER 2

Communication Patterns

Cloud native applications comprise a collection of microservices that are connected with one another, as well as external systems, through interservice communication techniques. With the proliferation of microservices and ever-increasing business requirements, building robust communication among microservices in cloud native applications is one of the hardest challenges in cloud native architectures.

This chapter will give you a broad understanding of the communication patterns and implementation technologies that you can use to build cloud native applications. These patterns can be used to build communication among microservices, other external systems, and consumer applications such as mobile and web apps. In this chapter, we focus mainly on foundational communication patterns for synchronous and asynchronous communication.

In *synchronous communication*, one microservice invokes another microservice and expects a response within a given time frame. For this, we use patterns such as Request-Response and Remote Procedure Calls (RPC). In *asynchronous communication*, microservices communicate by passing messages asynchronously with the help of an intermediary (known as a *message broker*), and we use patterns utilizing queue-based messaging and publisher-subscriber messaging. In most real-world cloud native applications, we can mix and match these communication patterns.

In addition to these foundational communication patterns, we'll also explore patterns related to defining the service interfaces of your cloud native applications' microservices so that the consumers of those microservices know how to interact with your service, either through synchronous or asynchronous communication techniques. Let's begin our discussion with synchronous messaging patterns.

Synchronous Messaging Patterns

When building cloud native applications, you may discover that one microservice needs to invoke one or more other microservices, and then wait for a timely response to complete its business logic. To build such microservices, we can use *synchronous messaging patterns*, in which the business logic of a given microservice is dependent on one or more other microservices or systems. For instance, if you are building an online retail application, the Search microservice that you build has to accept queries and send the responses rapidly by invoking the relevant downstream microservices or systems.

You can use multiple messaging patterns to build synchronous communication into your cloud native application. Let's dive into one of the most commonly used patterns: Request-Response.

Request-Response Pattern

The *Request-Response pattern* is probably the most commonly used communication pattern in cloud native applications, as well as in the space of distributed computing at large. This pattern requires both parties to act in a timely fashion to pass data between them.

How it works

In the Request-Response pattern (Figure 2-1), one microservice (which acts as the client) sends a request and waits for a response from one or more other microservices or systems. The business logic of the client application blocks until it receives the response, and the communication channel has to be kept open until the response is received by the client application.

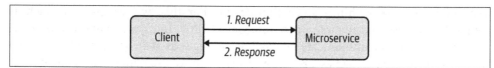

Figure 2-1. Request-Response pattern

The Request-Response pattern seeks to establish a connection between the client and the server application (microservice) and to exchange data between them in a synchronous way. The data exchanged is known as *messages*. Once a connection is established, the client sends a request for data to the microservice and waits until either it receives the response data, or the maximum time that the client intends to wait is reached (which is known as a *time-out*). Since this pattern is similar to querying a given entity, this style is sometimes referred to as a *query-based* interaction.

How it's used in practice

The Request-Response pattern of communication is often used for building cloud native applications containing business logic that is interactive (frequent exchange of messages) and requires an immediate response. Most external-facing services are implemented using this pattern. Since it is agnostic of the underlying network protocols and the data format of the request and response message, we can use a wide range of techniques to realize this pattern.

Microservices designed using HTTP and RESTful services are the most common realization of this pattern, which was popular in the early stages of cloud native architecture. However, now quite a few request-response communication techniques are in use based on disparate use cases and requirements. We discuss them in the latter part of the chapter when we dive into the implementation technologies of cloud native communication patterns.

Considerations

This synchronous Request-Response pattern is the most commonly used pattern when building communication among microservices in cloud native applications. However, having a greater number of synchronous request-response interactions results in more coupling among microservices. A service that sends a request and expects a response creates an implicit dependency on the services that it calls. This approach works well for a small number of services, but as the number of services connected via request-response messaging increases, we create a chain of dependent services. Each service in the chain can introduce a potential performance bottleneck or downtime, which impacts all other services in the chain.

Therefore, you should select this pattern whenever you need interactive communication among microservices or with external consumers or systems. For other use cases, choose asynchronous communication (which we'll explore later in this chapter). Often you will have to mix and match the Request-Response pattern with other communication patterns in real-world use cases.

Related patterns

The Request-Response communication pattern is commonly used with the following patterns:

Service Orchestration and API Gateway
> These patterns heavily use the request-response style of communication when building the composition of services and exposing services as managed APIs, respectively.

Request-Reply
> This pattern uses an intermediary to implement a similar style of communication with the use of a queue.

Now that you have a general understanding of Request-Response, let's look at the Remote Procedure Calls pattern.

Remote Procedure Calls Pattern

The *Remote Procedure Calls* (*RPC*) pattern is a synchronous communication pattern that enables distributed applications to invoke procedures of a remote application— just as if making a local procedure call. A given microservice can build a certain piece of business logic as a function and make it available for remote invocation by a consumer that resides in a separate process.

How it works

To understand how RPC works, imagine an online retail application that has a microservice for getting product details. We can expose that functionality as a remote procedure call so that external clients/consumers can invoke it as easily as making a local function call in their client application code. The underlying RPC framework handles all the complexities of the remote method invocation over the network and hides the details of the underlying network communication from the application developer. Implementing the RPC pattern allows you to use disparate technologies (different programming languages) to build your client and server applications.

Let's look at Figure 2-2 to understand how RPC works. In RPC, the first thing you would do as the service developer is to come up with a *service definition* that outlines the details of the remote methods that you expose to the consumers, service name, name resolution, and data types that the service uses to exchange information. The language used to specify the service definition is an interface definition language (IDL).

RPC implementations allow you to use the service definition to generate client- and server-side code that handles the low-level protocol details of the RPC communication. These generated code components are called server or client *stubs*. As a consumer or as the microservice's business logic developer, you don't need to worry about the implementation details of the RPC technology; you can fully rely on the abstractions provided by the stubs and focus more on the business logic of your applications.

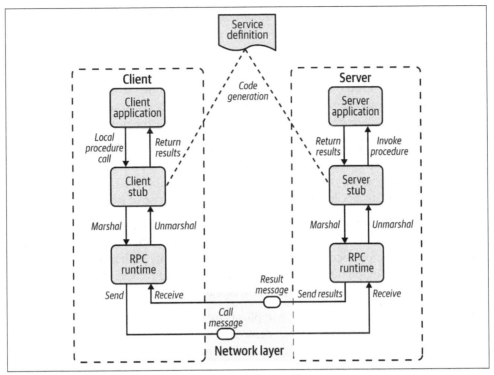

Figure 2-2. Implementation of Remote Procedure Calls pattern

When a client application wants to invoke a remote method by using RPC, the client application calls the client stub with the required parameters. This is a local function call, as the client stub resides within the client's process or address space. The data types used inside the client application to communicate with the remote service are provided as part of the client stub itself. Then the client stub serializes (or marshals) the details of the remote service call into an encoded binary message, and the RPC runtime component passes the message to the underlying network transport layer to invoke the remote server application.

On the server side, the network transport layer passes the call message to the RPC runtime, which invokes the corresponding server stub (internally, it uses request-response messaging on top of Transmission Control Protocol, or TCP). The server stub deserializes (or unmarshals) the binary message and resolves the server procedure, mapping parameters and data types. Then it can call the corresponding server application's remote procedure, where the server-side business logic resides.

Once the server's business logic is executed, it returns the response data types to the server stub (returning the expected data type from the local function), which marshals it to the reply message. Then the server hands over the message to the RPC runtime, which sends it back to the client application over the network transport layer.

Similar to the server side, the client stub unmarshals the return parameters, and execution returns to the client application.

How it's used in practice

In the context of cloud native applications, RPC can be used for most inter-microservices communications. Each microservice can be built as an RPC application, while each business capability is implemented as a remote procedure.

Numerous RPC technologies (such as Common Object Request Broker Architecture, or CORBA) have been used in distributed application development for decades. Most were directly built on top of TCP and were inherently complex. Therefore, the usage of such legacy RPC technologies has plummeted with the rise of RESTful services.

However, the RPC pattern has been reinvigorated with *gRPC*, a cloud native implementation of RPC that tries to overcome conventional limitations by using HTTP2 as the communication protocol (which is easier to interoperate with most of the existing communication components such as load balancers) and Protocol Buffers as the data serialization format (which is efficient and type safe).

Figure 2-3 illustrates a cloud native application built using multiple microservices implementing RPC-based interservice communication. Here we use gRPC as the RPC technology. RPC-based communication is often suitable for building the communication among services that are used internally.

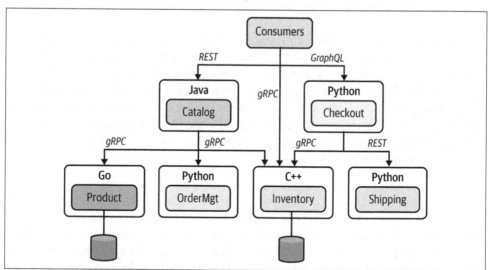

Figure 2-3. Using gRPC for microservice communication

While no technical limitation prevents you from using gRPC for external communication (such as services exposed to the web), most RPC technologies lack the support required in web clients. gRPC is the most commonly used RPC technique in the context of cloud native applications. We'll explore gRPC in detail later in this chapter.

Considerations

RPC is one of the most efficient and robust ways to build communication among microservices. Whenever you need to build synchronous communication among services, we recommend using cloud native RPC technologies such as gRPC. However, when the services need to be exposed to external consumers such as web and mobile applications, RPC may not be the best choice because these types of applications provide better support for other styles and data formats such as RESTful and JSON.

Related patterns

Here are some of the patterns that are related to Remote Procedure Calls:

Service composition and API management patterns
RPC is commonly used as a foundational pattern when realizing these other patterns (covered in Chapters 3 and 7, respectively).

Request-Response
This is an alternative approach for RPC.

Summary of Synchronous Messaging Patterns

Table 2-1 summarizes when to use—and when not to use—the synchronous messaging patterns, as well as their benefits.

Table 2-1. Synchronous messaging patterns

Pattern	When to use	When not to use	Benefits
Request-Response	Services need real-time responses. Service contracts need to be flexible. To interoperate with many types of consumers. Services are exposed to external consumers.	Low-latency and high-throughput communication is required. Strict contract-first interactions are required.	The most interoperable and standard communication pattern for implementing services exposed to external as well as internal consumers.
Remote Procedure Calls	High-performance communication among services is critical. To enforce a strict contract-first approach for building services. Service business logic needs to be completely independent from the underlying wire protocol and its semantics.	Service interoperability with multiple application types such as web or mobile apps is required. You have to enable loose contracts and flexibility for consumers.	Suitable for efficient and type-safe service-to-service communication.

Asynchronous Messaging Patterns

In asynchronous communication patterns, one microservice communicates with another microservice by sending data as messages without expecting a response. There may be no response at all, or the response may arrive asynchronously on a different channel (such as a separate queue).

With asynchronous messaging patterns, communication among microservices is facilitated by a third-party component known as a *message broker,* or *event broker.* This component receives messages from the source/producer microservice and sends them to the consumer. The consumers can consume the messages that they are interested in via the message broker.

 In this section, we discuss the foundational patterns related to asynchronous messaging. We dive into variants of asynchronous messaging patterns in detail in Chapter 5.

When building cloud native applications, the broker applications provide a robust messaging infrastructure with minimal business logic. The business logic of the microservices should always be implemented at each producer and consumer microservice, but not at the message-broker level. Given that the broker is a messaging infrastructure that doesn't have any business logic, it is common to use it as a centralized messaging platform (you don't always need a dedicated broker runtime for each asynchronous messaging pattern implementation).

You can choose from multiple asynchronous communication patterns to build cloud native applications. Let's begin our discussion with the Single-Receiver pattern.

Single-Receiver Pattern

In the *Single-Receiver pattern,* a given microservice delivers messages to exactly one target microservice, or to a system using a messaging infrastructure such as a message broker. The messages sent here are usually considered *commands* because the pattern ensures that the messages are delivered to a single consumer that is supposed to process them and perform an action.

For example, when we have to process an order in an online retail system, we place an asynchronous message in a message broker queue, so that the Order-Processing service can process it and perform actions. Since it describes the information exchange between one producer and a single receiver, this pattern is also called *point-to-point asynchronous messaging.*

How it works

The Single-Receiver pattern is built by publishing messages to a queue in the message broker. One consumer service or system then consumes messages from that queue. The producer service is interested only in whether the message is delivered successfully to the queue; it doesn't care when or whether the message is processed.

Since this pattern uses a queue to deliver messages from a producer to a consumer, it ensures the ordered delivery of the messages. The message broker offers the required message-delivery guarantees (such as at-least-once delivery) as part of the communication protocol it uses. Both producer and consumer can ensure the delivery of the message by using the semantics provided from the broker (such as acknowledgments after producing or receiving messages).

Figure 2-4 illustrates how two microservices of an online retail application communicate via the Single-Receiver pattern. In this example, the Checkout microservice publishes the order messages to a queue in the message broker. The OrderMgt service consumes those messages from the queue and performs the corresponding action.

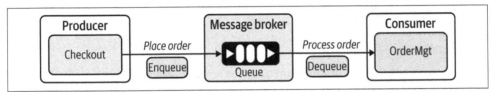

Figure 2-4. Single-Receiver pattern for implementing asynchronous message-based commands

When producing messages, the Checkout service can ensure that the message has been delivered to the queue. At the receiver side, the OrderMgt service can send an acknowledgment after processing the message from the queue. The message broker's queue ensures that the message is sent to only a single consumer. The Single-Receiver pattern is often used to implement guaranteed message-delivery use cases.

How it's used in practice

The Single-Receiver pattern can be implemented using a wide range of message broker solutions. While the messaging semantics are similar, the implementation technology differs from broker to broker. Advanced Message Queuing Protocol (AMQP) is the most widely accepted protocol that facilitates queue-based single-consumer messaging. Other variants of the Single-Receiver pattern are discussed in Chapter 5.

With AMQP, message brokers can support disparate (implemented in different programming languages) producer and consumer applications and establish the Single-Receiver pattern using queues. AMQP implementations such as RabbitMQ, Apache

ActiveMQ, and Apache ActiveMQ Artemis are commonly used to implement this pattern. Also, fully cloud-based messaging solutions such as Microsoft Azure Service Bus support this pattern through the broker solution, which is offered as a cloud service.

Considerations

A queue-based Single-Receiver pattern is a commonly used messaging technique in which end-to-end guaranteed message delivery is required. The broker that we select to implement this pattern plays a major role in reliability, scalability, and performance of the cloud native application. Therefore, it's important to select a broker technology that suits your exact requirements.

Most brokers that we can use to realize this pattern have roots in monolithic enterprise middleware. They tend to allow the developer to add quite a lot of business logic as part of message brokering (for example, routing, filtering, and content-aware delivery). Use them with caution in the context of cloud native applications. Our recommendation is to try to place business logic *outside* the broker and inside the microservices as much as possible.

Related patterns

Multiple patterns that are built on top of the base Single-Receiver pattern cater to various message-delivery semantics such as at-most-once and at-least-once delivery. In addition, variants such as the Fire and Forget pattern can be implemented without using a message broker. We explore this pattern in detail in Chapter 5.

Multiple-Receiver Pattern

Single-consumer-based asynchronous messaging works when you have one consumer to consume messages that you publish to a message broker. What if you have to send the same message to multiple consumers who are interested in a particular event? This is where the *Multiple-Receiver*, or *Publisher-Subscriber*, pattern comes into the picture.

In our cloud native applications, we often need to build microservices that execute business logic upon the occurrence of certain events, or that notify one or more other microservices when a particular event occurs. In these interactions, we can use the Multiple-Receiver pattern.

How it works

In the Multiple-Receiver pattern, messages are delivered to more than one consumer microservice. We also use a message broker or an event bus to facilitate the asynchronous message delivery. One microservice publishes a message to a *topic* in the event bus, and one or more microservices can subscribe to a given topic. The message is asynchronously delivered to all the subscribers of that topic.

The Multiple-Receiver pattern is implemented using an event bus (Figure 2-5). Returning to our online retailer example, here we see that the price update of a particular item is published to the price update topic by the Product Management microservice. Several other microservices (such as ShoppingCart, FraudDetection, and Subscription) are interested in learning about events related to the price update topic.

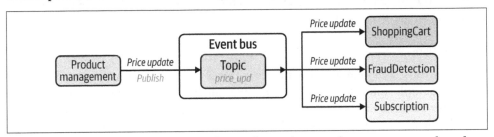

Figure 2-5. Multiple-Receiver pattern for implementing asynchronous message-based communication

The event bus is responsible for handling the publisher and subscription requests and delivering the message to the corresponding subscribers. The delivery guarantees are not as strict as in the Single-Receiver pattern. In most cases, the event bus simply delivers messages to available subscribers. If the subscribers need to receive messages when they are offline for a long time, we can leverage durable subscription techniques that are implemented in certain event bus solutions. Keep in mind that supporting durable subscription increases the load on the event bus, as it needs to keep all the messages sent to those topics for the subscribers.

How it's used in practice

The Multiple-Receiver pattern is implemented with the use of message broker solutions that support publisher-subscriber messaging. For example, conventional brokers (such as ActiveMQ, RabbitMQ, and Azure Service Bus) that support queue-based single-receiver models also support topic-based messaging. In addition, specific messaging technologies designed for event-based multiple-consumer scenarios such as Apache Kafka, Neural Autonomic Transport System (NATS), Amazon Simple Notification Service (SNS), and Azure Event Grid offer highly scalable event-driven messaging using the Multiple-Receiver pattern.

When it comes to a delivery mechanism, the Multiple-Receiver pattern is often implemented with support for persistent delivery, which means the events published by the producers are stored in a persistent store. However, when the events are published to subscribers, delivery of messages is not guaranteed by default to all subscribers, as some of them may not be reachable. Therefore, this pattern is used when delivery semantics such as at-least-once delivery are not required on the consumer side. However, certain brokers introduce such delivery guarantees with concepts such as *durable topics*: the broker logically persists an instance of each message for every durable consumer, since each durable consumer gets its own copy of the message.

As a general practice, if you want to send the same message to multiple parties with delivery semantics such as at-least-once delivery, then rather than using multiple consumers, you can use multiple queues for each consumer and publish messages as we did in the Single-Receiver pattern.

Considerations

The event bus component is generally used as a centralized runtime that is shared among multiple microservices. For example, all the implementations of multiple-consumer patterns may share the same broker instance. Therefore, it is important to keep the broker independent from the business logic (such as message routing based on certain properties of the message) and use it as a messaging infrastructure only. Then consumers will get more control over the consumption of the messages.

Also, as discussed earlier, we should bring in special message-delivery mechanisms such as durable subscription and durable topics only if the use case mandates it. At the event-bus level, we can include more-granular controls for the topic subscription and delivery of messages to the topics, and there is support for concepts such as hierarchical topics and routing rules. We explore those patterns in detail in Chapter 5.

Related patterns

Event-driven architecture uses the Multiple-Receiver pattern as one of its core approaches. In Chapter 5, we explore the various flavors of multiple-receiver messaging patterns.

Asynchronous Request-Reply Pattern

What we have discussed so far regarding asynchronous communication has mostly been about one-way messaging: we send data without expecting any response in return. But in some cases, producers need to send messages to a consumer via a broker and receive a reply from the consumer via the broker on a different communication channel. This is where the *Asynchronous Request-Reply pattern* comes into play.

How it works

In the Asynchronous Request-Reply pattern, we follow the same messaging model used in the Single-Receiver pattern: the producer microservice publishes messages to a queue in a message broker, and then the producer consumes that message from the queue. However, the message contains metadata specifying that it requires a reply, the location where the reply should be sent, and how to correlate the reply. The producer uses that information to send the reply back to the producer via a completely different channel established through a separate queue in the message broker.

In Figure 2-6, a producer microservice—Checkout—sends a request to a *request queue* in the message broker. Since we intend to process a reply, the message sent from the producer may contain a correlation ID and reply channel information. When a message is successfully sent to the queue, the producer ensures only that the message is successfully produced to the queue but doesn't worry about the reply. The reply is handled by a completely different flow in the producer: the producer initializes a separate subscription to a predefined *response queue* (also known as *callback queue*) that resides in the message broker.

On the consumer side, when the message is consumed, it obtains the reply channel information and correlation ID and places the reply on the response, or callback, queue. As we listen for it from the producer side, we can process the reply message asynchronously.

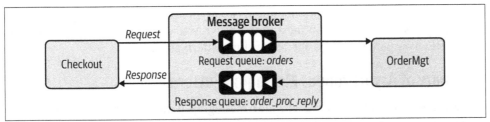

Figure 2-6. Asynchronous Request-Reply pattern implemented using a message broker

In this example, the Checkout service sends an order-processing request to the request queue with an order ID and reply queue name (order_proc_reply). Then the consumer OrderMgt service processes it and delivers the response to the response queue.

How it's used in practice

The Asynchronous Request-Reply pattern is not an alternative to the Request-Response pattern you learned about previously. This pattern serves a specific purpose; when you need to send back a reply that contains business data to a given asynchronous message, you need to use this pattern. Therefore, most of the messaging solutions that support the Single-Receiver pattern facilitate the Asynchronous Request-Reply pattern as well.

Broker implementations such as RabbitMQ, ActiveMQ, and Azure Service Bus support the Asynchronous Request-Reply pattern. We further discuss some of the other patterns that you can build on top of this one in Chapter 5.

Considerations

Because of its similarities with the Request-Response pattern, you may think the Asynchronous Request-Reply pattern is a better and more reliable alternative to synchronous request-response messaging, because we can use queues to ensure persistent messaging between the parties. However, keep in mind that these two patterns are used for completely different use cases.

The Asynchronous Request-Response pattern is a combination of two one-way messages. However, the performance implication due to using a queue for both request and response, and the overhead of correlating messages, need to be taken into account when applying this pattern. In the real world, we don't see this pattern used as frequently as the other asynchronous communication patterns that we've discussed.

Related patterns

This pattern is essentially a combination of two asynchronous single-receiver patterns built in opposite directions. So most of the delivery semantics that you apply for the Single-Receiver pattern can be applied for this pattern as well.

Summary of Asynchronous Messaging Patterns

Table 2-2 summarizes the asynchronous messaging patterns, detailing when to use them and when not to.

Table 2-2. Asynchronous messaging patterns

Pattern	When to use	When not to use
Single-Receiver	One microservice sends an asynchronous command to another microservice. For ordered message delivery. For guaranteed message delivery.	Efficient data transfer is required without delivery semantics such as at-least-once.
Multiple-Receiver	More than one consumer is interested in the same message/event.	Usually not suitable when you need guaranteed message delivery.
Asynchronous Request-Reply	For asynchronous messaging scenarios in which correlation is required between a request and a reply.	Shouldn't be used as a reliable messaging alternative to synchronous request-response patterns.

Service Definition Patterns

When building communication among cloud native applications, one of the most important aspects to consider is the *service definition*—how you define your microservice interface to its consumers. Service definition techniques, and how we use them, differ. Let's first focus our discussion on using service definitions in synchronous communication.

Service Definitions in Synchronous Communication

When we build synchronous services, we can publish the service definitions to a central location known as the *service registry*. This is more or less a metadata repository that the other microservices and developers can interact with. In defining the service interface, you can choose from a wide range of technologies, depending on the communication protocol you're using for synchronous communication (for example, RESTful with HTTP, gRPC, and so on).

How it works

The service definition is a way of declaring how a given service can be consumed by consumers/clients. It is something that will be shared with consumers prior to establishing the communication channel among the services where synchronous communication takes place.

As illustrated in Figure 2-7, microservices can publish their service definitions to a service registry (or they can be published manually by the microservice owners). Then the consumers of those microservices can connect to the service registry and obtain the service definitions (programmatically or manually by the developers). This step is known as *service discovery*.

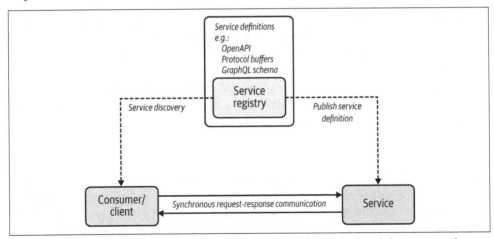

Figure 2-7. Using a service registry for storing service definitions and discovering them

The service definitions that the consumers obtain can be used to build the client application or generate the required client libraries to communicate with the server. The service definition contains the interfaces that a given service offers, as well as message formats and schema for data types exchanged between the client and microservices.

A service registry holds the service definitions and may offer additional capabilities such as user ratings, reviews, and support for various API collaboration requirements. We explore the Service Registry and Discovery pattern in detail in Chapter 3.

How it's used in practice

A service registry is often implemented as a metadata repository with an API to manage service definitions and other metadata. Some tools that can do this are Consul, etcd, and Apache ZooKeeper. In most deployments, we can run the service registry as a centralized component. The Service Registry and Discovery pattern is discussed in detail in Chapter 3, but for the context of service definition patterns, we can just assume it's a metadata repository for putting and retrieving service metadata.

The service definition techniques differ from one protocol to another. For instance, RESTful services use OpenAPI, gRPC uses Protocol Buffers, and GraphQL uses GraphQL schemas to define service interfaces. While some protocols (gRPC) mandate the use of a service definition, others don't require a service definition at all (REST). However, in the context of cloud native applications, since we are interacting with numerous microservices, it is always a good practice to use a service definition in each and every service that we develop, and to ensure that it is discoverable through a mechanism such as a service registry.

Service definitions for RESTful services with OpenAPI and Consul. You can define the business interface of a microservice in your cloud native application by using service definition specifications such as OpenAPI. You can then store that definition in a service registry such as Consul, so that the consumers of your service can obtain the metadata required to access the service. By using the OpenAPI definition, consumers can generate code, refer to documentation, understand service-level agreements, obtain supported security schemas, and so on. Service registries like Consul provide a uniform way to access the service metadata and act as the service catalog for obtaining information on any service that is part of your organization.

Considerations

The service definition and how to share that definition with the rest of the organization is tightly coupled to the overall governance aspects of building cloud native applications. We usually store service definitions in a central service registry so all the consumers of the microservices that we build can discover them. Therefore, the service registry should be capable of handling disparate sets of service definitions, such as the OpenAPI specification, gRPC service definitions, and GraphQL schemas.

With the introduction of service definitions, the build and the development life cycle of your microservice also changes. Often when you have a service definition, you can code-generate or validate your microservice implementation against the service definition. This ensures that every release of your microservice complies with the advertised service definition.

Related patterns

Service definition patterns are closely related to the Service Registry and Discovery pattern explained in detail in Chapter 3. In addition, we can apply this pattern along with synchronous Request-Response and Remote Procedure Calls covered previously in this chapter, and the API management patterns covered in Chapter 7.

Service Definition in Asynchronous Communication

In asynchronous communication, messages exchanged between producers and consumers contain structured data that is being serialized or deserialized using a *schema* that defines and validates the data exchanged between the parties. Since the communication happens asynchronously through a message broker or an event bus, the microservices that do the producing and consuming of messages should use a common schema. Similar to service definitions in a synchronous messaging scenario, the producer and consumer microservices have to use a central metadata registry to store the schemas.

How it works

Asynchronous communication patterns don't create any coupling between the producer and consumers. So we tend to think that we can publish any arbitrary message to the interested topic and expect the consumer to process it somehow. However, this is far from the reality.

To build robust communication among microservices that use asynchronous communication, you need to use a service definition that specifies the asynchronous messaging contract (which includes the type definitions of the messages exchanged between the producers and consumers). Often this contract contains the schema definition of the messages exchanged between producers and consumers.

When two microservices use asynchronous message-driven communication, the producer can validate the message against a schema (residing in the schema registry) while publishing the message to a queue or topic in a message broker. In our online retail application depicted in Figure 2-8, the Checkout service, publishing a message to a queue, will adhere to the service definition that contains the order schema in the registry when it serializes the messages. If the schema validation fails, the producer can't publish a message to the broker. Under the hood, the producer connects to the schema registry to retrieve the service definition with the schema and validate it.

The consumers follow the same pattern when they deserialize the message so that they read the message based on the schema provided in the registry. In this example, the OrderMgt service can use the order schema from the service registry.

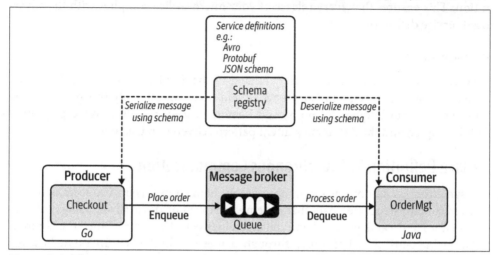

Figure 2-8. The service registry contains the service definitions and schemas for messages exchanged between producers and consumers.

When there's a mismatch of the data either being sent or consumed (for example, the producer type is different from the type that is expected by the consumer), it can be detected at the producer or consumer side during publishing or consumption of messages.

By using schema-based data serialization and deserialization, asynchronous message-based communication can drastically reduce the amount of metadata related to type information and field names that you have to pass along with every message.

How it's used in practice

In most early implementations of asynchronous communication, schemas and schema registries were not commonly used. However, with the proliferation of asynchronous communication among microservices, the necessity of having a clearly defined contract for messages exchanged between producers and consumers has increased. Therefore, many message broker solutions offer first-class support for a schema registry as part of producing and consuming messages.

Similar to the service definitions that we use in synchronous communication, we can use a central metadata repository such as a service registry, and for the schema definition techniques we can use Apache Avro, Protocol Buffers, or JSON schemas.

Depending on the type of broker you use, the schema definition technique may vary. For example, Kafka supports Avro, and Azure uses Azure Schema Registry in its Event Hubs messaging service. Emerging asynchronous service definition technologies such as AsyncAPI (*https://www.asyncapi.com*) can be used to specify the entire service contract rather than just the schema for the messages.

For applications that use event-driven architecture, the service definitions can leverage event-describing specifications, such as CloudEvents (*https://cloudevents.io*). In this way, we can simplify the event declaration and delivery across disparate microservices and other systems. We discuss these techniques in detail in Chapter 5.

Schema definitions with Kafka Schema Registry. Kafka supports the integration of message consumers and producers with the Kafka Schema Registry, in which you can store and retrieve your schema definitions for messages exchanged between producers and consumers in asynchronous messaging. You can store Avro, JSON, and Protocol Buffers schemas in the Kafka Schema Registry, and from your producers and consumer applications you can validate the schema compliance while producing or consuming messages.

The Schema Registry stores a versioned history of all schemas and provides serializers that plug into Kafka clients. These clients handle schema storage and retrieval for Kafka messages that are sent in any of the supported formats.

Cloud messaging services such as Amazon Kinesis and Azure Event Hubs also support this pattern, with seamless integration among their respective schema registry services.

Service definitions with AsyncAPI. Schema registries provide only the schema for messages exchanged between producers and consumers. However, these registries don't specify any contract details related to publishing or consuming messages. AsyncAPI tries to standardize the definition of the service contracts for producers and consumers in asynchronous messaging. Although it has not yet been widely adopted by the community, it has some promising characteristics of becoming the standard service definition for asynchronous messaging architectures.

Considerations

Most asynchronous messaging is implemented without using schema-based serialization and deserialization. This often leads to inconsistencies and data-type mismatching between producers and consumers. In addition, the amount of metadata that needs to be sent along with the message increases the message size, which slows the performance of asynchronous communication. Therefore, adopting schemas in asynchronous messaging is vital for ensuring the reliability and safety of cloud native applications.

We discussed schema validation on both the producer and consumer side. This inherently introduces performance overhead, as each message needs to go through a validation process. Also, pulling the schema from the registry may require a caching mechanism to avoid performance bottlenecks.

Related patterns

Service definition patterns are closely related to the Service Registry and Discovery pattern detailed in Chapter 3. We can apply this pattern along with Asynchronous Request-Reply and Remote Procedure Calls (covered previously in this chapter) as well as the API management patterns (covered in Chapter 7).

Now that we have covered all the foundational communication patterns for building cloud native applications, let's wrap up the chapter by discussing technologies that enable the patterns we've discussed.

Technologies to Implement Synchronous Messaging Patterns

Most implementations of the Request-Response pattern leverage protocols such as HTTP while using different data representations and exchange techniques to transfer data between microservices.

RESTful Services

RESTful services are one of the most popular ways to build a cloud native application's microservices using the Request-Response pattern. They are built on top of the REST architectural style. The REST model uses a navigational scheme to represent objects and services over a network. These are known as *resources*—objects with a type, associated data, relationships to other resources, and a set of methods that operate on them (for example, an order is a resource in the context of an online retail application where you can perform multiple actions). A client can access (request) the resource by using the unique URI, and a representation of the resource is returned (as the response).

REST doesn't depend on any of the implementation protocols, but the most common implementation is HTTP. When accessing RESTful resources with HTTP, the URI of the resource serves as the resource identifier, and GET, PUT, DELETE, POST, and HEAD are the standard HTTP operations to be performed on that resource. Therefore, all the requests are sent in the form of those HTTP operations.

Figure 2-9 shows a real-world implementation of a RESTful service: an Order service in an online retail application.

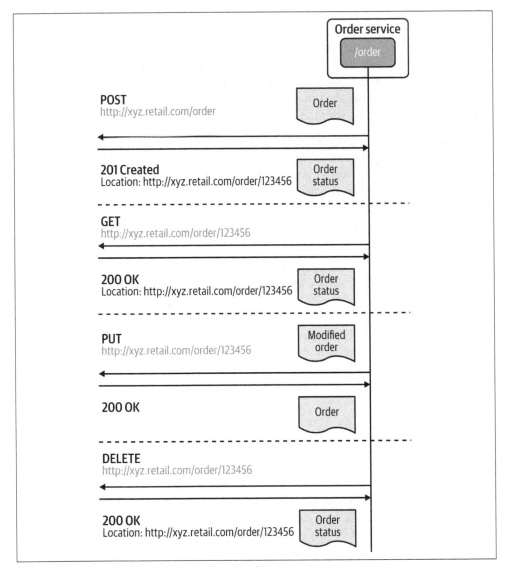

Figure 2-9. An example RESTful service and its interactions

In this example, we have represented an Order as a resource, and all requests sent in the form of HTTP operations are executed against that entity. The format of the request and response data is an implementation detail that's agnostic of the REST architectural style. Often JSON, Extensible Markup Language (XML), and other text-based data formats are used. For example, we can send an order-creation request by using an HTTP POST message to the order resource located at a given URL. Similarly, we can retrieve, update, or delete the order resource by sending HTTP GET, PUT, and DELETE requests, respectively.

GraphQL

GraphQL is another technology that is becoming popular for building interprocess communication using the Request-Response pattern. Unlike RESTful services, GraphQL is based on the concept of sending a query as a request to the microservice. The query represents the data that the client is interested in, and the microservice's logic fulfills those queries with the existing data and business logic.

GraphQL allows clients to determine which data they want, how they want it, and in what format. This is different from RESTful services, where the client doesn't have control over the response data that it receives. GraphQL primarily uses *queries, mutations*, and *subscriptions* as the main interaction styles with consumers and services. With a query, the client can request the data it needs from the server, while mutations are mostly used to modify data on the server. GraphQL also supports other messaging styles such as asynchronous event-driven communication via subscriptions.

Figure 2-10 shows how a real GraphQL microservice works. Here, the client sends the request to the microservice via the GraphQL queries and decides what data it wants in the response. If a given service has multiple entities, you don't have to send explicit requests to retrieve them, but a single GraphQL query can do that for you. GraphQL requests are served over HTTP under the hood. A standard GraphQL request is sent as an HTTP POST request; it should use the application/JSON content type and include a JSON-encoded body (queries can be sent as an HTTP GET request with query parameters as well).

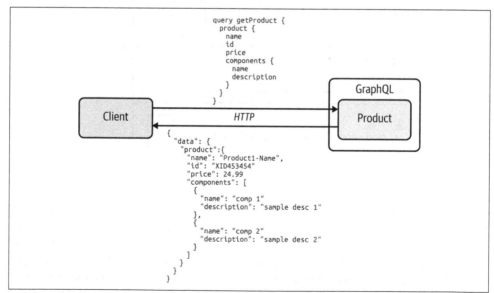

Figure 2-10. An example GraphQL service and its interactions

GraphQL is commonly used for external-facing microservices or APIs that are directly exposed to consumers (clients such as mobile applications), and for clients that need more control over the data that they consume from the server. In addition to Request-Response, GraphQL supports other messaging patterns such as publisher-subscriber messaging.

In comparison to REST, GraphQL offers an efficient way to fetch data without over-fetching (retrieving redundant data not required for the consumer) or under-fetching (retrieving only a portion of required data, which results in subsequent requests to fetch the remaining data). With GraphQL, the consumer can fetch the exact data needed in a single request. GraphQL provides other advantages including validation and type checking, detailed error handling, and backward-compatible versioning.

WebSocket

One technology used to implement the synchronous Request-Response pattern is the *WebSocket protocol*, which can simply be introduced as TCP over the web. However, it is more powerful than just a simple request-response protocol, as it supports full duplex (allows communication in both directions) and asynchronous messaging once the connection is established. WebSocket uses a single TCP connection for traffic in both directions and uses HTTP as the initial handshaking protocol (Figure 2-11). Therefore, it can work with the existing infrastructure and works on top of HTTP for the initial handshake. It acts like raw TCP sockets afterward.

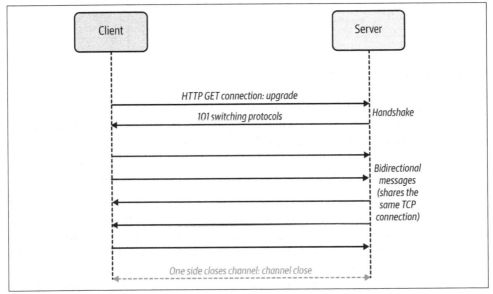

Figure 2-11. An example of WebSocket communication

WebSocket doesn't mandate a specific data serialization format for messages, so you can choose any message format you like. WebSocket is useful for building microservice applications that use synchronous request-response communication as well as duplex messaging between the server and the client applications.

gRPC

gRPC is an RPC-based communication technology. It makes connecting distributed heterogeneous microservices as easy as making a local function call. gRPC is designed to be an internet-scale interprocess communication technology that can overcome most of the shortcomings of conventional RPC technologies. It uses an efficient binary data serialization format, Protocol Buffers, to marshal and unmarshal data exchanged between the client and server applications. Also gRPC is implemented on top of HTTP2, which makes it an interoperable and efficient RPC technology. It offers language plug-ins for all the popular programming languages so you can build polyglot cloud native applications. Figure 2-12 illustrates the key components of a gRPC-based communication between two microservices.

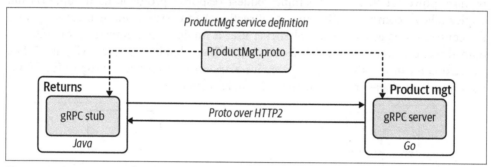

Figure 2-12. An example of microservices communication using gRPC

When you develop a gRPC application, the first thing to do is define a service interface. As we've discussed, a service interface definition indicates how your service can be consumed by consumers, which methods allow consumers to call remotely, and which method parameters and message formats are used when invoking those methods. gRPC uses Protocol Buffers to specify the service interface definitions of gRPC-based microservices.

Using the service definition, you can generate the server and client stubs. As we covered earlier, the methods that you specify in the service interface definition can be remotely invoked by the client side as easily as making a local function call. The underlying gRPC framework handles all the complexities normally associated with enforcing strict service contracts, data serialization, network communication, authentication, access control, and observability.

Apache Thrift, another RPC framework similar to gRPC, uses its own interface definition language and offers support for a wide range of programming languages. gRPC is more opinionated than Thrift and offers first-class support for HTTP2. gRPC implementations on HTTP2 leverage the protocol capabilities to achieve efficiency and support for messaging patterns such as streaming.

Summary of Synchronous Messaging Technologies

Table 2-3 compares the synchronous message technologies that we've discussed.

Table 2-3. Synchronous messaging technologies

Synchronous messaging technology	When to use
RESTful services	The business use case fits the resource-oriented model (in which you can represent business entities and functionalities as HTTP resources and operations). The service needs to interoperate with disparate sets of clients (web clients, mobile clients). The service needs to negotiate to support various content types (JSON, CSV, XML) based on client requests. You need human-readable text-based message formats.
GraphQL	Clients want to determine the data they want, how they want it, and the data format. You want a well-defined yet flexible schema for interservice communication. You want to reduce the number of service calls needed to retrieve business data from a service.
gRPC	You require low-latency and high-throughput interservice communication. You want type-safe and robust data exchange between microservices. The client or the server application needs to build a streaming business operation.
WebSocket	You have to implement full-duplex efficient messaging between services using your own data formats.

Technologies to Implement Asynchronous Messaging Patterns

Let's discuss some of the most commonly used technologies for implementing asynchronous messaging patterns in this section. We'll begin our discussion with an overview of AMQP.

AMQP

The *Advanced Message Queuing Protocol (AMQP)* is the most commonly used protocol for implementing the Single-Receiver messaging pattern. AMQP facilitates reliable communication of asynchronous messaging among producers, brokers, and consumers. It ensures rapid and reliable message delivery, and message acknowledgments for both producing and consuming services. Message acknowledgments can be used on both the producer and consumer side. When a producer delivers a message to a queue, the broker sends acknowledgments, and when a message is delivered to a consumer, the consumer notifies the broker, either automatically or when the application code decides to do so. In message acknowledgments mode, the broker will completely remove a message from a queue only when it receives a notification for that message (or group of messages).

AMQP is a language-agnostic protocol, so you can use it to build asynchronous message-based communication among microservices or applications that use disparate programming languages and frameworks.

We discuss several other patterns in which AMQP becomes useful and some message brokers that implement this protocol in Chapter 5.

Kafka

Apache Kafka is a distributed open source event bus/broker solution built on the concept of maintaining messages/events as a distributed commit log. The messages in Kafka are stored durably, in order, and can be read deterministically by multiple consumers at their own speed. Kafka is designed to be a highly scalable and distributed event broker. As such, it tries to give more control of messaging to producers and consumers while providing a robust, reliable, efficient, and scalable infrastructure. Kafka is a good choice when building a cloud native application that uses asynchronous communication patterns with heavy business logic that resides within the service logic itself.

As Kafka does not remove the events from the log upon delivery, it enables the replay of events. It uses an event *sequence number* to enable consumers to track their position in the stream to allow for selective replay. Kafka does not support protocols such as AMQP, Streaming Text Oriented Messaging Protocol (STOMP), or Message Queuing Telemetry Transport (MQTT), and it does not provide event queue semantics. Still, it is widely adopted for building event-driven architectures because of its high-performance characteristics and event-delivery guarantees. Kafka also provides extensions for implementing stream-processing systems.

NATS

NATS (*https://nats.io*) is a simple, open source messaging infrastructure specifically built for cloud native applications. Its key objectives are ease of use for developers and operators, high performance, high availability, lightweight messaging, and support for polyglot applications. NATS facilitates message-delivery semantics such as at-most-once and at-least-once for the Single-Receiver and Multiple-Receiver patterns. Like Kafka, it also uses logs for storing events, uses event sequence numbers to track events, and provides the ability to replay.

It does not have support for protocols such as AMQP, STOMP, or MQTT. But because of its lightweight nature, scalability, and native integration with Docker, Kubernetes, service meshes, and other cloud native technologies, it has become one of the first message brokers that is truly cloud native. It also supports event streaming, and command-and-control management for Internet of Things (IoT) and edge systems.

We explore a wide range of other asynchronous messaging technologies that are useful in building event-driven cloud native applications in Chapter 5.

Testing

A cloud native application consists of multiple collaborating microservices that use different communication patterns. Therefore, testing strategies for these applications depend heavily on the underlying communication patterns that we use.

For synchronous communication, we can often isolate a given service and verify the capabilities by running tests against that service interface. As part of the tests, we send test requests to the service and verify that we get the expected responses, throughput, error messages, and so on. If the service calls multiple other services (these patterns are discussed in detail in Chapter 3) and systems, we can still verify the composite business capability by running tests against that composite service.

However, for asynchronous communication, the testing strategy needs to be drastically changed. Unlike with synchronous messaging, we cannot test the service just by sending a request and evaluating the response. Even the simplest producer and consumer asynchronous messaging scenario requires messages to be published to a message queue (or topics) in the broker; then the consumer subscribes to it, and then it processes the message at the consumer side. Because all these entities are decoupled, it's really hard to verify the end-to-end asynchronous messaging functionality with unit tests. We need to break down the scenario so that the producer service ensures that the required message is published to the broker and verifies it by consuming the message it has produced to the broker in the tests. The consumer can test its business logic by consuming identical messages from the broker.

While this process verifies the functionality of the producer and consumer to a certain extent, to ensure the proper execution of the end-to-end use case, we need to test producer, broker, and consumer all at once in a single deployment. This is essentially an integration test that scaffolds up the testing environment with the required configuration for producer and consumer services. We can automate such tests by using Docker Compose or a Kubernetes deployment.

Security

Implementing communication patterns in a secure way is a key requirement of any application that you build. Depending on the communication pattern that you use, the way you secure a cloud native application may differ. For synchronous messaging, we can use Transport Layer Security (TLS) to secure the communication channels between each microservice. This is applicable to any synchronous messaging technique such as RESTful services, gRPC, or GraphQL. Synchronous messaging communication patterns can be used along with other identity and access management patterns such as delegated authorization with OAuth 2.0 and federated identity with JSON Web Token (JWT). The details of these technologies are beyond the scope of this book, but we highly recommend *Microservices for the Enterprise* by Kasun Indrasiri and Prabath Siriwardena (Apress) for more details.

In asynchronous messaging, we don't have a notion of service-to-service security as we have in synchronous communication. Rather, we secure the connectivity between the producer and the broker, as well as the broker and the consumer. To secure the communication by authenticating producers and consumers, we can expose broker endpoints via TLS, so that both producers and consumers use secured channels for producing and consuming messages. And we can implement authorization to access the broker by using technologies such as access control lists (ACLs), which are supported in most message brokers. We explore event-driven and streaming-architecture-specific security considerations in Chapters 5 and 6.

Observability and Monitoring

Observability of cloud native applications is more or less independent of the type of communication technology we use. We simply have to use or import the agents or plug-ins related to metrics, tracing, logging, and service visualization in our application code. The underlying observability tools will take care of collecting, analyzing, and presenting the data related to observability.

For synchronous communication, all the technologies that we discussed in this chapter offer first-class support for integrating with observability tools. Therefore, minimal work is required from the cloud native application developers to build observable services. For asynchronous communication, certain aspects of observability such as tracing may require additional input from the application (such as correlation IDs) to determine the flow of messages, as it involves intermediaries such as message brokers. The low-level details of how observability and monitoring are implemented for cloud native applications are beyond the scope of this book.

DevOps

When it comes to automating and integrating the processes between software development and IT operations, most platforms and tools seamlessly work with the foundational communication patterns covered in this chapter. In particular, all the synchronous communication patterns integrate flawlessly with platforms such as Kubernetes as well as the cloud services offered from the main cloud providers.

For asynchronous communication patterns, the deployment style, workload state, and scaling and high-availability needs may be drastically different from that of synchronous communication. For example, scaling a broker deployment in a Kubernetes cluster requires extra effort (such as setting up a broker deployment using stateful storage and so on) compared to running an application that uses synchronous messaging. Most asynchronous messaging solutions offer some abstractions (for example, Kubernetes operators for Kafka (*https://strimzi.io*) and RabbitMQ (*https://oreil.ly/ L44RJ*)) to simplify the DevOps tasks or offer the solution as a cloud service so that most of the DevOps-related work is included as part of the cloud service itself.

All the generic DevOps best practices can be applied when we build cloud native applications. We highly recommend Martin Fowler's online Software Delivery Guide (*https://oreil.ly/NI0c6*), which identifies various delivery strategies and DevOps patterns that you can apply to cloud native applications.

Summary

Cloud native communication patterns are applied when microservices of a cloud native application communicate with one another and with external systems. With the proliferation of microservices and increasing business requirements, we need to use a wide range of communication patterns when building cloud native applications. The two main categories of these patterns are synchronous and asynchronous.

In synchronous patterns, the client or consumer microservice/application expects a timely response from the microservice that it invokes. Most of the commonly used patterns such as Request-Response and Remote Procedure Calls fall under this category.

Asynchronous communication is all about delivering messages between the producers and consumers by using an intermediate messaging infrastructure called a message broker or event hub. The Single-Receiver and Multiple-Receiver patterns are the two main types within this category. The Single-Receiver pattern has a queue-based message delivery mechanism that is commonly used for ordered and reliable delivery of messages between a producer and a single consumer. The Multiple-Receiver pattern enables more than one consumer to receive the same message.

The service definition of a cloud native application also plays an important role in establishing which communication patterns you use. While service definition techniques may drastically differ from one protocol to another, the way we use the schemas from a central service registry is similar for all communication patterns.

This chapter has provided an overview of the fundamental communication patterns of cloud native applications. The next chapter covers how to build connectivity among the microservices of a cloud native application and how to create composition by integrating those services and systems.

Connectivity and Composition Patterns

Cloud native applications are inherently a distributed collection of microservices connected via interservice communication. When building real-world cloud native applications, it is critical to establish interservice connectivity, to integrate multiple services to create business capabilities, and to present these connected services as managed capabilities.

In this chapter, we explore a wide range of patterns that we can use to build connectivity among microservices (as well as with other existing systems) in a cloud native application. We also look at creating business functionalities by using *service composition* patterns to integrate services. Let's begin our discussion with connectivity patterns for building cloud native applications.

Connectivity Patterns

native *connectivity patterns* allow you to build connectivity among microservices as well as with the other systems in your cloud native application. As we discussed in Chapter 1, a cloud native application consists of microservices and may also connect with existing proprietary or legacy systems, external services such as software-as-a-service (SaaS) applications, databases, messaging infrastructure such as message brokers, and more.

 In Chapter 2, we primarily discussed how interservice communication takes place between microservices of a cloud native application. In this section, our main focus is on the styles that we can use to connect those services. Here we will use foundational communication patterns as well as other supporting technologies to connect our microservices when building cloud native applications.

In addition to the connectivity requirements related to the business capabilities of your cloud native application, you may need to consider the connectivity requirements for nonfunctional capabilities such as security, observability, reliability, and load balancing. This requires you to connect the microservices of your cloud native application with other systems such as identity management services and observability tools. Therefore, having the ability to seamlessly and efficiently connect all these services and systems is important when building cloud native applications. In this section, we'll explore key patterns that are useful when building the connectivity between your microservices and other systems.

Service Connectivity Pattern

The *Service Connectivity pattern* is a high-level, composite pattern that can be used in building cloud native applications. This pattern explains how a cloud native application is formed by connecting microservices and existing systems, and how these services interface with the consumers of the application.

How it works

The Service Connectivity pattern provides a generic way to connect different components such as microservices, external systems, and APIs exposed to consumers. This pattern uses one or more foundational communication patterns such as synchronous or asynchronous communication to establish the connectivity in your cloud native applications. It is applied to the backend implementation of any of the business capabilities of your cloud native application. We explore the patterns related to frontend and backend connectivity later in this chapter.

You can mix and match the most suitable communication patterns to build the Service Connectivity pattern (Figure 3-1). These services can connect with other systems such as databases, message brokers, or any external system. The business capabilities that we choose to present to consumers are exposed as managed APIs using the API gateway layer.

In Figure 3-1, microservices are connected to multiple other services via synchronous communication. These services can use patterns such as Request-Response or RPC to build the connectivity. Other services may require asynchronous communication via an event or message broker to build queue-based Single-Receiver communication or publisher-subscriber-based Multiple-Receiver communication.

In addition to these interactions, the microservices need to connect with external services and databases. The API management layer that sits on top of all the business capabilities of a cloud native application makes sure that all these capabilities are offered as managed APIs to consumers. (We'll dive into API management patterns in Chapter 7.) In certain cases, you may also want to apply techniques such as event stream processing to process data from external and internal event-streaming sources. (Chapter 6 covers these patterns in detail.)

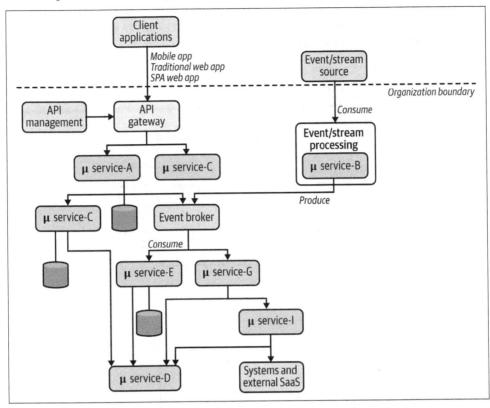

Figure 3-1. Service Connectivity pattern

So, the key idea of the Service Connectivity pattern is that it should be used as a high-level pattern that connects services and systems to realize the end-to-end business capabilities of a cloud native application.

How it's used in practice

As we discussed earlier, the Service Connectivity pattern is used in almost all cloud native applications. Any application that has more than one microservice or system needs to use this pattern to connect them and build the business capabilities. In most real-world use cases, the Service Connectivity pattern leverages several foundational communication patterns to connect the required microservices and other systems.

Figure 3-2 shows a sample use case of an online retail application built using this pattern. As the Service Connectivity pattern outlines how to connect services and systems using foundational communication patterns, this example uses multiple communication patterns to build various parts of the use case. For instance, communication with external-facing services (Catalog and Order) inherently use request-response messaging using REST and GraphQL, while some of the internal service interactions (communication between the Order and Payments services) were done asynchronously using a Kafka broker.

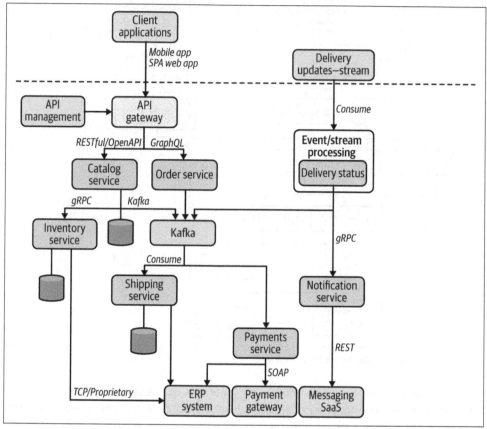

Figure 3-2. Using the Service Connectivity pattern in an online retail application

An API gateway is used to expose our online retail application's APIs to external consumers such as mobile clients or web portals. Most of the internal microservice connectivity is implemented with RPC using protocols such as gRPC. The required proprietary and legacy systems are used to build the business capability by calling them through microservices. For example, the Inventory service calls a proprietary enterprise resource planning (ERP) system in this example. Certain parts of the application, such as the Delivery Status service in this scenario, consume an external event stream and process those events.

Considerations

As you can see in Figure 3-1, the more microservices and systems that we have to connect, the greater the complexity of the entire cloud native application. Therefore, before applying this pattern, we need to make sure that we are using the appropriate service granularities. If you are seeing too many interactions among microservices, that's a sign that your service design scope is too fine-grained. If that's the case, you need to revisit the microservice design phase again and redefine the scope of the services so that they are directly mapped to the business capabilities, rather than framed features or utilities.

Also, as we discussed in Chapter 2, the foundational communication patterns used in our application need to be determined by the business use case. For example, an interactive business capability such as searching for items in an online retail store needs a synchronous Request-Response communication pattern, while placing orders requires a more durable guaranteed delivery messaging pattern such as the asynchronous Single-Receiver pattern. Therefore, we need to spend quality time identifying or defining service interaction styles and the underlying protocols to use. This is usually something that you will do as part of the microservice design phase itself. When it comes to third-party systems, you don't have much control over them and will have to rely on the interaction interfaces and protocols they offer.

When building service interactions, we need to make sure that we don't leak any infrastructure (or anything else that is not related to business logic) to our application's connectivity logic. If we do, our application's business logic gets coupled to the infrastructure or the environment, and we lose the application's portability. The service connectivity capabilities that are not mandatory for the application behavior need to be implemented at other layers (such as sidecars), which we will explore later in this chapter.

Related patterns

The Service Connectivity pattern provides a high-level view of how a typical cloud native application is formed by connecting its microservices and supporting systems. Most of the foundational cloud native communication patterns covered in Chapter 2 as well as other patterns that we'll explore throughout this chapter are closely related; we use them inside the Service Connectivity pattern.

Service Abstraction Pattern

When a microservice in a cloud native application needs to interact with another microservice or an external system, it is preferable to use an abstraction that hides the details of the underlying implementation, location, and deployment structure. That is the key idea behind the *Service Abstraction pattern*. This pattern uses a service to abstract one or more underlying services.

How it works

A given microservice or any other external system in a cloud native application can be represented as a service, so that it hides all the implementation details. For example, a given service may have multiple runtime instances running in different locations, with different Domain Name System (DNS) names and Internet Protocol (IP) addresses, and so on. If we don't use an abstraction to represent that microservice, all the clients or other services that consume it need to know the implementation details of the target service or system. Therefore, we can introduce a service abstraction in front of the microservices or systems in a cloud native application (Figure 3-3).

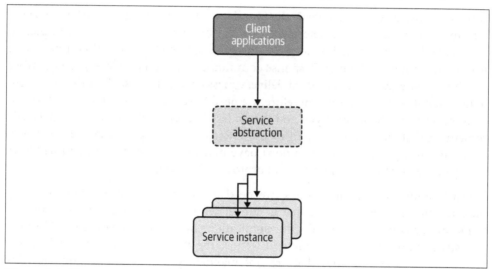

Figure 3-3. The service is an abstraction that hides the implementation details of the underlying microservice or the system

A service groups a set of runtime instances of the same microservice or the system (it can even be a monolithic system that our cloud native application needs to interact with). The underlying instances can come and go, and their IP addresses can change without affecting consumers. Here are some of the key benefits of using the Service Abstraction pattern:

- It allows you to use a stable or fixed location (IP) to represent your microservice or system within the cloud native application.

- It can provide a built-in service-discovery capability, so that the consumer applications refer to the service by using a generic naming scheme that hides the implementation details (for example, *http://hostname:port/checkout*). This is the key idea behind the Service Registry and Discovery pattern, which allows us to represent all the microservices and systems in our cloud native application at a central location so other consumers can discover existing services or register new services.

- It can seamlessly provide load balancing and failover.
- Dynamic scaling of the microservice or system is possible when using a service abstraction, as the underlying instances can come and go as needed.

Let's look at how the Service Abstraction pattern is used in cloud native applications.

How it's used in practice

The notion of the service abstraction is often built along with the service or the system. Using a service abstraction for any service instance or system has been used even in the SOA era. However, it was widely adopted with the rise of containers (Docker) and Kubernetes.

Kubernetes services. Certain platforms, such as Kubernetes, use a service abstraction as a fundamental construct. This makes life easier for the developers to represent all the microservices and systems that need to interact with Kubernetes services.

A Kubernetes service groups a set of pod endpoints into a single resource. You can configure how you access that service in various ways (for example, load balancing or cluster IP). Figure 3-4 shows how the Catalog service abstraction deployed on Kubernetes groups Catalog service instances into pods. It exposes a stable endpoint to consumers, while we can dynamically change the location and number of pods backing the Catalog service. With the Kubernetes Catalog service of the online retail application, you get a stable cluster IP address that clients inside the cluster can use to invoke the service. A client sends a request to the stable IP address in the Kubernetes cluster, and the request is routed to one of the pods in the Catalog service.

The Kubernetes service also provides seamless load balancing among the grouped pods. Kubernetes allows you to define various types of Kubernetes services to control the way you expose your microservice or any other system. For instance, if you use the service type LoadBalancer, Kubernetes automatically creates a cloud network load balancer of the underlying cloud platform (AWS, Azure, GCP, and so forth). This load balancer provides an externally accessible IP address that sends traffic to the correct port on your cluster nodes, provided your cluster runs in a supported environment and is configured with the correct cloud load-balancer package.

As we discussed earlier, with the Service Abstraction pattern, you can expose any other monolithic or proprietary systems that are consumed by your cloud native application as a service as well. For example, Kubernetes allows you to use the service type ExternalName that provides an internal alias for an external DNS name. As shown in Figure 3-4, if there's a monolithic deployment of a Kafka broker, you can represent it as an external system and consume that as a Kubernetes service for your microservices.

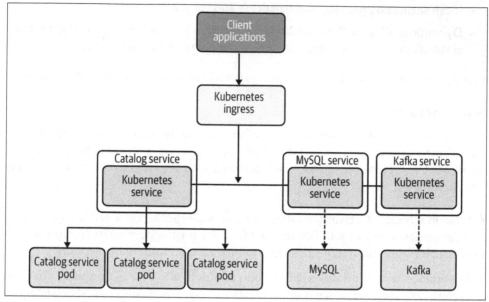

Figure 3-4. Kubernetes groups a set of pods, or any external system, to a single abstraction known as a service

Considerations

Service Abstraction is more or less a mandatory pattern that you need to use when building cloud native applications. The power of the service abstraction is critical to achieve the scalability, redundancy, and encapsulation (hiding the implementation details) of your microservices and other systems. While implementation of the Service Abstraction pattern without using an underlying platform is possible, we recommend using a platform such as Kubernetes that already supports service abstractions as a first-class construct.

Related patterns

Service Abstraction is commonly used with most of the connectivity patterns in this chapter. For example, service abstractions are used in the Service Registry and Discovery pattern, which we discuss next.

Service Registry and Discovery Pattern

When you build cloud native applications, you need a place to keep the information about the services that you create. This enables consumers to find out all the details of the services. The *Service Registry and Discovery pattern* can be used for this.

How it works

Once you represent all the entities in a cloud native application as services (through the Service Abstraction pattern), you need to keep information about these services so consumers can obtain that data and access them. The repository containing this service information and metadata is the service registry. Often we keep service information such as service URLs, service interface definitions (for example, OpenAPI specs or gRPC Protobuf definitions), service-level agreements, and other information that is useful to the service consumers. A service registry typically uses a canonical representation of a service so that we can define any service metadata at the service-registry level, despite the technologies that we use to implement them.

A service registry is implemented as another service that offers a registry repository API and discovery API. The service consumers/client applications can get the service information by accessing the service registry API (Figure 3-5). Service owners/developers can register the service by providing its details. The owners are responsible for updating and maintaining the service information at the service registry. The service consumers then use that service registry to learn how to consume the service.

We can implement the Service Registry and Discovery pattern in two ways. In the first approach, called *client-side service discovery*, the client is responsible for service discovery (Figure 3-5).

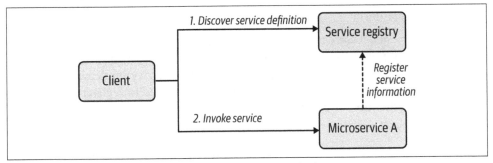

Figure 3-5. Service Registry and Discovery—client-side discovery

The information that we store in the service registry can be a service definition or service contracts. Once consumers obtain this information, they can invoke the corresponding service by processing the service information. The consumption of the service registry can happen during both runtime and development time. We can use it at runtime to determine the endpoint address or security policies of a given service, and we can use it at development time to obtain the service contract and build the consumer application according to the service contract.

In certain scenarios, we can offload the service discovery task to an intermediate component such as a load balancer. This service discovery mechanism is known as *server-side discovery*. In this scenario, the consumer/client simply sends the request to the load balancer with a reference to the service that it wants to invoke and the corresponding message (Figure 3-6).

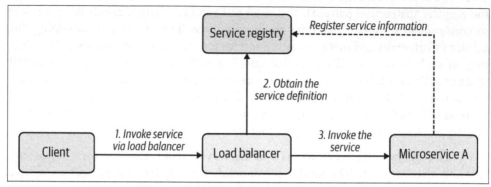

Figure 3-6. Service Registry and Discovery—server-side discovery

The load balancer is preconfigured to work with the service registry so that when a request is made for a given service, the load balancer retrieves the service information from the registry (such as the service endpoint URL) and uses it to invoke the service. (In most cases, the load balancer caches the service information rather than invoking the registry per each request.)

How it's used in practice

Service Registry and Discovery is a mandatory pattern for building any real-world cloud native application because of the immutable nature of microservices. To use this pattern in practice, we can use a dedicated service registry implementation such as Consul, as shown in Figure 3-7. All the microservices need to register with the service registry at the time of deployment. We can also configure them to send heartbeats to the registry to detect any unavailable services.

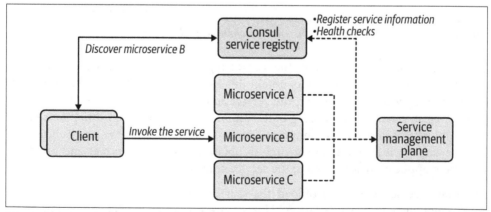

Figure 3-7. Service Registry and Discovery with Consul

If you use a separate service management or governance plane to manage the service life cycles, you can use the service registry as the service repository for that management plane. The service registry can be configured to work with either client-side discovery or server-side discovery using a load balancer.

Service discovery in Kubernetes. If you are using Kubernetes to invoke one service from another service, you don't need to worry about the actual location of the service that you are invoking. Kubernetes by default uses DNS names to discover the pods. Therefore, if you want to call the Bar service from the Foo service, in the Foo service's code you can just refer to *http://bar:<port>* as the service endpoint. Kubernetes will resolve and map the name to the actual endpoint. Kubernetes internally uses etcd as the distributed key-value store that is used as the service registry. However, this built-in registry component does not provide the same level of capabilities for managing the service metadata as a dedicated service registry such as Consul. Therefore, if you have complex service registry and discovery requirements, you can use a dedicated service registry alongside Kubernetes.

Considerations

Service Registry and Discovery is an essential pattern for building cloud native applications. However, this doesn't mean you should have a full-blown service registry and discovery solution from day one. For the most part, the primitive capabilities of Service Registry and Discovery are offered in the platforms used to build cloud native applications, such as Kubernetes. If you are using a cloud service, such as AWS, Azure, or GCP, Service Registry and Discovery will be supported as part of the cloud service. Therefore, you should invest in a dedicated service discovery and registry solution if the your use case absolutely requires you to have advanced Service Registry and Discovery capabilities such as managing service dependencies and associations, health checks, and leader election.

Related patterns

Service Registry and Discovery is a foundational pattern used along with most of the connectivity patterns in this chapter. In the context of API management, when you have to expose certain capabilities as APIs, we use a dedicated API registry known as the *API developer portal*, which is similar to a service registry. But it's a dedicated API repository to store the business capabilities that you expose to your consumers, and not all services are published to the developer portal.

Resilient Connectivity Pattern

When you are building connectivity among microservices as well as the other systems in your cloud native application, you need to use a network. In distributed computing, the network is always considered to be unreliable. Therefore, we need to make sure that we connect microservices and systems by using resilient connectivity techniques.

How it works

The *Resilient Connectivity pattern* allows you to design a resilient interaction between the microservice and the other services or systems it invokes, so that if a failure occurs, the system will be able to handle it or recover from it. For example, suppose you have two microservices in your cloud native application: Microservices A and B. Microservice A invokes Microservice B via network communication, and we need to make sure that communication happens resiliently.

The logic that invokes Microservice B should be able to handle the failures that could occur, recover from them if possible, or gracefully take actions to avoid the failure in the future. The key idea here is that Microservice A contains resilient communication logic that is executed as part of the service runtime.

Depending on the nature of the failure that could occur during interservice communication, we may implement the resilient communication logic in different ways, but the high-level architecture implementing resilient communication can be generalized as shown in Figure 3-8.

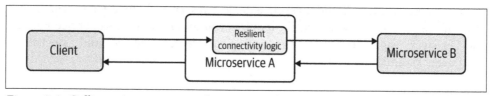

Figure 3-8. Calling microservices and systems resiliently

How it's used in practice

The Resilient Connectivity pattern is implemented to handle multiple communication requirements. Let's discuss the various styles of resilient communication.

The various applications of the Resilient Connectivity are sometimes defined as separate patterns. For more information, consider reviewing the patterns defined by Michael Nygard in *Release It!* (Pragmatic Bookshelf).

Time-out. A *time-out* is used when one service calls another one and waits for a timely response or acknowledgment. If we don't use a time-out when invoking another service or system, the caller service waits indefinitely for a response from the target service. That behavior hinders the responsiveness of the cloud native application; even if a failure occurs, the application takes an indefinite time to detect it. So, if we implement the caller service's connectivity logic that can decide when to stop waiting for a response, we call that time duration the *time-out*. Once we reach a time-out on the caller side, we can specify time-out handling logic that can gracefully handle the situation.

In Figure 3-9, Microservice A calls Microservice B by using resilient communication logic that has a time limiter specifying a time-out of 20 milliseconds (ms). However, the network latency is 10 ms, and Microservice B's processing time is 30 ms. Since the round-trip time of 40 ms (30 + 10) is greater than the time-out (20 ms), the time-out handling logic is invoked.

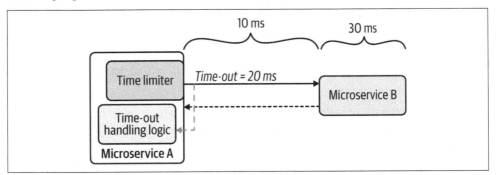

Figure 3-9. Resilient connectivity with time-outs

We need to be realistic when setting time-out values, because if the time-out is too low or too high, we won't get satisfactory results. Consider the typical network latency and target service's processing time prior to setting the time-out value.

A time-out helps services isolate misbehavior or the anomaly of another service or system, so it does not have to become your service's problem.

Retry. When services communicate over a network, intermittent failures can occur. The key idea behind retry logic is to provide a way to get the expected response, despite network disruption, after trying to invoke the same service one or more times. As part of the *retry* resilient connectivity logic, we can specify the number of total retries that the service should invoke and the duration between retries.

Figure 3-10 shows Microservice A calling Microservice B with retry resilient connectivity logic. Microservice A will trigger three retries in 10-second intervals until it successfully receives the response.

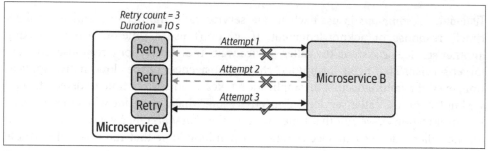

Figure 3-10. Retry logic trying to invoke the same service a specified number of times at given intervals

In addition to the retry logic, we may also define logic that we want to execute if the maximum retry count is reached for a given service invocation.

Deadlines. Deadlines are another resilient connectivity technique, similar to time-outs. With time-outs, you define a duration of time that the resilient communication logic of a given service should wait. With *deadlines,* you specify a fixed point in time that a given invocation should complete (for example, at 7:50 p.m. on...). The deadline technique is useful when you have a chain of services that a given request goes through.

In Figure 3-11, the client calls the ProductMgt service, which calls the Inventory service. At the time the client initiates the request, it can set a deadline for each request, and that deadline is propagated across all downstream services. As part of the resilient connectivity logic, each service checks the deadline of a given message. If it has expired, the service invokes the deadline-exceeded logic.

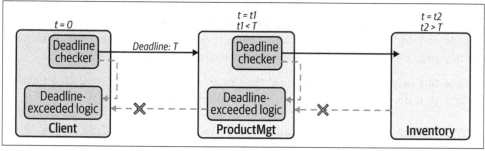

Figure 3-11. Deadlines

The deadline checker at each service is responsible for deadline validation as well as the propagation of deadline data across the board. When you are setting a deadline from the requester side, it should be included in predefined metadata of a request/message (which can be a message header or part of the message payload).

Circuit breaker. When invoking other services or systems, if the target service keeps on failing, further invocation of that service may cause more damage and cascading failures. To handle these scenarios, we can introduce a *circuit breaker* for the resilient connectivity logic of the caller microservice. A circuit breaker will prevent any further invocation of a target service if the previous service invocations have failed and the circuit state reaches a certain threshold.

Under normal circumstances, the circuit is in the *closed* state, and the invocation of the microservice takes place without any issue. However, when failures occur that match the circuit-breaker opening criteria, the circuit goes to an *open* state, preventing the invocation. Figure 3-12 illustrates this process.

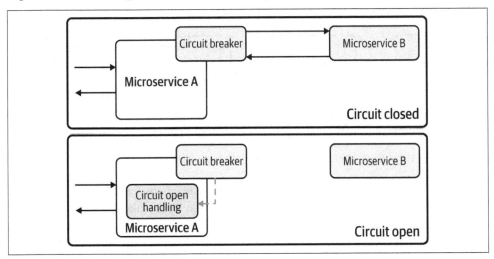

Figure 3-12. Circuit breaker

As part of the circuit-breaker configuration, we can specify multiple parameters to change its behavior. When an invocation failure occurs, the circuit breaker maintains the closed state and updates the *threshold count*. Based on the threshold count, or frequency of the failure count, it opens the circuit. When the circuit is open, the real invocation of the external service is prevented, and the circuit breaker generates and returns an error immediately without invoking the target service.

When the circuit is in an open state for a certain time period, we can apply a self-resetting behavior by trying the service invocation again after a suitable interval and resetting the breaker should it succeed. This time interval is known as the *circuit reset time-out*. When this time-out is reached, we usually say the circuit is in a *half-open state*, in which the circuit breaker allows one or more invocations of the external service as a trial. The circuit breaker changes the state to closed again if the trial succeeds, or it changes the state to open if the trial fails.

The circuit breaker is a mechanism for degrading the performance of a system when it is not operating as expected. This prevents any further damage to the system or cascading failures. We can configure the circuit breaker with the various back-off mechanisms, time-outs, reset intervals, error codes that trigger open states, error codes that trigger an ignore response, and so on.

Fail-fast.   In distributed computing, a fast failure response is considered much better than a slow failure response. The key idea behind *fail-fast* is to detect any failures or anomalies related to service connectivity as quickly as possible. The resilient communication logic can be implemented in such a way that we validate the request prior to sending it to the target service so that we can detect any failures without even invoking the target service or system (see Figure 3-13).

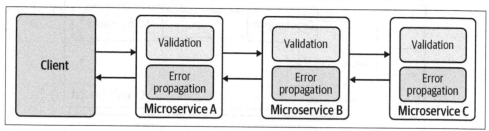

Figure 3-13. Validation of request to achieve fail-fast services

We can detect failures in many ways, and they may change from one use case to another. In some use cases, we can detect failures just by looking at the message content. We can also check system resources—including thread pools, connections, socket limits, and databases—and the state of the downstream components of the request life cycle.

In most cloud native applications, resilient connectivity styles can be used either individually or as a combination (for example, time-out and circuit breaker together).

Considerations

Resilient connectivity is essential in building cloud native applications. We may opt to implement it as part of the service's business logic (using libraries designed for building resilient connectivity) or as a separate runtime (known as a *sidecar*, which we'll discuss next), or the underlying cloud service can provide these capabilities out of the box (we just need to configure them). These resilient connectivity styles can be used together with various communication patterns, such as synchronous or asynchronous, that we explored in Chapter 2.

Related patterns

The Resilient Connectivity pattern is often used along with the Sidecar and Service Mesh patterns that we explore later in this chapter. Most of the techniques that we've discussed can be used in concert with most of the patterns related to interservice communication.

Sidecar Pattern

The *Sidecar pattern* is a generic pattern in which you run a colocated container (application or microservice) along with your main microservice. Sidecar containers extend and enhance capabilities of the main container. In the context of service connectivity, the Sidecar pattern is often used to implement the interservice and intersystem connectivity logic outside your main microservice.

How it works

Let's look at how the Sidecar pattern is used in the context of service connectivity. Suppose we have two microservices; Microservice A and B, and we need to establish interservice communication between the two (Figure 3-14). The typical approach would be to build the interservice communication along with the business logic of the service. If the communication logic requires complex network communication that is independent of the business capabilities of the service, the service developers may have to spend considerable time implementing that inside the service. And when we build multiple microservices, we may have to duplicate the same capability over and over again and with multiple programming languages or frameworks.

The Sidecar pattern allows you to offload the interservice communication logic to a separate runtime that is colocated with the main microservice. When we use containers to deploy cloud native applications, a sidecar is often implemented as a colocated container with the main container that runs the business logic.

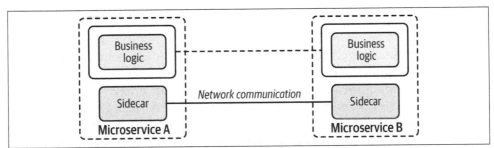

Figure 3-14. Using a sidecar to offload interservice communication

When you use a sidecar for interservice communication, the business logic of each service doesn't need to worry about the underlying network communication, as the sidecar is already providing it. As the developer, you have to plug the sidecar into your main container and configure the sidecar to achieve the preferred interservice communication logic. The main container calls the colocated sidecar component (for example, via localhost), and the sidecar takes care of the external-facing communication. With this approach, no microservice should talk to other services or systems directly.

The runtime that we choose to use as the sidecar should support all the commodity features (such as secured communication, traffic routing, and service discovery) that are required for interservice communication. And we should be able to configure the sidecar by using a high-level configuration language (for example, YAML or JSON). The sidecar and main microservice share the same life cycle. It's important to keep in mind that a sidecar can be used for any purpose that enhances the capability of the main microservice. But in this section, we focus on the service connectivity aspect of sidecar.

How it's used in practice

In general, the Sidecar pattern is often realized with the use of a platform such as Kubernetes, mainly because we can easily encapsulate a sidecar-based microservices application as a Kubernetes pod. So, it's a multicontainer pod—one with the main container and the other with the sidecar. We can manage and scale the entire application as a single unit, while we have clear separation of concerns between the business logic and the extension or enhancement logic.

The Sidecar pattern is used in multiple ways when we build the connectivity between microservices or other external systems.

Sidecar proxy.   We can use the sidecar as a *proxy* to mediate the inbound and outbound communication to the main microservices that the sidecar is attached to. Since the sidecar is being used as a proxy, the main container calls the sidecar that runs on localhost as it invokes the external service or system. Then the sidecar proxy requests the additional network communication feature, such as security or service discovery logic.

Figure 3-15 shows an application of this approach in a typical cloud native application. Two microservices—Checkout and Inventory—communicate with each other using Envoy (*https://www.envoyproxy.io*) as the sidecar proxy. Communication between the two services takes place over the Envoy proxy through HTTP. The inventory service also uses Envoy to connect to the MongoDB database. In this case, the Inventory service uses the MongoDB wire protocol (over TCP/IP) to connect to Envoy proxies that request to MongoDB.

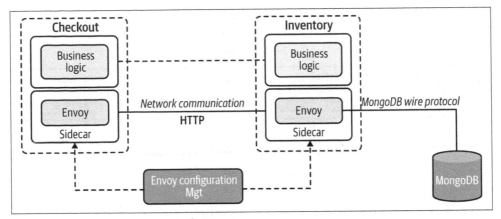

Figure 3-15. Using Envoy as a sidecar

The sidecars can be configured using Envoy's configuration management APIs to change the behavior of the sidecar proxy. For example, the communication between the two services that takes place via the Envoy proxy can be made secure and reliable with the use of Envoy features. Similarly, we can externally monitor the communication between the Inventory service and MongoDB by allowing Envoy to sniff the communication (by using Envoy's MongoDB sniffing filters) and report to an external monitoring tool.

Sidecar bridge. In the sidecar proxy approach, the proxy didn't alter the inbound and outbound protocols. It simply connected the main container to the external services and systems using the same protocol. However in the sidecar bridge approach, we use the sidecar to bridge two different protocols.

For example, suppose your main container wants to communicate with only HTTP and still wants to connect with messaging systems such as Kafka. The main container and sidecar use completely different protocols as well as completely different messaging patterns. We can use a sidecar bridge to achieve communication between the two.

The example in Figure 3-16 uses Dapr (*https://dapr.io*) as the sidecar. Microservice A calls the sidecar APIs through HTTP to produce messages to Kafka. The sidecar is configured to connect with the Kafka service, which is transparent to the microservices. On the consumer side, Microservice B registers (using HTTP API) with the Dapr sidecar to receive messages that are published to a given topic. The Dapr sidecar then subscribes to that topic in Kafka by using the Kafka protocol. So, when there's a new message for that topic in Kafka, the Dapr sidecar receives the message and then forwards it to Microservice B via HTTP.

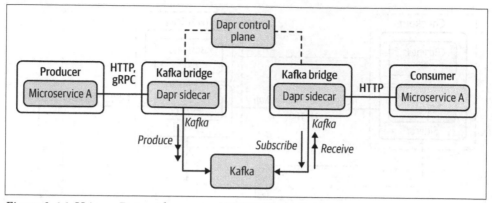

Figure 3-16. Using a Dapr sidecar as an HTTP-Kafka bridge

As you can see, the use of a protocol-bridging sidecar vastly simplifies the business logic of the microservice. As a developer, you can now focus on the microservices' business logic while the sidecar takes care of connecting the microservice to a wide range of systems and services with minimal effort.

Considerations

The Sidecar pattern is one of the most popular patterns used in cloud native application development. The capabilities that it brings can greatly enhance and extend the main container. However, keep in mind that using this pattern comes with a price. Here are some of the key considerations to be aware of when using this pattern:

- Using a sidecar along with a microservice multiplies the number of instances you need to manage and run. If you have four microservice instances, then with a sidecar you need to run eight instances.

- Management of sidecar containers needs to be done via a dedicated control plane component. While it is possible to invoke the configuration API via standard protocols such as HTTP or gRPC, it is more efficient and easier to manage sidecars via a dedicated control plane component.

- Sidecar configuration can rapidly grow to complex logic. The more services and systems that you connect with, the more complex the sidecar configuration that you need to manage.

- Never implement any business-logic-related capability inside the sidecar. That would violate the key purpose of the Sidecar pattern; the leaking of business logic to multiple layers also may have adverse consequences such as management and ownership nightmares.

With the overwhelming success and usage of the Sidecar pattern, some platforms (such as Kubernetes) are planning to support sidecars as a first-class construct in the platform in the future.

Related patterns

The Sidecar pattern is closely related to, and extended, when implementing the Service Mesh pattern, which we discuss next.

Service Mesh Pattern

The *Service Mesh pattern* is essentially an extension of the Sidecar pattern, to be used as the communication infrastructure of a cloud native application.

The main motivations behind the Service Mesh pattern are the challenges that we started to encounter when building the connectivity between microservices and systems of a cloud native application. As we discussed in Chapter 1, we used to use the centralized ESB architecture to connect services and systems. With the elimination of ESB, now the microservices themselves need to take care of the interservice communication logic.

Figure 3-17 depicts the two architectures: ESB on the left, and microservices on the right. Say you need to call multiple downstream services in a resilient manner (including time-outs and retries) and expose the functionality of another microservice. With the ESB architecture (left), you can use the built-in capabilities of ESB for building reliable communication with minimal effort. However, when you use microservices architecture (right), the interservice communication logic must be part of the microservices you build. Your microservice code needs to take care of both the business logic and the connectivity logic.

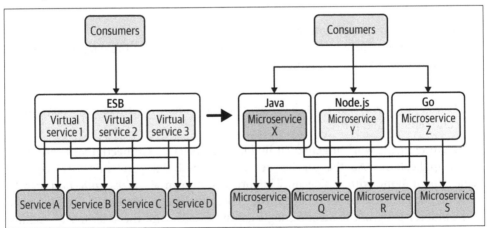

Figure 3-17. Interservice communication: from ESB (left) to microservices (right)

Building this network communication logic as part of your microservices drastically complicates the business logic and increases the development time for all your microservices. You will have to rely on external libraries (for example, Resilience4j) to build these interservice communication features. Also, if you use multiple technologies or programming languages, you will have to duplicate the effort across multiple technology stacks (for example, the circuit breaker has to be implemented in Java, Node.js, or Go).

Since most of the interservice communication requirements are generic across all microservice implementations, we can think about offloading all such tasks to a different layer such as the sidecar, so we can keep the service code independent. This is the key idea behind the Service Mesh pattern.

How it works

The Service Mesh pattern allows you to have an interservice communication infrastructure between your microservices and other systems. With a service mesh, a given microservice won't directly communicate with the other microservices. Rather, all service-to-service communications take place through a sidecar proxy. As illustrated in Figure 3-18, the Service Mesh pattern introduces the following components to provide a simple, scalable, and configurable communication infrastructure:

Service Mesh sidecar proxy
    This is known as the *data plane,* in which all the interservice communication logic is applied to the messages exchanged between services and systems.

Control plane
    Sidecar proxies are controlled through the control plane. This centralized component provides a rich and simple API to control sidecar proxies of the data plane.

Service Mesh configuration language
    This is the configuration API that allows you to configure the data plane to control the interservice communication logic.

Built-in support
    This support provides reliability, security, observability, service discovery, policy enforcement, and more.

These components work together in building interservice connectivity in our cloud native applications. As the service developer, you build your microservices and deploy them along with a sidecar. This process, known as *sidecar injection*, can be done manually or can be automatically injected during deployment. As we discussed in the Sidecar pattern, the business logic communicates with the sidecar via localhost communication (which is denoted as Primitive Network Functions in Figure 3-18).

Then the sidecar takes care of connecting with any external system. Both the sidecar and main container are deployed as a single unit (for example, in a Kubernetes pod).

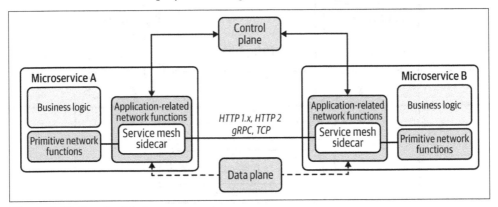

Figure 3-18. Service Mesh components

Service Mesh implementations define a configuration language or API to control the various capabilities and control the data plane via that configuration. The control plane connects all sidecars to a central location and enables the developers to manage their services that run on top of the service mesh. The capabilities such as reliability, security, observability, service discovery, and policy enforcement are applied at the data-plane level while they are controlled through the control plane.

How it's used in practice

The Service Mesh pattern is used in complex microservices deployments where we need to manage an increasingly large number of microservices. Often the service mesh is built on top of a container orchestration layer such as Kubernetes to reduce the overhead of managing containers and to use the abstractions provided by Kubernetes such as services and pods. Quite a few service mesh implementations are available: Istio and Linkerd are the most popular. Each service mesh has its own configuration language and API.

Figure 3-19 shows the component architecture of Istio. For any microservice that you develop, you can enable Istio sidecar injection so that sidecar proxies can intercept all network communication between microservices and other systems. Then, using the Istio control plane, you can configure and manage the communications.

The control plane consists of *Istiod* components that provide service discovery, configuration, and certificate management. The sidecar proxies are managed by Istiod, and users control the mesh behavior via Istiod.

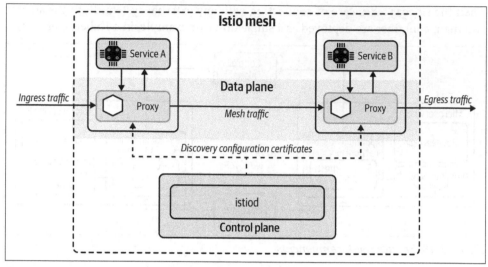

Figure 3-19. Component architecture of Istio service mesh

Key features of Istio include the following:

Automatic load balancing
> For HTTP, gRPC, WebSocket, and TCP traffic

Traffic control
> Includes routing rules, retries, failovers, and fault injection

Policy enforcement
> A pluggable policy layer and configuration API supporting access controls, rate limits, and quotas

Observability
> Metrics, logs, and traces for all traffic within a cluster

Security
> Service-to-service communication in a cluster with strong identity-based authentication and authorization

In addition to standalone service mesh offerings, cloud vendors such as Google Cloud offer Istio as a managed service.

Considerations

Although the Service Mesh pattern is a popular concept these days, adopting it in the real world to build cloud native applications should be done with caution. Here's why:

- Managing a service mesh deployment can be overwhelmingly complex. The complexity comes from the sidecar architecture (in which we need to run one extra container for each service instance) as well as from the architecture of the service mesh implementation (we need to manage multiple service mesh components that interact with each other).

- A service mesh is often built on top of containers and container orchestration platforms such as Kubernetes. This may double the complexity that it brings in.

- Running and managing a fleet of sidecar proxies carries a major performance overhead.

- Service Mesh doesn't offer first-class support for asynchronous event-driven communication yet.

Service Mesh as a service offering is quite pragmatic, and you will be able to overcome most of the operational complexity of managing it yourself.

Related patterns

The Service Mesh pattern is closely related to the Service Connectivity and Sidecar patterns (described in this chapter).

Sidecarless Service Mesh Pattern

As you have seen in the previous section, the service mesh requires a fleet of sidecar proxies for each microservice instance that you run in your cloud native application. This is one reason for the slow adoption of the Service Mesh pattern. The *Sidecarless Service Mesh pattern* tries to solve that problem by eliminating the need for a sidecar. The application of this pattern is still in its early stages, but because of its unique advantages, it's quite a promising pattern in the context of microservices connectivity.

How it works

The key idea behind the Sidecarless Service Mesh pattern is this: if the control plane can manage and control the network communication of the sidecar proxy, why not directly do it with the client component of the main container? Suppose two microservices need to communicate with each other, as shown in Figure 3-20. Similar to the Service Mesh pattern, we can use a control plane to manage and configure the communication (mesh traffic) between microservices. Rather than using a dedicated sidecar proxy to handle the interservice communication, we can embed the sidecar proxy logic to the microservice runtime itself. For example, Microservice A's runtime contains the business logic as well as the logic related to the mesh traffic. The embedded runtime understands the control plane configuration commands that come through using a control plane communication protocol.

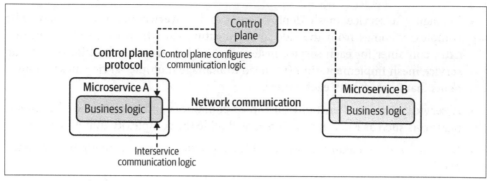

Figure 3-20. Sidecarless service mesh

As you can see in the figure, the control plane defines the configuration API and the control plane protocol. The technology that we use to build both microservices implements a client application that understands the control plane configuration protocol. For example, in this use case, suppose Microservice A is using a Java client to build the interservice communication. If we build the support to control that client component via the control plane configuration protocol, all the interservice communication capabilities can be applied at the microservice level itself (same runtime) while being centrally managed via the control plane. However, this requires each implementation technology to support the control plane API and apply the network communication logic at each network communication layer.

How it's used in practice

The Sidecarless Service Mesh pattern can be used to implement various aspects of microservices communication. It can be used to implement a full-blown service mesh or to implement a selected set of features offered from a service mesh.

Sidecarless gRPC services in Google Traffic Director.   One of the first implementations of the Sidecarless Service Mesh pattern was realized with Google Cloud's Traffic Director. As shown in Figure 3-21, Traffic Director is the control plane that manages microservices-based applications running in the system and can control Envoy sidecar proxies via Envoy's configuration API xDS. In the sidecarless deployment of gRPC-based microservices, the gRPC client side implements Envoy's configuration protocol xDS so that the control plane can control the communication flows through the gRPC client.

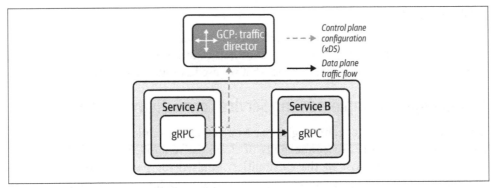

Figure 3-21. Sidecarless Service Mesh

Traffic Director gives the gRPC clients information about which services to contact, how to load-balance requests to multiple instances of a server, and what to do with requests if a server is not running. As long as you use a gRPC client that implements Envoy xDS API, you no longer need to have a sidecar proxy to bring the service mesh capabilities to your gRPC applications. In this case, the gRPC client implements only a selected set of features of a service mesh, but we can further improve it to support all its other features.

When it comes to the development experience of microservices that you deploy on top of a sidecarless service mesh, an implementation of a control plane configuration API is transparent to the service developers. It is implemented in the framework's or client library's network communication logic.

Considerations

Sidecarless Service Mesh is an emerging pattern that tries to overcome the limitations of the conventional sidecar-based service mesh architecture. The main complexity it introduces is that the libraries that we are using need to have support for the service mesh control plane APIs and implement the network communication logic as part of that client library itself.

For example, suppose you want to use the circuit-breaking capability when you call an external service. The client library that you use to build the microservices that invoke the other service then needs to offer support for the xDS protocol for the control plane, as well as implement the actual circuit-breaking logic as part of the client library. Therefore, the adoption of this pattern largely depends on availability of such network communication libraries for a wide range of programming languages.

Related patterns

Sidecarless Service Mesh is an alternative to the Service Mesh pattern with a sidecar proxy. The patterns related to resilient communication are often implemented at the control plane–compliant client libraries that we use to build the microservices.

Technologies for Implementing Service Connectivity Patterns

Let's discuss some of the technologies that you can use to implement the connectivity patterns in this section. For connectivity of cloud native applications, platforms such as Kubernetes offer most of the capabilities required for patterns such as Service Abstraction, Service Registry and Discovery, and Sidecar. Similarly, these features are built-in capabilities of cloud services such as AWS, Azure, and GCP.

Kubernetes primarily drives the use of the Service Abstraction pattern in the context of container and container orchestration. However, many cloud services use the notion of a service in most of their offerings. The scope and capabilities of the service may be dramatically different based on the context and use case. For example, server-less platforms such a Knative (*https://knative.dev*) use service abstraction to deploy an application, while service mesh solutions such as Istio use a virtual service (*https://oreil.ly/uqnMz*) abstraction, which is a unit of application behavior bound to a unique name in a service registry. An Istio service consists of multiple network endpoints implemented by workload instances running on pods, containers, and VMs. Therefore, we need to choose the implementation technology by looking at the actual use case for which we need service abstraction.

The service mesh solutions offer built-in support for resilient communication, security, observability, service discovery, and traffic routing. The service mesh technology space is growing rapidly, but Istio and Linkerd are the most popular implementations out there. The production-level adoption of service mesh is still low because of the complexity of managing it and resource consumption due to having a sidecar per each service instance. Some cloud vendors such as GCP offer managed service mesh offerings, which makes life easier for users.

If you are not using a service mesh, or the underlying platform (cloud services) doesn't support its features (such as resilient communication or service discovery), then those features need to be implemented at the microservice level by using dedicated client libraries. You need to choose a library that enables resilient communication for the service development technology you're using. Several libraries are available for various programming languages (for example, we can use Reslience4j (*https://oreil.ly/KgIvr*), Quarkus (*https://oreil.ly/dNdm2*), or Micronaut (*https://oreil.ly/tPonw*) for Java, and frameworks such as Go kit (*https://oreil.ly/ZZYpw*) for Go).

If you plan to use the sidecar architecture to implement certain connectivity patterns, you can use Envoy (*https://www.envoyproxy.io*), which supports a wide range of them.

Also, projects such as Dapr (*https://github.com/dapr/dapr*) offer higher-level abstractions related to connectivity such as sidecar bridges. Sidecarless architectures are also at a very primitive stage, and cloud vendors such as Google Cloud support sidecarless architecture for a selected set of protocols such as gRPC. The control plane configuration protocols such as Envoy's xDS (*https://oreil.ly/pQ18U*) play a vital role in the success of the sidecarless architecture.

Summary of Connectivity Patterns

Table 3-1 lists the connectivity patterns, and details when and when not to use them.

Table 3-1. Connectivity patterns

Pattern	When to use	When not to use
Service Connectivity	This is a generic pattern that you can use to build connectivity in almost all the cloud native applications.	(Not applicable.)
Service Abstraction	Usually, you need to explicitly use it if you are using Kubernetes or a cloud service. Useful when you connect cloud native applications with existing monolithic systems.	Not required to specifically use this pattern when you are fully dependent on a cloud service or a serverless platform.
Service Registry and Discovery	A fully fledged service registry and discovery solution is required if you have several dozen services consumed by a wide range of clients across the organization and beyond. For most use cases, the foundational service registry and discovery offered from platforms such as Kubernetes should be sufficient. If you use a cloud service such as AWS, Azure, or GCP, most of the capabilities are available out of the box.	If the number of services that you need to connect is small, having a full-blown service registry and discovery service doesn't make sense. You will still need a primitive service discovery mechanism (for example, DNS) to encapsulate service location and deployment details.
Service Resilience	Often required when building a reliable cloud native application that connects with multiple services and systems. Essential for connecting legacy systems with cloud native applications. Explicitly implement resilience if the underlying cloud service or deployment (for example, service mesh) doesn't support resilient connectivity.	Not required to explicitly use if you are building the application on top of a service mesh, cloud service, or using a serverless platform (they offer out-of-the-box support for resilient connectivity for the most part).
Sidecar	Useful when you have to decouple the business logic from the connectivity logic. If the connectivity logic is too complex, offloading it to a separate runtime makes sense. You use polyglot technologies that require the same connectivity features.	Not suitable if your DevOps don't have the capacity to handle the complexity of sidecar architecture. If you don't use container orchestration, it's overwhelmingly complex to support sidecar architecture.
Service Mesh	You have to connect numerous microservices to achieve resilience, traffic routing, secured communication, service discovery, and observability.	(Same as Sidecar pattern.)

Pattern	When to use	When not to use
Sidecarless Service Mesh	Useful if the sidecar architecture hinders performance. The underlying implementation technology supports sidecarless interaction with control planes.	Still at very early stages. So, it is better to avoid it unless the pattern is offered from the technology stack or cloud provider (for example, GCP Traffic Director).

Service Composition Patterns

In a cloud native application, the interaction among microservices is what builds the business capabilities of that application. (For example, in our online retail application example, the Order microservice needs to interact with the Catalog microservice and the Payment microservice, and so on.) When building any business capability, you have to connect one or more microservices and other systems. In the previous section, we discussed patterns related to connecting services and systems at a more operational or infrastructure level. In this section, we focus on the patterns that you can use when realizing the business logic of a service, as well as how to create composite capabilities by using multiple services or systems.

Service composition is all about how you implement a business use case by plumbing, or integrating, multiple services and systems. It's important to keep in mind that the services that we build use existing services, and should have a clear business scope and be driven by clear business requirements. We cannot simply create composite services by randomly connecting them. For instance, if you want to support a certain business capability (such as order management), you should come up with the API of the composite service and the downstream services and systems that you want to integrate with. Next we'll discuss three common service composition patterns: Service Orchestration, Service Choreography, and Saga.

Service Orchestration Pattern

Service Orchestration is a well-known composition pattern from the era of SOA. In the context of cloud native applications, when we have to build a business capability by invoking multiple services and systems, the composition logic is implemented in a single microservice. This pattern, for the most part, uses synchronous communication and operates in a stateless way.

How it works

Service Orchestration implements the business logic of a microservice by invoking and integrating one or more microservices and systems. Suppose you are building a new business capability implemented as Microservice Z (Figure 3-22). It requires the integration of several existing microservices such as Microservices A, B, and C. You can build the business logic of Microservice Z so that it invokes Microservices A, B, and C with the required messages and finally sends the response back to the consumer of Microservice Z. The downstream services may use disparate message formats and communication protocols. Therefore, Microservice Z needs to handle all that complexity. The entire composition logic is self-contained within Microservice Z's scope.

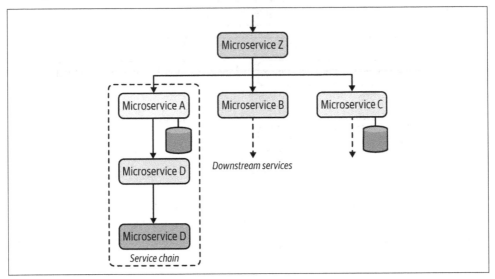

Figure 3-22. Service Orchestration logic implemented in Microservice Z

The downstream services can use either synchronous or asynchronous communication. These downstream services may call several other downstream services too. This style of communication is known as *service chaining*. From the perspective of composite services such as Microservice Z, the existence of multiple chained downstream services is irrelevant.

How it's used in practice

Service Orchestration is commonly used in most cloud native applications, as microservices need to integrate with one or more other microservices or systems when implementing a given business capability. As discussed earlier, before the cloud native era, we used to use technologies such as ESBs or workflow engines to build this integration logic. In the context of cloud native applications, we rarely use conventional monolithic solutions such as ESBs or workflow engines to build orchestration logic. Instead, we build a microservice that orchestrates the composition logic.

Figure 3-23 shows a typical service orchestration scenario within a real-world online retail application. The Order service's business logic requires the orchestration of the calls to four microservices: Catalog, Inventory, Shipping, and Customers (CRM). As you can see, these service invocations are using disparate communication protocols such as REST over HTTP, gRPC, and SOAP. When we are building this kind of microservice, the orchestration logic is implemented as part of the Order service's business logic.

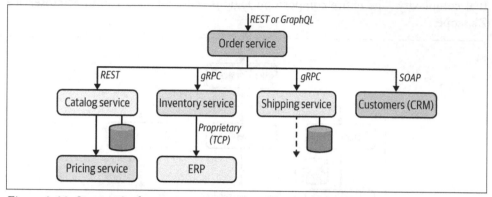

Figure 3-23. Service Orchestration in a real-world service composition use case

When making technology choices to implement such a service, we can use a generic programming language (such as Java, Go, or C#) or a cloud native integration framework such as Apache Camel that has a lot of abstractions to simplify the service integration.

Considerations

When using Service Orchestration, we need to be aware of several considerations:

- Use this pattern if it can be directly mapped to a business capability that aggregates the capabilities of several other downstream capabilities. Otherwise, you will be creating a monolithic service with multiple business capabilities.

- Service Orchestration is straightforward to implement in scenarios that are stateless, so we don't need to worry about preserving the state of the orchestration.

- It is better to limit the number of service calls in a composition. For instance, if you have to orchestrate calls among more than four or five services, that's a sign of business scope issues with the service, or perhaps the downstream services may be too granular.

- Service Orchestration centralizes the composition logic to a single service, and that service is tightly coupled to all the downstream services that it connects with.

Avoid using a conventional monolithic technology such as an ESB or a workflow engine to implement the orchestration logic, as they are not designed for building cloud native applications.

The composite services that we develop by using Service Orchestration are exposed to the consumers via an API management layer, which we will explore in Chapter 7.

Related patterns

Service Orchestration is used alongside other service composition patterns such as Service Choreography; most use cases require a hybrid of both patterns. Most of the foundational communication patterns introduced in Chapter 2 can be applied when building service orchestrations.

Service Choreography Pattern

When building service compositions, we don't always want to centralize the composition logic to a single service. In some cases, we need to build it across multiple services. The *Service Choreography pattern* creates service compositions by using asynchronous communication between microservices and other systems.

How it works

At the heart of the Service Choreography pattern, we build a business use case that requires interaction among multiple microservices and other systems by creating asynchronous event-driven communication links with the use of a message broker (or event hub). The interaction logic is dispersed across multiple microservices, and no direct coupling occurs between microservices. Unlike in the Service Orchestration pattern, microservices do not actively invoke other microservices, but operate more or less in a reactive mode based on the events and messages coming into the service. Hence the microservices that we use in Service Choreography are also known as *reactive microservices*. (Some of the core concepts in Service Choreography are closely related to the event-driven architecture patterns that we explore in Chapter 5.)

Microservices interact with one another through the events coming in from, and events published to, the broker (Figure 3-24).

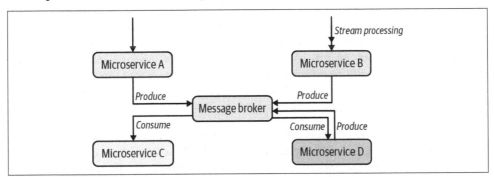

Figure 3-24. Service Choreography pattern

The composition logic is formed by publishing messages to queues or topics and the consumer microservices subscribing to them. By using asynchronous messaging patterns such as Single-Receiver (queue-based) or Multiple-Receiver (pub-sub with topics), we can create distributed asynchronous composition logic across multiple microservices.

In Figure 3-24, Microservice A receives an event and publishes the resulting event to a queue in the broker. Another service consumes that message from the queue and executes the service's business logic upon the receipt of that message. Similarly, we can publish the same event to multiple consumers via a topic. A given service operates autonomously and is responsible only for processing the event and publishing the result to the broker. Also in a Service Choreography scenario, services can process a stream of events and publish results to the broker (in this example, Microservice B). Based on the requirements, the messaging among these services can have additional reliability guarantees such as at-least-once (Chapter 5 covers these guarantees in detail).

It's important to note that in the Service Choreography pattern, we use the message broker as a *primitive messaging infrastructure*. We don't put any business logic (such as routing based on a certain criteria) inside the broker. All the logic should reside inside either producer or consumer microservices.

How it's used in practice

The realization of the Service Choreography pattern doesn't require any specific technology or framework. It requires only the coordination between the service and system using asynchronous messaging via a message broker.

In an online retail application designed as a cloud native application, multiple services exchange events based on the business use case that we need to support (Figure 3-25). For example, the Order service gets an order-place event and enqueues it in the broker. Then the Payment service that listens to that queue processes the order and verifies the payment. The result of the payment verification is also sent to another queue, which the Shipping service listens to. When that event reaches the Shipping service, it knows that the payment is already verified, and we are good to proceed with the shipping process. Similarly, the Delivery Status service receives a stream of events, and the results are published as events to a topic in the broker. Several services may be subscribed to that topic (such as Delivery Trends and Order Status), and they will receive messages via pub-sub.

It is also possible to use multiple and disparate broker solutions to facilitate communication among services. It is not mandatory to stick to a single broker, but based on the use case, you can use multiple message broker solutions to implement different types of asynchronous communication. For instance, you can use an AMQP-based broker for implementing reliable and guaranteed delivery between services, while you can use a broker such as Kafka for pub-sub and highly scalable use cases that have fewer constraints on delivery guarantees.

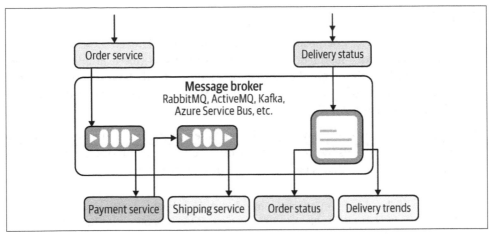

Figure 3-25. Service Choreography in action with queue- and topic-based asynchronous messaging

Considerations

Some of the key considerations to be aware of when adopting the Service Choreography pattern include the following:

- Service composition logic is dispersed across multiple microservices. Unlike in Service Orchestration, you can't understand the business logic of a choreography scenario by just looking at a single service.

- Services are loosely coupled. Adding or removing services is much easier with the Service Choreography pattern compared to Service Orchestration.

- Because of the event-driven and asynchronous nature of the Service Choreography pattern, you can implement it by using a serverless platform. For instance, you can model all the event-driven microservices as serverless functions.

Related patterns

Service Choreography is often used along with Service Orchestration in a hybrid way. Most use cases require both synchronous and asynchronous service interactions. When realizing Service Choreography, we use asynchronous communication patterns such as the Single-Receiver and Multiple-Receiver patterns introduced in Chapter 2.

Saga Pattern

When we create service compositions by using multiple microservices, we may have to execute those service interactions in a transactional way (for example, if one service interaction fails, the rest of the service interactions should be rolled back). As the transaction boundary of such a scenario spans multiple microservices and other systems, this is known as a *distributed transaction*.

The *Saga pattern* provides a way to build distributed transactions that span multiple microservices. It does this by using corresponding compensation operations to undo every service interaction that is part of a single distributed transaction.

 The Saga pattern was introduced in a paper (*https://oreil.ly/ MCjoW*) published in 1987 by Hector Garcia-Molina and Kenneth Salem.

The Saga pattern can be applied in both the Service Orchestration and Service Choreography patterns that we discussed in previous sections.

How it works

The Saga pattern aims to build distributed transactions across multiple microservices and other systems by breaking a given transaction into a sequence of subtransactions and corresponding compensating transactions. All transactions in a Saga either complete successfully, or, in the event of a failure, compensating transactions are executed to roll back all subtransactions.

Before diving into the details of how the Saga pattern is implemented, let's first understand the nature of the problem that Saga solves. The Saga pattern solves the problem of building distributed transactions across multiple microservices in a cloud native application.

Distributed transactions use a central process called a *transaction manager* to orchestrate the steps of a transaction. The main protocol used in implementing distributed transactions is known as a *two-phase commit (2PC)*.

Distributed transactions have inherent limitations, though, which hinder their usage with 2PC for most microservice use cases that require transactions. Some of the limitations of distributed transactions using 2PC are listed here:

- The transaction manager is the single point of failure. Pending transactions will never complete if the transaction manager is unavailable.

- If a given participant fails to respond, the entire transaction will be blocked.

- The 2PC protocol assumes that if a given participant has agreed to commit a transaction by responding Yes to the transaction manager, then it can definitely commit the transaction too. This is not the case with most of the practical scenarios. The participant may fail to commit a transaction although it has responded Yes.

Given the distributed and autonomous nature of microservices, using a distributed transaction/two-phase commit for implementing transactional business use cases is a complex, error-prone task that can hinder the scalability of the entire system.

For example, suppose we need to build a service composition scenario across multiple microservices (Figure 3-26). This composition logic must be implemented in such a way that all the invocations are done in a single transaction, which means all the transactions (T1, T2, and T3) must be executed together or not at all. The composite business capability can be built into another microservice (Microservice X) that is responsible for the execution of the distributed transaction.

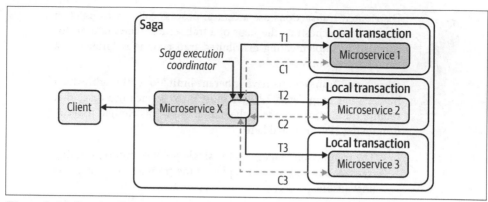

Figure 3-26. Service Composition with distributed transactions using the Saga pattern

The Saga pattern breaks this distributed transaction scenario into multiple local transactions and groups them together to execute and introduce compensating operations to roll back each subtransaction. In Figure 3-26, Microservice X is responsible for implementing the distributed transaction, and each downstream microservice can execute a local transaction (such as transactionally adding data to a database or publishing a message to a queue). To roll back these local transactions, each microservice offers a *compensating operation.*

Microservice X executes composition logic (in this case, an orchestration of multiple services) implemented through a component called the *Saga Execution Coordinator* (*SEC*). This is a stateful invocation of all the required service calls (transactions T1, T2, and T3). If one of those invocations fails, the SEC logic of Microservice X can execute the corresponding compensating operations (C1, C2, and C3) to roll back everything.

Saga at the conceptual level is trivial, and most centralized workflow solutions such as Business Process Model and Notation (BPMN) solutions are built using the same terminology. But for cloud native applications, we need to implement the Saga pattern for microservices that are distributed and ephemeral (microservices can come and go, so we need to persist the transaction state). Thus, the implementation of the Saga pattern in the context of cloud native applications requires having a Saga log, which is a distributed log that the SEC component of the composite microservice interacts with.

In the Saga log, we persist every transaction during execution of the given composition logic. The log contains various state-changing operations such as Begin Saga, End Saga, Abort Saga, Begin T-i, End T-i, Begin C-i, End C-i, and so on. Using these state-changing events that are persisted in a distributed log, we can roll back to any state that we want in the case of a failure. Microservice X in our scenario, in which the SEC logic is implemented, can be ephemeral because the Saga log allows us to re-create the state when booting up a new instance of the same microservice.

The SEC component orchestrates all the logic and is responsible for the execution of the Saga pattern. The SEC writes and interprets the records of a Saga log but doesn't maintain any in-memory state. When realizing Saga patterns, we need to use a framework or technology that allows us to create the SEC inside our microservice logic, and the SEC has to connect to a distributed log that is used to maintain the state of the composition logic.

The Saga pattern is most commonly applied on top of the Service Orchestration pattern. It is possible to use the same compensating operations when using the Service Choreography pattern as well. However, in that case, there is no central SEC, but each microservice interacts with the broker transactionally. All the operations, including compensating operations, are carried out as messages/events published to a broker and events received from the broker. The transaction boundary spans only a given microservice and the broker entity (for example, a queue) that interacts with it.

How it's used in practice

The Saga pattern is used when we're building business capabilities that need distributed transactions across multiple microservices and systems. Let's look at a real-world use case of a travel-booking service (Figure 3-27). Suppose we need to build a business capability that allows customers to book their airline, hotel, and car rental in a single transaction. The airline, hotel, and car-rental functionalities are implemented as microservices. Each service performs its own local transaction, such as adding an airline reservation to a database, publishing the hotel booking to a broker, and adding the car-rental reservation to a database.

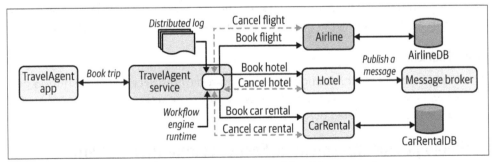

Figure 3-27. Application of Saga pattern in a travel-booking scenario

To implement the Saga pattern, the microservices that the travel-booking service invokes should support corresponding compensating transactions such as Cancel Flight, Cancel Hotel, and Cancel Car Rental. It's the responsibility of each microservice to ensure the safety of all the local transactions. The travel-booking service therefore uses a distributed log to record transactions and to implement the business logic. Most of the tasks related to state persistence of Saga execution and restoring after a restart are handled by the underlying Saga implementation. The business logic focuses on only the invocation of underlying business functionalities and compensating operations whenever required.

Frameworks and workflow engines such as Camunda (*https://camunda.com*) and Apache Camel (*https://oreil.ly/C1via*), and cloud services such as Azure (*https://oreil.ly/V5fOR*), support implementation of the Saga pattern using serverless functions and event brokers.

Considerations

The application of the Saga pattern for building service composition with distributed transactions should be done only when absolutely necessary. In most cases, you can avoid distributed transactions across multiple services. If your use case inherently requires distributed transactions (such as xyz), you need to be aware of these considerations when using the Saga pattern:

- The implementation of the Saga pattern requires a Saga framework or a workflow engine solution that supports stateful execution (that is, the Saga Execution Coordinator) of the business transaction between services. Implementing everything from scratch is generally not recommended because of the complexity involved.

- Running an observability solution alongside a Saga implementation is essential, as we have to debug and troubleshoot complex business transactions across distributed services.

- A Saga implementation framework should be backed by a scalable distributed log, as a single transaction may emit a multitude of events to the Saga log.

Related patterns

The Saga pattern is most commonly applied on top of the Service Orchestration pattern when creating service compositions. Most of the local transactions done by each service leverage data-related patterns, covered in Chapter 4.

Technologies for Implementing Service Composition Patterns

The service composition patterns are implemented using multiple types of implementation technologies. In most cloud native applications, we can create compositions by using a microservice development framework such as Spring Boot (*https://oreil.ly/0kkRx*), Quarkus (*https://oreil.ly/RFg5Z*), Micronaut (*https://oreil.ly/4YzhX*), or Go kit (*https://oreil.ly/5fayD*), or by simply using the programming language (Go, Python, Node, C#) directly. However, if the composition requires heavy lifting when it comes to integrating services with multiple protocols and messaging patterns, using a dedicated composition or integration framework such as Apache Camel (*https://camel.apache.org*) is a better option. The conventional integration platform vendors (MuleSoft (*https://oreil.ly/OSkwl*), Red Hat Fuse (*https://oreil.ly/qNQxd*), and WSO2 Micro Integrator (*https://oreil.ly/f6izc*)) also offer cloud native variants of their platform that can be used to build service composition patterns. Such offerings are also available as *integration platform as a service (iPaaS)*, a fully managed service for creating service compositions (for example, Boomi (*https://boomi.com*), Azure Logic Apps (*https://oreil.ly/NjbIw*), and MuleSoft Anypoint Platform (*https://oreil.ly/wk6fP*)). For workflows and Saga implementations, you can use dedicated workflow engines such as Camunda (*https://oreil.ly/gZV8n*), Netflix Conductor (*https://oreil.ly/SrIpO*), or Uber's Cadence (*https://cadenceworkflow.io*), to execute service composition in a stateful and transactional way

Summary of Service Composition Patterns

Table 3-2 summarizes the service composition patterns, and indicates when to use and when to not use each.

Table 3-2. Service composition patterns

Pattern	When to use	When not to use
Service Orchestration	The business use case requires one service to handle all the interactions with other services and systems. Usually suitable for interactive services.	Not suitable if the coupling between services is a concern. Not suitable when the majority of your use case is based on asynchronous messaging for events.
Service Choreography	You require service composition across event-driven microservices. You want to build fully decoupled microservices in a cloud native application.	Not well suited for interactive services such as APIs that are exposed to consumers.
Saga	Distributed transactions across multiple microservices are essential.	Not useful when the services cannot offer compensating operations that can execute transactionally. You shouldn't adopt it unless you have a framework or solution that can build the Saga execution for you. (Implementing Saga from scratch is overwhelmingly complex.)

Summary

Cloud native applications are distributed applications that consist of a collection of microservices and systems. In this chapter, we explored patterns that allow you to build connectivity among microservices as well as the other systems in your cloud native application in an efficient, resilient, secure, and scalable manner. You also learned how to use patterns to create services that require composition of multiple services and systems to realize the business capability that you want to implement. In

Chapter 7, we'll delve deeper into how these capabilities can be presented to consumers as managed APIs.

CHAPTER 4

Data Management Patterns

Data is the key for all applications. Even a simple echo service depends on the data in the incoming message in order to send a response. This chapter is all about data and its management in cloud native applications.

First, we'll focus on data architecture, explaining how data is collected, processed, and stored in cloud native applications. Then, we'll look at understanding data by categorizing it through multiple dimensions, based on how it is used in an application, its structure, and its scale. We'll discuss possible storage and processing options and how to make the best choice given a specific type of data.

We'll then move on to explaining various patterns related to data, focusing on centralized and decentralized data, data composition, caching, management, performance optimization, reliability, and security. The chapter also covers various technologies currently used in the industry to effectively implement these cloud native applications' development patterns.

This knowledge of data, patterns, and technologies together will help you design cloud native applications for your specific use case and for the type of data that your applications deal with.

Data Architecture

Cloud native applications should be able to collect, store, process, and present data in a way that fulfills our use cases (Figure 4-1).

Here, *data sources* are cloud native applications that feed data such as user inputs and sensor readings. They sometimes feed data into *data-ingestion systems* such as message brokers or, when possible, directly write to data stores. Data-ingestion systems can transfer data as events/messages to other applications or data stores; through these we will be able to achieve reliable and asynchronous data processing. (Chapter 5 provides more details about data-ingestion systems.)

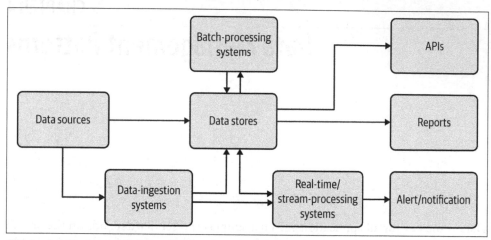

Figure 4-1. Data architecture for cloud native applications

The *data stores* are the critical part of this architecture; they store data in various formats and at scale to facilitate the use case. They are used as the source for generating reports and also used as the base of data APIs. We present more detail about data stores in the following sections.

Real-time and stream-processing systems process events on the fly and produce useful insights for the use case, as well as provide alerts and notifications when they happen. Chapter 6 covers these in detail. *Batch-processing systems* process data from data sources in batches, and write the processed output back to the data stores so it can be used for reporting or exposed via APIs. In these cases, the processing system may be reading data from one type of store and writing to another, such as reading from a filesystem and writing to a relational database. Batch processing of cloud native data is similar to traditional batch data processing, so we do not go into the details here.

Just as cloud native microservices have characteristics such as being scalable, resilient, and manageable, cloud native *data* has its own unique characteristics that are quite different from traditional data processing practices. Most important, cloud native data can be stored in many forms, in a variety of data formats and data stores. They are not expected to maintain a fixed schema and are encouraged to have duplicate data to facilitate availability and performance over consistency. Furthermore, in cloud native applications, multiple services are not encouraged to access the same database; instead, they should call respective service APIs that own the data store to access the data. All these provide separation of concerns and allow cloud native data to scale out.

Types and Forms of Data

Data, in its multiple forms, has a huge influence on applications—cloud native or not. This section discusses how data alters the execution of an application, the formats of this data, and how data can be best transmitted and stored.

Application behavior is influenced by the following three main types of data:

Input data

Sent as part of the input message by the user or client. Most commonly, this data is either JSON or XML messages, though binary formats such as gRPC and Thrift are getting some traction.

Configuration data

Provided by the environment as variables. XML has been used as the configuration language for a long time, and now YAML configs have become the de facto standard for cloud native applications.

State data

The data stored by the application itself, regarding its status, based on all messages and events that occurred before the current time. By persisting the state data and loading it on startup, the application will be able to seamlessly resume its functionality upon restart.

Applications that depend only on input and configuration (config) data are called *stateless applications*. These applications are relatively simple to implement and scale because their failure or restart has almost no impact on their execution. In contrast, applications that depend on input, config, and state data—*stateful applications*—are much more complex to implement and scale. The state of the application is stored in data stores, so application failures can result in partial writes that corrupt their state, which can lead to incorrect execution of the application.

Cloud native applications fall into both stateful and stateless categories. Chapter 3 covered stateless applications. This chapter focuses on stateful applications.

Cloud native applications use various forms of data, which are generally grouped into the following three categories:

Structured data

Can fit a predefined schema. For example, the data on a typical user registration form can be comfortably stored in a relational database.

Semi-structured data

Has some form of structure. For example, each field in a data entry may have a corresponding key or name that we can use to refer to it, but when we take all the entries, there is no guarantee that each entry will have the same number of fields or even common keys. This data can be easily represented through JSON, XML, and YAML formats.

Unstructured data

Does not contain any meaningful fields. Images, videos, and raw text content are examples. Usually, this data is stored without any understanding of its content.

Data Stores

We have to choose the data store type for cloud native data, based on the use case of the application. Different use cases use different types of data (structured, semi-structured, or unstructured) and have varying scalability and availability requirements. With the diverse storage options available, different data stores provide different characteristics, such as one providing high performance while another provides high scalability. At times we may even end up using more than one data store at the same time to achieve different characteristics. In this section, we look at common types of data stores, and when and how they can be used in cloud native applications.

Relational Databases

Relational databases are ideal for storing structured data that has a predefined schema. These databases use Structured Query Language (SQL) for processing, storing, and accessing data. They also follow the principle of defining *schema on write*: the data schema is defined before writing the data to the database.

Relational databases can optimally store and retrieve data by using database indexing and normalization. Because these databases support atomicity, consistency, isolation, and durability (ACID) properties, they can also provide transaction guarantees. Here, *atomicity* guarantees that all operations within a transaction are executed as a single unit; *consistency* ensures that the data is consistent before and after the transaction; *isolation* makes the intermediate state of a transaction invisible to other transactions; and, finally, *durability* guarantees that after a successful transaction, the data is persistent even in the event of a system failure. All these characteristics make relational databases ideal for implementing business-critical financial applications.

Relational databases do not work well with semi-structured data. For example, if we are storing product catalog data for an ecommerce site and the initial input contains product detail, price, some images, and reviews, we can't store all this data in a relational store. Here we need to extract only the most important and common fields such as product ID, name, detail, and price to store in a relational database, while storing the list of product reviews in NoSQL and images in a filesystem. However, this approach could impose performance degradation due to multiple lookups when retrieving all the data. In such cases, we recommend storing critical unstructured and semi-structured data fields such as the product thumbnail image as a blob or text in the relational data store to improve read performance. When taking this approach, always consider the cost and space consumption of relational databases.

Relational databases are a good option for storing cloud native application data. We recommend using a relational database per microservice, as this will help deploy and scale the data along with the microservice as a single deployment unit. It is important to remember that relational databases are not scalable by design. In terms of scaling, they can support only primary/secondary architecture, allowing one node for write operations while having multiple worker nodes for read operations.

Therefore, we recommend using relational databases in cloud native applications when the number of records in the store will never exceed the limit that the database can efficiently process. If we can foresee that the data will constantly grow, such as with the number of orders, logs, or notifications stored, then we may need to deploy data-scaling patterns to relational data stores that we discuss later in this chapter, or we should look for other alternatives.

NoSQL Databases

The term *NoSQL* is usually misunderstood as *not SQL*. Rather, it is better explained as *not only SQL*. This is because these databases still have some good SQL-like query support and behaviors along with many other benefits, such as scalability, and the ability to store and process semi-structured data. NoSQL databases follow the principle of *schema on read*: the schema of the data is defined only at the time of accessing the data for processing, and not when it is written to the disk.

These databases are best suited to handling big data, as they are designed for scalability and performance. As NoSQL stores are distributed in nature, we can use them across multiple cloud native applications. To optimize performance, data stored in NoSQL databases is usually not normalized and can have redundant fields. When the data is normalized, table joins will need to be performed when retrieving data, and this can be time-consuming because of the distributed nature of these databases. Further, only a few NoSQL stores support transactions while compromising their performance and scalability; therefore, it is generally not recommended to store data in NoSQL stores that need transaction guarantees.

The usage of NoSQL stores in cloud native applications varies, as there are various types of NoSQL stores, and unlike relational databases, they do not have behavioral commonalities. These NoSQL stores can be categorized by the way they store data and by the consistency and availability guarantees they provide.

Some common NoSQL stores categorized by the way they store data are as follows:

Key-value store
> This holds records as key-value pairs. We can use this for storing login session information based on session IDs. These types of stores are heavily used for caching data. Redis is one popular open source key-value data stores. Memcached and Ehcache are other popular options.

Column store
> This stores multiple key (column) and value pairs in each of its rows, as shown in Figure 4-2. These stores are a good example of *schema on read*: we can write any number of columns during the write phase, and when data is retrieved, we can specify only the columns we are interested in processing. The most widely used column store is Apache Cassandra. For those who use big data and Apache Hadoop infrastructure, Apache HBase can be an option as it is part of the Hadoop ecosystem.

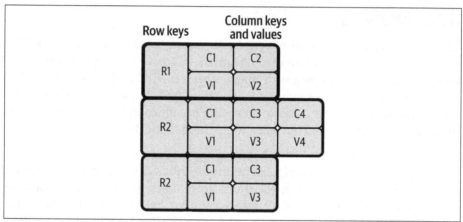

Figure 4-2. Column store

Document store
> This can store semi-structured data such as JSON and XML documents. This also allows us to process stored documents by using JSON and XML path expressions. These data stores are popular as they can store JSON and XML messages, which are usually used by frontend applications and APIs for communication. MongoDB, Apache CouchDB, and CouchBase are popular options for storing JSON documents.

Graph store
> These store data as nodes and use edges to represent the relationship between data nodes. These stores are multidimensional and are useful for building and querying networks such as networks of friends in social media and transaction

networks for detecting fraud. Neo4j, the most popular graph data store, is heavily used by industry leaders.

Many other types of NoSQL stores, including object stores and time-series data stores, can help store and query use-case-specific specialized data. Some stores also have multimodel behavior; they can fall into several of the preceding categories. For example, Amazon DynamoDB can work as a key-value and document store, and Azure Cosmos DB can work as a key-value, column, document, and graph store.

NoSQL stores are distributed, so they need to adhere to the CAP theorem; *CAP* stands for *consistency, availability, and partition tolerance*. This theorem states that a distributed application can provide either full availability or consistency; we cannot achieve both while providing network partition tolerance. Here, *availability* means that the system is fully functional when some of its nodes are down, *consistency* means an update/change in one node is immediately propagated to other nodes, and *partition tolerance* means that the system can continue to work even when some nodes cannot connect to each other. Some stores prioritize consistency over availability, while others prioritize availability over consistency.

Say we need to keep track of and report the number of citizens in the country, and missing the latest data in the calculation will not cause significant error in the final outcome. We can use a data store that favors *availability*. On the other hand, when we need to track transactions for business purposes, we need to choose a data store that favors *consistency*.

Table 4-1 categorizes NoSQL data stores in terms of consistency and availability.

Table 4-1. NoSQL data stores favoring consistency and availability

	Favor consistency	Favor availability
Key-value stores	Redis, Memcached	DynamoDB, Voldemort
Column stores	Google Cloud Bigtable, Apache HBase	Apache Cassandra
Document stores	MongoDB, Terrastore	CouchDB, SimpleDB
Graph stores	Azure Cosmos DB	Neo4j

Though some favor consistency and others favor availability, still other NoSQL data stores (such as Cassandra and DynamoDB) can provide both. For example, in Cassandra we can define consistency levels such as One, Quorum, or All. When the consistency level is set to One, data is read/written to only one node in the cluster, providing full availability with eventual consistency. During eventual consistency, data is eventually propagated to other nodes, and reads can be outdated during this period. On the other hand, when set to All, data is read/written from all nodes before the operation succeeds, providing strong consistency with performance degradation. But when using Quorum, it reads/writes data from only 51% of the nodes. Through this, we can ensure that the latest update will be available in at least one node, providing both consistency and availability with a minimum performance overhead.

Therefore, we recommend that you understand the nature of the data and its use cases within cloud native applications before choosing the right NoSQL data store. Remember that the data format, as well as the consistency and availability requirements of the data, can influence your choice of data store.

Filesystem Storage

Filesystem storage is the best for storing unstructured data in cloud native applications. Unlike NoSQL stores, it does not try to understand the data but rather purely optimizes data storage and retrieval. We can also use filesystem storage to store large application data as a cache, as it can be cheaper than retrieving data repeatedly over the network.

Though this is the cheapest option, it may not be an optimal solution when storing text or semi-structured data, as this will force us to load multiple files when searching for a single data entry. In these cases, we recommend using indexing systems such as Apache Solr or Elasticsearch to facilitate search.

When data needs to be stored at scale, distributed filesystems can be used. The most well-known open source option is Hadoop Distributed File System (HDFS), and popular cloud options include Amazon Simple Storage Service (S3), Azure Storage services, and Google Cloud Storage.

Data Store Summary

We've discussed three types of data stores: relational, NoSQL, and filesystem. Cloud native applications should use relational data stores when they need transactional guarantees and when data needs to be tightly coupled with the application.

When data contains semi-structured or unstructured fields, they can be separated and stored in NoSQL or filesystem stores to achieve scalability while still preserving transactional guarantees. The applications can choose to store in NoSQL when the data quantity is extremely large, needs a querying capability, or is semi- structured, or the data store is specialized enough to handle the specific application use case such as graph processing.

In all other cases, we recommend storing the data in filesystem stores, as they are optimized for data storage and retrieval without processing their content. Next, we will see how this data can be deployed, managed, and shared among cloud native applications.

Data Management

Now that we've covered the types of data and corresponding data stores used for developing cloud native applications, this section discusses how your data and data store can be deployed, managed, and shared among those applications. Data can be managed through centralized, decentralized, or hybrid techniques. We'll delve deeply into each option next.

Centralized Data Management

Centralized data management is the most common type in traditional data-centric applications. In this approach, all data is stored in a single database, and multiple components of the application are allowed to access the data for processing (Figure 4-3).

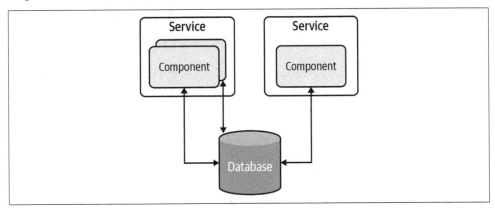

Figure 4-3. Centralized data management in a traditional data-centric application

This approach has several advantages; for instance, the data in these database tables can be normalized, providing high data consistency. Furthermore, as components can access all the tables, the centralized data storage provides the ability to run stored procedures across multiple tables and to retrieve results faster. On the other hand, this provides tight coupling between applications, and hinders the ability to evolve the applications independently. Therefore, it is considered an antipattern when building cloud native applications.

Decentralized Data Management

To overcome problems with centralized data management, each independent functional component can be modeled as a microservice that has separate data stores, exclusive to each of them. This *decentralized data management* approach, illustrated in Figure 4-4, allows us to scale microservices independently without impacting other microservices.

These databases do not introduce the coupling that can make change riskier and more difficult. Although application owners have less freedom to manage or evolve the data, segregating it in each microservice so that it's managed by its teams/owners not only solves data management and ownership problems, but also improves the development time of new feature implementations and release cycles.

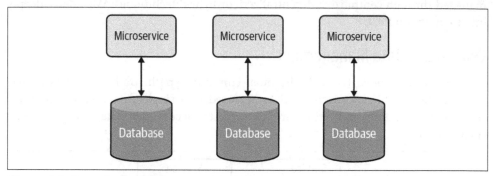

Figure 4-4. Decentralized data management

Decentralized data management allows services to choose the most appropriate data store for their use case. For example, a Payment service may use a relational database to perform transactions, while an Inquiry service may use a document store to store the details of the inquiry, and a Shopping Cart service may use a distributed key-value store to store the items picked by the customer.

Hybrid Data Management

Apart from the benefits of using a single database that we discussed in the preceding section, there are other operational advantages it can provide. For example, it helps achieve compliance with modern data-protection laws and ease security enforcement as data resides in a central place. Therefore, it is advisable to have all customer data managed via a few microservices within a secured bounded context, and to provide ownership of the data to one or a few well-trained teams to apply data-protection policies.

On the other hand, one of the disadvantages of decentralized data management is the cost of running separate data stores for each service. Therefore, for some small and medium organizations, we can use a *hybrid data management* approach (Figure 4-5). This allows multiple microservices to share the same database, provided these services are governed by the same team and reside in the same bounded context.

But when using hybrid data management, we have to make sure that our services do not directly access tables owned by other services. Otherwise, this will increase the system's complexity and make it difficult to separate data into multiple databases in the future.

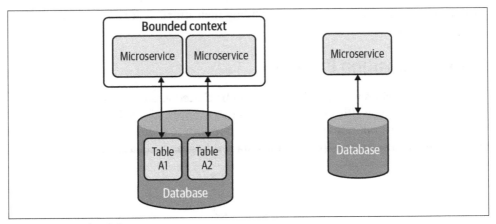

Figure 4-5. Hybrid data management

Data Management Summary

In this section, we looked at how cloud native applications are modeled as independent microservices, and how we achieve scalability, maintainability, and security, by exclusively using separate data stores for each microservice (Figure 4-6).

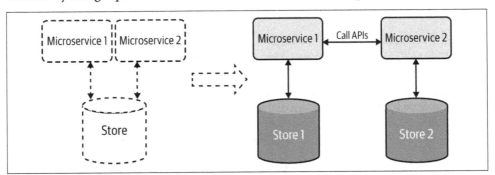

Figure 4-6. Cloud native applications, depicted at right, have a dedicated data store for each microservice.

We've seen how applications communicate with each other via well-defined APIs, and we can use this approach to retrieve data from respective applications without accessing their data stores directly.

Now that we've covered the types and formats of data, as well as storage and management options, let's dig into the data-related patterns that we can apply when developing our cloud native applications. The *data management patterns* provide a good way to understand how to better handle data with respect to data composition, scalability, performance optimization, reliability, and security. Relevant data management patterns are discussed in detail next, including their usage, real-world use cases, considerations, and related patterns.

Data Composition Patterns

This section describes ways in which data can be shared and combined in a meaningful way that helps you efficiently build cloud native applications. Let's consider a simple cloud native application and its data store, shown in Figure 4-7. Here the application's microservice fully owns the data residing in its data store.

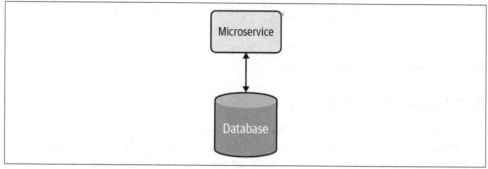

Figure 4-7. Basic cloud native microservice

When the service is under high load, it can introduce high latency due to longer data-retrieval time. This can be mitigated by using a cache (Figure 4-8). This reduces the load on the database when multiple read requests occur and improves the overall performance of the service. More information on caching patterns and other performance optimization techniques are discussed in detail later in this chapter.

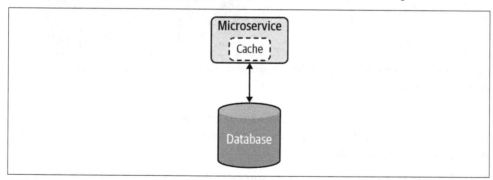

Figure 4-8. Cloud native microservice with cache

When the functionality of the service becomes more complex, the service can be split into smaller microservices (Figure 4-9). During this phase, relevant data will also be split and moved along with the new services, as having multiple services share the same data is not recommended.

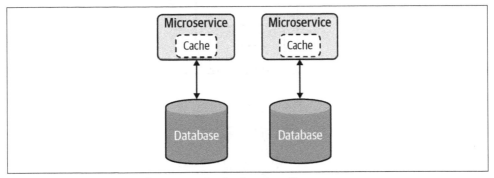

Figure 4-9. Segregation of microservice by functionality

At times, splitting the data in two might not be straightforward, and we might need an alternative option for sharing data in a safe and reusable manner. The following Data Service pattern explains in detail how this can be handled.

Data Service Pattern

The *Data Service pattern* exposes data in the database as a service, referred to as a *data service*. The data service becomes the owner, responsible for adding and removing data from the data store. The service may perform simple lookups or even encapsulate complex operations when constructing responses for data requests.

How it works

Exposing data as a data service, shown in Figure 4-10, provides us more control over that data. This allows us to present data in various compositions to various clients, apply security, and enforce priority-based throttling, allowing only critical services to access data during resource-constraint situations such as load spikes or system failures.

These data services can perform simple read and write operations to a database or even perform complex logic such as joining multiple tables or running stored procedures to build responses much more efficiently. These data services can also utilize caching to enhance their read performance.

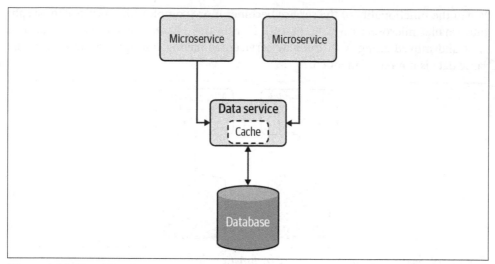

Figure 4-10. Data Service pattern

How it's used in practice

This pattern can be used when we need to allow access to data that does not belong to a single microservice, or when we need to abstract legacy/proprietary data stores to other cloud native applications.

Allow multiple microservices to access the same data.   We can use this pattern when the data does not belong to any particular microservice; no microservice is the rightful owner of that data, yet multiple microservices are depending on it for their operation. In such cases, the common data should be exposed as an independent data service, allowing all dependent applications to access the data via APIs.

For example, say an ecommerce system has Order and Product Detail microservices that need to access discount data. Because the discount does not belong to either of those microservices, a separate service should be created to expose discount data. Now, both Order and Product Detail microservices should access the new discount data service via APIs for information.

Expose abstract legacy/proprietary data stores.   We can also use this pattern to expose legacy on-premises or proprietary data stores to other cloud native applications. Let's imagine that we have a legacy database to record all business transactions for our proprietary on-premises application. In this case, if we need our cloud native applications to access that data, we need to use its C# database driver and make sure all of them know the table and structure of the database to access the data.

It might be not a good idea to access the database directly through the driver, as this will force us to write all our cloud native applications in C#, and all our applications should also embed the knowledge of the table. Instead, we can create a single data service that fronts the legacy database and exposes that data via well-defined APIs. This will allow other cloud native applications to access the data via APIs and decouple themselves from the underlying database table and programming language. This will also allow us to migrate the database to a different one in the future without affecting services that are depending on the data service.

Considerations

When building cloud native applications, accessing the same data via multiple microservices is considered an antipattern. This will introduce tight coupling between the microservices and not allow the microservices to scale and evolve on their own. The Data Service pattern can help reduce coupling by providing managed APIs to access data.

This pattern should not be used when the data can clearly be associated with an existing microservice, as introducing unnecessary microservices will cause additional management complexity.

Related patterns

The following patterns, all covered in this chapter, are related to the Data Service pattern:

Caching pattern
> Provides an opportunity to optimize the efficiency of data retrieval by using local or distributed caching when exposing data via a service.

Performance optimization patterns
> Apart from caching data, these execute complex queries such as table joins and running stored procedures directly in the database to improve performance.

Materialized View pattern
> Accessing data via an API can still be performance-intensive. For use cases that need joins to be performed with data that resides in stores belonging to other services, having that data replicated in its local store and building a materialized view can help improve query performance.

Vault Key pattern
> Along with API security, knowing who is accessing the data can help identify the caller and enforce adequate security and data protection.

Composite Data Services Pattern

The *Composite Data Services pattern* performs data composition by combining data from more than one data service and, when needed, performs fairly complex aggregation to provide a richer and more concise response. This pattern is also called the *Server-Side Mashup pattern*, as data composition happens at the service and not at the data consumer.

How it works

This pattern, which resembles the Service Orchestration pattern from Chapter 3, combines data from various services and its own data store into one composite data service. This pattern not only eliminates the need for multiple microservices to perform data composition operations, but also allows the combined data to be cached for improving performance (Figure 4-11).

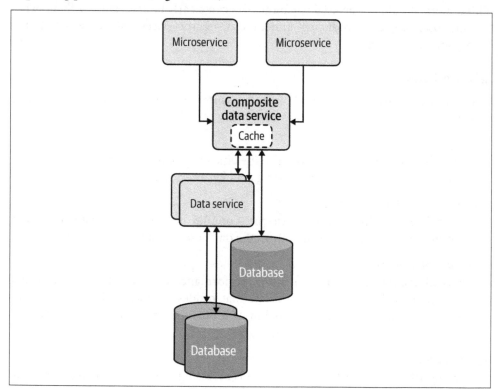

Figure 4-11. Composite Data Services pattern

How it's used in practice

This pattern can be used when we need to eliminate multiple microservices repeating the same data composition. Data services that are fine-grained force clients to query multiple services to build their desired data. We can use this pattern to reduce duplicate work done by the clients and consolidate it into a common service.

Let's take an ecommerce system that calculates product inventory by aggregating various data services exposed by different fulfillment stores. In this case, introducing a common service to combine data from all fulfillment services can be beneficial, as this will help remove the duplicate work, reduce the complexity of each client, and help the composite data services evolve without hindering the clients.

When such data is cached at the composite data service, the response time for inventory information can also be improved. This is because, in a given time frame, most of the microservices will be accessing the same set of data, and caching can drastically improve their read performance.

Considerations

Use this pattern only when the consolidation is generic enough and other microservices will be able to reuse the consolidated data. We do not recommend introducing unnecessary layers of services if they do not provide meaningful data compositions that can be reused. Weigh the benefits of reusability and simplicity of the clients against the additional latency and management complexity added by the service layers.

Related patterns

The Composite Data Services pattern is related to the following (both covered in this chapter):

Caching pattern
    Provides an opportunity to optimize the efficiency of data retrieval and helps achieve resiliency by serving data from the cache when backends are not available.

Client-Side Mashup pattern
    Allows the data mashup to happen at the client side, such as in the user's browser. This can be a good solution when asynchronous data loading is feasible and when meaningful data composition can be performed with partial data.

Client-Side Mashup Pattern

In the *Client-Side Mashup pattern*, data is retrieved from various services and consolidated at the client side. The client is usually a browser loading data via asynchronous Ajax calls.

How it works

This pattern utilizes asynchronous data loading, as shown in Figure 4-12. For example, when a browser using this pattern is loading a web page, it loads and renders part of the web page first, while loading the rest of the web page. This pattern uses client-side scripts such as JavaScript to asynchronously load the content in the web browser.

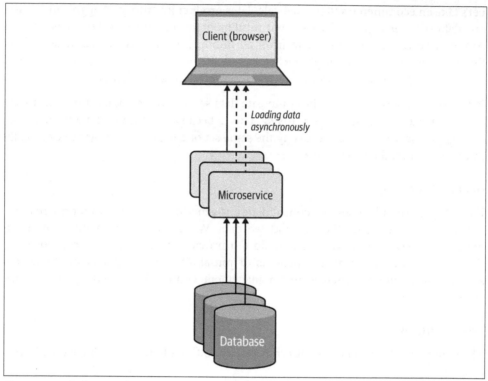

Figure 4-12. Client-Side Mashup at a web browser

Rather than letting the user wait for a longer time by loading all content on the website at once, this pattern uses multiple asynchronous calls to fetch different parts of the website and renders each fragment when it arrives. These applications are also referred to as *rich internet applications (RIAs)*.

How it's used in practice

This pattern can be used when we need to present available data as soon as possible, while providing more detail later, or when we want to give a perception that the web page is loading much faster.

Present critical data with low latency. Let's take a use case of an ecommerce system like Amazon; when the user loads a product detail page, we should be able to present all the critical data that the user expects, with the lowest latency. Getting these product reviews and loading images can take time, so we render the page with basic product details with the default image, and then use Ajax calls to load other product images and reviews, and update the web page dynamically. This approach will allow us to deliver the most critical data to the user much faster than waiting for all data to be fetched.

Give a perception that the web page is loading faster. If we are retrieving loosely related HTML content and building the web page while the user is loading it, and if we can allow the user to view part of the content while the rest is being loaded, then we can give the perception that the web site is loading faster. This keeps the user engaged with the website until the rest of the data is available and can ultimately improve the user experience.

Considerations

Use this pattern only when the partial data loaded first can be presented to the user or used in a meaningful way. We do not advise using this pattern when the retrieved data needs to be combined and transformed with later data via some sort of a join before it can be presented to the user.

Related patterns

The Client-Side Mashup pattern is related to the following patterns (covered in this chapter):

Composite Data Services pattern
> This is useful when content needs to be mashed synchronously and the composite data is common enough to be used by multiple services.

Caching pattern
> Provides an opportunity to cache data to improve the overall latency.

Summary of Data Composition Patterns

This section outlined commonly used patterns of data composition in cloud native application development. Table 4-2 summarizes when we should and should not use these patterns and the benefits of each.

Table 4-2. Data composition patterns

Pattern	When to use	When not to use	Benefits
Data Service	Data is not owned by a single microservice, yet multiple microservices are depending on the data for their operation.	Data can clearly be associated with an existing microservice, as introducing unnecessary microservices can also cause management complexity.	Reduces the coupling between services. Provides more control/security on the operations that can be performed on the shared data.
Composite Data Services	Many clients query multiple services to consolidate their desired data, and this consolidation is generic enough to be reused among the clients.	Only one client needs the consolidation. Operations performed by clients cannot be generalized to be reused by many clients.	Reduces duplicate work done by the clients and consolidates it into a common service. Provides more data resiliency by using caches or static data.
Client-Side Mashup	Some meaningful operations can be performed with partial data; for example, rendering nondependent data in web browsers.	Processing, such as a join, is required on the independently retrieved data before sending the response.	Results in more-responsive applications. Reduces the wait time.

Data Scaling Patterns

When load increases in cloud native applications, either the service or the store can become a bottleneck. The patterns for scaling services are discussed in Chapter 3. Here, we will see how to scale data. When the data can be categorized as big data, we can use NoSQL databases or distributed filesystems. These systems do the heavy lifting of scaling and partitioning the data and reduce the development and management complexity.

Nevertheless, consistency and transactional requirements of business-critical applications may still require us to use relational databases, and as relational databases do not scale by default, we might need to alter the application architecture to achieve data scalability. In this section, we'll dive deep into the patterns that can help us facilitate the scaling of data stores to optimally store and retrieve data.

Data Sharding Pattern

In the *Data Sharding pattern*, the data store is divided into *shards*, which allows it to be easily stored and retrieved at scale. The data is partitioned by one or more of its attributes so we can easily identify the shard in which it resides.

How it works

To shard the data, we can use horizontal, vertical, or functional approaches. Let's look at these three options in detail:

Horizontal data sharding

Each shard has the same schema, but contains distinct data records based on its sharding key. A table in a database is split across multiple nodes based on these sharding keys. For example, user orders can be shared by hashing the order ID into three shards, as depicted in Figure 4-13.

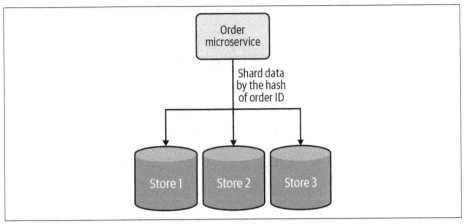

Figure 4-13. Horizontal data sharding using hashing

Vertical data sharding

Each shard does not need to have an identical schema and can contain various data fields. Each shard can contain a set of tables that do not need to be in another shard. This is useful when we need to partition the data based on the frequency of data access; we can put the most frequently accessed data in one shard and move the rest into a different shard. Figure 4-14 depicts how frequently accessed user data is sharded from the other data.

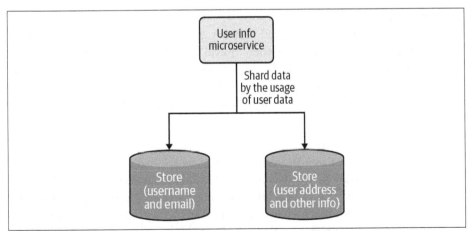

Figure 4-14. Vertical data sharding based on frequency of data access

Functional data sharding

Data is partitioned by functional use cases. Rather than keeping all the data together, the data can be segregated in different shards based on different functionalities. This also aligns with the process of segregating functions into separate functional services in the cloud native application architecture. Figure 4-15 shows how product details and reviews are sharded into two data stores.

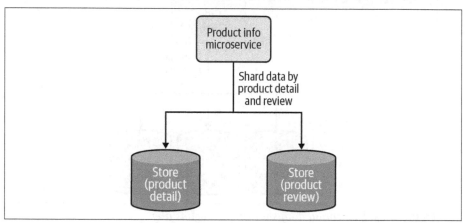

Figure 4-15. Functional data sharding by segregating product details and reviews into two data stores

Cloud native applications can use all three approaches to scale data, but there is a limit to how much the vertical and functional sharding can segregate the data. Eventually, horizontal data sharding needs to be brought in to scale the data further. When we use horizontal data sharding, we can deploy one of the following techniques to locate where we have stored the data:

Lookup-based data sharding

A lookup service or distributed cache is used to store the mapping of the shard key and the actual location of the physical data. When retrieving the data, the client application will first check the lookup service to resolve the actual physical location for the intended shard key, and then access the data from that location. If the data gets rebalanced or resharded later, the client has to again look up the updated data location.

Range-based data sharding

This special type of sharding approach can be applied when the sharding key has sequential characters. The data is shared in ranges, and as in lookup-based sharding, a lookup service can be used to determine where the given data range is available. This approach yields the best results for sharding keys based on date and time. A data range of a month, for example, may reside in the same shard, allowing the service to retrieve all the data in one go, rather than querying multiple shards.

Hash-based data sharding

Constructing a shard key based on the data fields or dividing the data by date range may not always result in balanced shards. At times we need to distribute the data randomly to generate better-balanced shards. This can be done by using hash-based data sharding, which creates hashes based on the shard key and uses them to determine the shard data location. This approach is not the best when data is queried in ranges, but is ideal when individual records are queried. Here, we can also use a lookup service to store the hash key and the shard location mapping, to facilitate data loading.

For sharding to be useful, the data should contain one or a collection of fields that uniquely identifies the data or meaningfully groups it into subsets. The combination of these fields generates the shard/partition key that will be used to locate the data. The values stored in the fields that contribute to the shard key should be fixed and never be changed upon data updates. This is because when they change, they will also change the shard key, and if the updated shard key now points to a different shard location, the data also needs to be migrated from the current shard to the new shard location. Moving data among shards is time-consuming, so this should be avoided at all costs.

How it's used in practice

This pattern can be used when we can no longer store data in a single node, or when we need data to be distributed so we can access it with lower latency.

Scale beyond a single node. This pattern can be useful when resources such as storage, computation, or network bandwidth become a bottleneck. A system's ability to vertically scale is always limited when adding more resources such as disk space, RAM, or network bandwidth; sooner or later, the application will run out of resources. Instead of working on short-term solutions, partitioning the data and scaling horizontally will help you scale beyond the capacity of a single node.

Segregate data to improve data-retrieval time. We can segregate data by combining multiple data fields to generate special shard keys. For example, let's imagine we have an online fashion store and have created a shard key that combines a dress type and brand in order to store data. If we know the type and brand of the dress that we are searching for, we will be able to map that to the relevant shard and quickly retrieve the data. But if we know only the type and size of the dress, we cannot construct a valid shard key. In this case, we need to search all shards to find the match, and this can greatly impact our performance.

This problem can be overcome by building hierarchical shard keys. For example, we can build the key with the dress `type` / `brand`. If we know the dress type, we can look up all shards that have that dress `type` and then search them for the particular dress `size`. This restricts the number of shards that we need to search and improves performance. If we need even better performance for the `type` and `size` combination, we can create secondary indexes using them. These secondary shard keys can help us retrieve the data with low latency. But the use of secondary indexes can increase the data modification cost, as now we also need to update the secondary shard keys when data is updated.

We can also shard the data by date and time ranges. For example, if we are processing orders, we are likely more interested in recent orders than old ones. We can shard data by time ranges and store the most recent orders (such as last-month or last-quarter orders) in a hot shard and the rest in a set of archived shards. This can help retrieve the critical data with efficiency. In this case, we should also periodically move the data from the hot shard to archive shards when it becomes old.

Geographically distribute data. When the clients are geographically distributed, we can shard the data by region and move the relevant data closer to them. For example, in a retail website use case, details about products sold in each region can be stored and served locally. This will help serve more requests at a lower turnaround time.

Some clients may be interested in buying products from around the world, so we might need to retrieve data from multiple shards distributed across regions to fulfill a request. For this use case to work efficiently, we need to model the clients in such a way that they can issue a fan-out request to all the shards and retrieve data concurrently. For example if a user is searching the products, we can send a fan-out request and just respond with the first 10 fastest entries we receive, but if the user is searching for the lowest-price options by name, we might need to wait for the response to arrive from all shards before showing the results. Note that we might be able to improve the performance with caching. We discuss that later in this chapter.

Considerations

When we use this pattern, it is important to balance the shards as much as possible in order for the load to distribute evenly. It is also necessary to monitor the load in each shard and perform a rebalance if the load is not distributed evenly. Imbalance can happen over time, due to new data skew with insertions, deletions, or a change in querying behavior. Keep in mind that with big data, rebalancing of data stores can take a couple of hours to days.

To facilitate rebalancing, we recommend making the shards reasonably smaller. In the initial days of the system, when the data and load are low, all shards can live in the same node. Eventually, when load increases, one or a collection of shards can be migrated to other nodes. This not only allows greater scalability in the long run, but also makes each shard migration relatively small, allowing the data rebalancing to happen faster with less interruption to the whole system.

It is also important to have multiple copies of shards to gracefully handle failures. Even when a node is down, we will have access to the same data in another node, and this can help us perform maintenance without making the full system unavailable.

When it comes to processing data aggregation across shards, different aggregations behave differently. Aggregations such as sum, average, minimum, and maximum can process the data in isolation at each partition, retrieve the results, and combine them to determine the final results. In contrast, aggregation operations such as median require the whole data at once, so this cannot be implemented with high precision when using sharded data.

We don't recommend using auto-incrementing fields when generating shard keys. Shards do not communicate with each other, and because of the use of auto-incrementing fields, multiple shards may have generated the same keys and refer to different data with those keys locally. This can become a problem when the data is redistributed during data-rebalancing operations.

Furthermore, it is important to select shard keys that will result in fairly balanced shards. Without balanced shards, the expected scalability cannot be achieved. The largest shard is always going to be the worst-performing one and will eventually cause bottlenecks.

Related patterns

The Data Sharding pattern is related to the following (both covered in this chapter):

Materialized View pattern
This can be used to replicate the dependent data of each shard to the local stores of the service, to improve data-querying performance and eliminate multiple lookup calls to data stores or services. This data can be replicated with only eventual consistency, so this approach is useful only if consistency on the dependent data is not business-critical for the applications.

Data Locality pattern
Having all the relevant data at the shard will allow the creation of indexes and execution of stored procedures for efficient data retrieval.

Command and Query Responsibility Segregation Pattern

The *Command and Query Responsibility Segregation (CQRS) pattern* separates updates and query operations of a data set, and allows them to run on different data stores. This results in faster data update and retrieval. It also facilitates modeling data to handle multiple use cases, achieves high scalability and security, and allows update and query models to evolve independently with minimal interactions.

How it works

We can separate commands (updates/writes) and queries (reads) by creating different services responsible for each (Figure 4-16). This not only facilitates running services related to update and reads on different nodes, but also helps model services appropriate for those operations and independently scale the services.

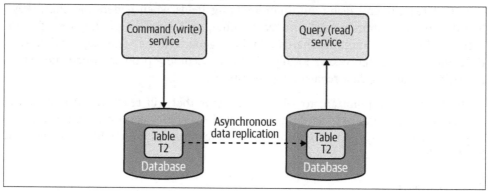

Figure 4-16. Separating command and query operations

The command and query should not have data store–specific information but rather have high-level data relevant to the application. When a command is issued to a service, it extracts the information from the message and updates the data store. Then it will send that information as an event asynchronously to the services that serve the queries, such that they can build their data model. The Event Sourcing pattern using a log-based queue system like Kafka can be used to pass the events between services. Through this, the query services can read data from the event queues and perform bulk updates on their local stores, in the optimal format for serving that data.

How it's used in practice

We can use this pattern when we want to use different domain models for commands and queries, and when we need to separate updates and data retrieval for performance and security reasons. Let's look at these approaches in detail next.

Use different domain models for command and query. For a retail website, we may be storing the product detail and inventory information in a normalized relational database. This might be our best choice to efficiently update inventory information upon each purchase. But this may not be the best option for querying this data via a browser, as joining and converting the data to JSON can be time-consuming. If that is the case, we can use this pattern to asynchronously build a query data set, such as a document store storing data in JSON format, and use that for querying. Then we will have separate optimized data models for both command and query operations.

Because command and query models are not tightly coupled, we can use different teams to own command- and query-related applications, as well as allow both models to evolve independently according to the use case.

Distribute operations and reduce data contention. This pattern can be used when cloud native applications have performance-intensive update operations such as data and security validations, or message transformations, or have performance-intensive query operations containing complex joins or data mapping. When the same instance of the data store is used for both command and query, it can produce poor overall performance due to higher load on the data store. Therefore, by splitting the command and query operations, CQRS not only eliminates the impact of one on the other by improving the performance and scalability of the system, but also helps isolate operations that need higher security enforcement.

Because this pattern allows commands and queries to be executed in different stores, it also enables the command and query systems to have different scaling requirements. In the retail website use case, we have more queries than commands, and have more product detail views than actual purchases. Hence, we can have most services support query operations and a couple of services perform the updates.

Considerations

Because this pattern segregates the command and query operations, it can provide high availability. Even if some command or query services become unavailable, the full system will not be halted. In this pattern, we can scale the query operations infinitely, and with an appropriate number of replications, the query operations can provide guarantees of zero downtime. When scaling command operations, we might need to use patterns such as Data Sharding to partition data and eliminate potential merge conflicts.

CQRS is not recommended when high consistency is required between command and query operations. When data is updated, the updates are sent asynchronously to the query stores via events by using patterns such as Event Sourcing. Hence, use CQRS only when eventual consistency is tolerable. Achieving high consistency with synchronous data replication is not recommended in cloud native application environments as it can cause lock contention and introduce high latencies.

When using this pattern, we may not be able to automatically generate separate command and query models by using tools such as object-relational mapping (ORM). Most of these tools use database schemas and usually produce combined models, so we may need to manually modify the models or write them from scratch.

 Though this pattern looks fascinating, remember that it can introduce lots of complexity to the system architecture. We now need to keep various data sources updated by sending events via the Event Sourcing pattern, as well as handle event duplicates and failures. Therefore, if the command and query models are quite simple, and the business logic is not complex, we strongly advise you to not use this pattern. It can introduce more management complexity than the advantages it can produce.

Related patterns

The following are related to CQRS:

Event Sourcing pattern
> Allows command services to communicate updates to query services, and allows both command and query models to reside on different data stores. This provides only eventual consistency between command and query models and adds complexity to the system architecture. Chapter 5 covers this pattern in detail.

Materialized View pattern
> Recommended over the CQRS pattern to achieve scalability, when command and query models are simple enough; Materialized View is covered in the next section.

Data Sharding pattern
> Helps scale commands by partitioning the data (as covered previously in this chapter). As query operations can simply be replicated, applying this pattern for queries may not produce any performance benefit.

API security
> Can be applied to enforce security for both command and query services.

Summary of Data Scaling Patterns

This section outlined commonly used patterns of data scaling in cloud native application development. Table 4-3 summarizes when we should and should not use these patterns and the benefits of each.

Table 4-3. Data scaling patterns

Pattern	When to use	When not to use	Benefits
Data Sharding	Data contains one or a collection of fields that uniquely identify the data or meaningfully group the data into subsets.	Shard key cannot produce evenly balanced shards. The operations performed in the data require the whole set of data to be processed; for example, obtaining a median from the data set.	Groups shards based on the preferred set of fields that produce the shard key. Creates geographically optimized shards that can be moved closer to the clients. Builds hierarchical shards or time-range-based shards to optimize the search time. Uses secondary indexes to query data by using nonshard keys.
Command and Query Responsibility Segregation (CQRS)	Applications have performance-intensive update operations with: • Data validations • Security validations • Message transformations For performance-intensive query operations such as complex joins or data mapping.	High consistency is required between command (update) and query (read). Command and query models are closer to each other.	Reduces the impact between command and query operations. Stores command and query data in two different data stores that suit their use cases. Enforces separated command/query security policies. Enables different teams to own applications that are responsible for command and query operations. Provides high availability.

Performance Optimization Patterns

In distributed cloud native applications, data is often the most common cause of bottlenecks. Data is difficult to scale, as consistency requirements can cause lock contention and synchronization overhead. All of this results in systems that perform poorly.

One primitive way of improving performance is by indexing data. Though this improves lookup performance, overuse of indexes can impair both read and write performance. For every write operation, all indexes need to be updated, causing databases to perform multiple writes. Similarly, when it comes to reads, data stores might not be able to load all indexes and keep them in memory. Each query might need to perform a couple of read operations, resulting in more time to fetch data.

Data denormalization is also a good technique for simplifying read models, as it can eliminate the need for joins and drastically improve read performance. This can be especially useful when we combine this approach with the CQRS pattern, as writers can use normalized data stores to maintain high consistency while allowing queries to read from denormalized data with efficiency.

In addition to these simple techniques, let's discuss how to improve performance by moving data closer to the execution, moving execution closer to the data, reducing the amount of data being transferred, or by storing preprocessed data for future use. This section discusses such patterns in detail.

Materialized View Pattern

The *Materialized View pattern* provides the ability to retrieve data efficiently upon querying, by moving data closer to the execution and prepopulating materialized views. This pattern stores all relevant data of a service in its local data store and formats the data optimally to serve the queries, rather than letting that service call dependent services for data when required.

How it works

This pattern replicates and moves data from dependent services to its local data store and builds materialized views (Figure 4-17). It also builds optimal views to efficiently query the data, similar to the Composite Data Services pattern.

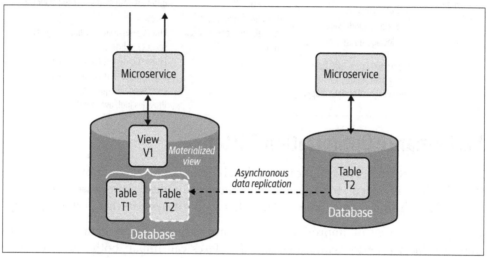

Figure 4-17. Service built with the Materialized View pattern

This pattern asynchronously replicates data from the dependent services. If databases support asynchronous data replication, we can use it as a way to transfer data from one data store to another. Failing this, we need to use the Event Sourcing pattern and use event streams to replicate the data. The source service pushes each insert, delete, and update operation asynchronously to an event stream, and they get propagated to the services that build materialized views, where they will fetch and load the data to their local stores. Chapter 5 discusses the Event Sourcing pattern in detail.

How it's used in practice

We can use this pattern when we want to improve data-retrieval efficiency by eliminating complex joins and to reduce coupling with dependent services.

Improve data-retrieval efficiency.   This pattern is used when part of the data is available locally and the rest needs to be fetched from external sources that incur high latency. For example, if we are serving a product detail page of an ecommerce application that, indeed, retrieves comments and ratings from a relatively slow review service, we might be rendering the data to the user with high latency. Through this pattern, the overall rating and precalculated best and worst comments can be replicated to the product detail service's data store to improve data-retrieval efficiency.

Even when we bring data into the same database, at times joining multiple tables can still be costly. In this case, we can use techniques like relational database views to consolidate data into an easily queryable materialized view. Then, when we need to retrieve product details, the detail service can serve the data with high efficiency.

Provide access to nonsensitive data hosted in secure systems.   In some use cases, our caller service might depend on nonsensitive data that is behind a security layer, requiring the service needs to authenticate and go through validation checks before retrieving the data. But through this pattern, we can replicate the nonsensitive data relevant to the service and allow the caller service to access the data directly from its local store. This approach not only removes unnecessary security checks and validations but also improves performance.

Considerations

Sometimes the dependent data may be stored in different types of data stores, or those stores can contain lots of unnecessary data. In this case, we should replicate only the relevant subset of data and store it in a format that can help build the materialized view. This will improve overall query performance by using data locally, and reduce bandwidth usage when transferring the data. We should always use asynchronous data replication, as synchronous data replication can cause lock contention and introduce high latencies.

The Materialized View pattern not only improves service performance by reducing the time to retrieve data, but also simplifies the service logic by eliminating unnecessary data processing and the need to know about dependent services.

This pattern also provides resiliency. As the data is replicated to the local store, the service will be able to perform its operations without any interruption, even when the source service that provided the data is unavailable.

We do not recommend using this pattern when data can be retrieved from dependent services with low latency, when data in the dependent services is changing quickly, or when the consistency of the data is considered important for the response. In these cases, this pattern can introduce unnecessary overhead and inconsistent behavior.

This pattern is not ideal when the amount of data that needs to be moved is huge or the data is updated frequently. This can cause replication delays and high network bandwidth, affecting accuracy and performance of the application. Consider using the Data Locality pattern (covered next) for these use cases.

Related patterns

The following are related to the Material View pattern; all but the last are covered in this chapter:

Data Locality pattern
Enables efficient data retrieval by moving the execution closer to the data.

Composite Data Services pattern
This can be used instead of the Materialized View pattern when data compositions can be done at the service level, or when dependent services have static data that can be cached locally at the service.

Command and Query Responsibility Segregation (CQRS) pattern
The Materialized View pattern can be used to serve query responses in the CQRS pattern. The command—the modifications to the data—will be done through the dependent service, and the query—the serving of the read requests—can be performed by query services constructing the materialized views.

Event Sourcing pattern
Provides an approach to replicate data from one source to another. Changes on dependent data are pushed as events through event streams, which are stored sequentially at a reliable log-based event queue such as Kafka, and then the services that serve the data read those event streams and constantly update their local storage to serve updated information. Chapter 5 covers this pattern.

Data Locality Pattern

The goal of the *Data Locality pattern* is to move execution closer to the data. This is done by colocating the services with the data or by performing the execution in the data store itself. This allows the execution to access data with fewer limitations, helping to quicken execution, and to reduce bandwidth by sending aggregated results.

How it works

Moving execution can improve performance more than moving data. When enough CPU resources are available, adding a service dedicated to the query at the data node, as shown in Figure 4-18, can improve performance by processing most of the data locally rather than transferring it over the network.

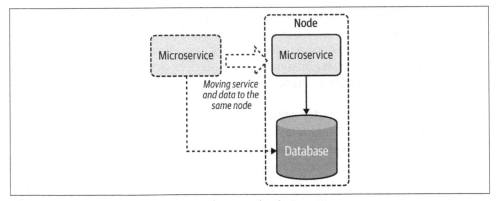

Figure 4-18. Moving a microservice closer to the data store

When the service cannot be moved to the same node, moving the service to the same region or data center can help better utilize the bandwidth. This approach can also help the service cache results and serve from them more efficiently.

We can also move execution closer to the data by moving it to the data store as stored procedures (Figure 4-19). This is a great way to utilize the capabilities of relational databases to optimize data processing and retrieval.

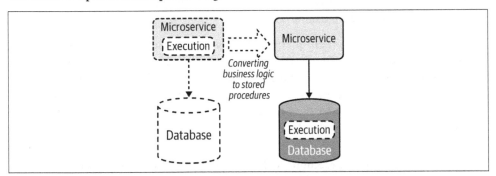

Figure 4-19. Moving execution to data stores as stored procedures

How it's used in practice

This pattern encourages coupling execution with data to reduce latency and save bandwidth, enabling distributed cloud native applications to operate efficiently over the network.

Reduce latency when retrieving data. We can use this pattern when we need to retrieve data from one or more data sources and perform some sort of join. To process data, a service needs to fetch all the data to its local memory before it can perform a meaningful operation. This requires data to be transferred over the network, introducing latency. By moving the service closer to the data store (or when there are multiple stores involved, moving it to the store that contributes to the most input) will reduce data being transferred via the network, thus reducing data-retrieval time. We can also use this pattern for composition services that perform joins by consuming data from data stores and other services. By moving these services closer to the data source, we can improve their overall performance.

Reduce bandwidth usage when retrieving data. This pattern is especially useful when we need to retrieve data from multiple sources to perform data aggregation or filtering operations. The output of these queries will be significantly smaller than their input. By running the execution closer to the data source, we need to transfer only a small amount of data, which can improve bandwidth utilization. This is especially useful when data stores are huge and clients are geographically distributed. This is a good approach when cloud native applications are experiencing bandwidth bottlenecks.

Considerations

Applying the Data Locality pattern can also help utilize idle CPU resources at the data nodes. Most data nodes are I/O intensive, and when the queries they perform are simple enough, they might have plenty of CPU resources idling. Moving execution to the data node can better utilize resources and optimize overall performance. We should be careful to not move all executions to the data nodes, as this can overload them and cause issues with data retrieval.

This pattern is not ideal when queries output most of their input. These cases will overload the data nodes without any savings to bandwidth or performance. Deciding when to use this pattern depends on the trade-off between bandwidth and CPU utilization. We recommend using this pattern when the gains achieved by reducing the data transfer are much greater than the additional execution cost incurred at the data nodes.

Transfer the execution to the data store only when that data store is exclusively used by the querying microservice. Running stored procedures in a shared database is an antipattern, as it can cause performance and management implications. Also be aware that change management of databases is nontrivial, and if not done carefully, the update of the stored procedure could incur downtime. Move execution to the data store only with caution, and prefer having the business logic in the microservice when there is no significant performance improvement.

Related patterns

The following patterns, covered in this chapter, are related to the Data Locality pattern:

Materialized View pattern
> Provides an alternative approach for this pattern, by moving data closer to the place of execution. This pattern is ideal when the data is small or when CPU-intensive operations such as complex joins and data transformations are needed during reads.

Caching pattern
> Complements this pattern by storing preprocessed data and serving it during repeated queries.

Caching Pattern

The *Caching pattern* stores previously processed or retrieved data in memory, and serves this data for similar queries issued in the future. This not only reduces repeated data processing at the services, but also eliminates calls to dependent services when the response is already stored in the service.

How it works

A *cache* is usually an in-memory data store used to store previously processed or retrieved data so we can reuse that data when required without reprocessing or retrieving it again. When a request is made to retrieve data, and we can find the necessary data stored in the cache, we have a *cache hit*. If the data is not available in the cache, we have a *cache miss*.

When a cache miss occurs, the system usually needs to process or fetch data from the data store, as well as update the cache with the retrieved data for future reference. This process is called a *read-through cache operation*. Similarly, when a request is made to update the data, we should update it in the data store and remove or invalidate any relevant previously fetched entries stored in the cache. This process is called a *write-through cache operation*. Here, invalidation is important, because when that data is requested again, the cache should not return the old data but should retrieve updated data from the store by using the read-through cache operation. This reading and updating behavior is commonly referred to as a *cache aside*, and most commercial caches support this feature by default.

Caching data can happen on either the client or server side, or both, and the cache itself can be local (storing data in one instance) or shared (storing data in a distributed manner).

Especially when the cache is not shared, it cannot keep on adding data, as it will eventually exhaust available memory. Hence, it uses eviction policies to remove some records to accommodate new ones. The most popular eviction policy is *least recently used (LRU)*, which removes data that is not used for a long period to accommodate new entries. Other policies include *first in, first out (FIFO)*, which removes the oldest loaded entry; *most recently used* (*MRU*), which removes the last-used entry; and trigger-based options that remove entries based on values in the trigger event. We should use the eviction policy appropriate for our use case.

When data is cached, data stored in the data store can be updated by other applications, so holding data for a long period in the cache can cause inconsistencies between the data in the cache and the store. This is handled by using an expiry time for each cache entry. This helps reload the data from the data store upon time-out and improves consistency between the cache and data store.

How it's used in practice

This pattern is usually applied when the same query can be repeatedly called multiple times by one or more clients, especially when we don't have enough knowledge about what data will be queried next.

Improve time to retrieve data. Caching can be used when retrieving data from the data store requires much more time than retrieving from the cache. This is especially useful when the original store needs to perform complex operations or is deployed in a remote location, and hence the network latency is high.

Improve static content loading. Caching is best for static data or for data that is rarely updated. Especially when the data is static and can be stored in memory, we can load the full data set to the cache and configure the cache not to expire. This drastically improves data-retrieval time and eliminates the need to load the data from the original data source.

Reduce data store contention. Because it reduces the number of calls to the data store, we can use this pattern to reduce data store contention or when the store is overloaded with many concurrent requests. If the application consuming the data can tolerate inconsistencies, such as data being outdated by a few minutes, we can also deploy this pattern on write-intensive data stores to reduce the read load and improve the stability of the system. In this case, the data in the cache will eventually become consistent when the cache times out.

Prefetch data to improve data-retrieval time. We can preload the cache fully or partially when we know the kind of queries that are more likely to be issued. For example, if we are processing orders and know that the applications will mostly call last week's data, we can preload the cache with last week's data when we start the service. This can provide better performance than loading data on demand. When preloading is omitted, the service and the data store can encounter high stress, as most of the initial requests will result in a cache miss.

This pattern also can be used when we know what data will be queried next. For example, if a user is searching for products on a retail website, and we are rendering only the first 10 entries, the user likely will request the next 10 entries. Preloading the next 10 entries to the cache can save time when that data is needed.

Achieve high availability by relaxing the data store dependency. Caching can also be used to achieve high availability, especially when the service availability is more important than the consistency of the data. We can handle service calls with cached data even when the backend data store is not available. As shown in Figure 4-20, we can also extend this pattern by making the local cache fall back on a shared or distributed cache, which in turn can fall back to the data store when the data is not present. This pattern can incorporate the Resilient Connectivity pattern with a circuit breaker discussed in Chapter 3 for the fallback calls so that they can retry and gracefully reconnect when the backends become available after a failure.

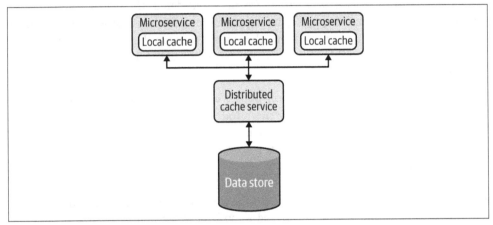

Figure 4-20. Multilayer cache fallback

When using a shared cache, we can also introduce a secondary cache instance as a standby and replicate the data to it, to improve availability. This allows our applications to fall back to the standby when the primary cache fails.

Cache more data than a single node can hold. Distributed caching systems can be used as another alternative option when the local cache or shared cache cannot contain all the needed data. They also provide scalability and resiliency by partitioning and replicating data. These systems support read-through and write-through operations and can make direct calls to the data stores to retrieve and update data. We can also scale them by simply adding more cache servers as needed.

Though distributed caches can store lots of data, they are not as fast as the local cache and add more complexity to the system. We might need additional network hops to retrieve data, and we now need to manage an additional set of nodes. Most important, all nodes participating in the distributed cache should be within the same network and have relatively high bandwidth among one another; otherwise, they can also suffer data-synchronization delays. In contrast, when the clients are geographically distributed, a distributed cache can bring the data closer to the clients, yielding faster response times.

Considerations

The cache should never be used as the single source of truth, and it does not need to be designed with high availability in mind. Even when the caches are not available, the application should be able to execute their expected functionalities. Because caches store data in memory, there is always a possibility of data loss, so data stores are the ones that should be used to persist data for long-term use.

In some cases, most of the data contributing to a response message will be static, and only a small portion of the data will be frequently updated. If constructing the static part of the data is expensive, it may be beneficial to split the records in two, as static and dynamic parts, and then store only those static parts in the cache. When building the response, we can combine the static data stored in the cache and the dynamically generated data.

As an alternative to cache eviction policies, we can also make local caches to support data overflow. This overflow data is written to the disk. You should use this approach only when reading the data from the disk is much faster than retrieving data from the original data store. This approach can introduce additional complexity, as now we also need to manage the cache overflow.

 The cache time-out should be set at an optimum level, not too long or too short. While setting a too-long cache time-out can cause higher inconsistencies, setting a too-short time-out is also detrimental, as it will reload the data too often and defeat the purpose of caching data. However, setting a long time-out can also be beneficial when the cost of data retrieval is significantly higher than the cost of data being inconsistent.

The biggest disadvantage of caching data locally is that when services scale, each service will have its own local cache and will sync data with the data stores at different times. One might get an update before the other, and that can lead to a situation where caches in different microservices are not in sync. Then, when the same query is sent to two services, they could respond with different values, because cache invalidation happens only at the service that processes the original update request, and caches in other microservices are not aware of this invalidation. This situation can also occur when the data is replicated at the data store level, as the caches in the microservices are unaware of those updates.

We can mitigate this problem, as shown in Figure 4-21, by invalidating all the caches during data updates by either informing the cache nodes about the update via a messaging system, as in the Publisher-Subscriber pattern, or by using the Event Sourcing pattern. Both patterns are covered in Chapter 5.

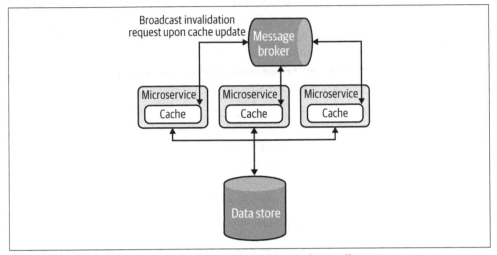

Figure 4-21. Using the message broker to invalidate cache in all services

 Introducing unnecessary layers of cache can cause high memory consumption, reduce performance, and cause data inconsistencies. We highly recommend performing a load test when introducing any caching solution, and especially monitoring the percentage of cache hits, along with performance, CPU, and memory usage. A lower cache-hit percentage can indicate that the cache is not effective. In this case, either modify the cache to achieve a higher percentage of cache hits or choose other alternatives. Increasing the size of the cache, reducing cache expiry, and preloading the cache are options that we can use to improve cache hits.

Whenever possible, we recommend batch data updates to caches, as is done in data stores. This optimizes bandwidth and improves performance when the load is high. When multiple cache entries are updated at the same time, the updates can follow either an optimistic or a pessimistic approach. In the *optimistic approach*, we assume that no concurrent updates will occur and check the cache only for a concurrent write before updating the cache. But in the *pessimistic approach*, we lock the cache for the full update period so no concurrent updates can occur. The latter approach is not scalable, so you should use this only for very short-lived operations.

We also recommend implementing forceful expiry or reload of the cache. For instance, if the client is aware of a potential update through other means, we can let the client forcefully reload the cache before retrieving data. We can achieve this by introducing a random variable as part of the cache key when storing the data. The client can use the same key over and over again, and change it only when needing to force a reload. This approach is used by web clients against browser caching, for example. Because browsers cache data against a request URI, by having a random element in the URI, the clients can forcefully reload the cached entry by simply changing that random URI element when they are sending the request. Be careful in using this technique with third-party clients because they can continuously change the random variable requesting forceful reload, and overload the system. But if the clients are within the control of the same team, this can be a viable approach.

Some commercial cache services can provide data security by using the Vault Key pattern, covered later in this chapter. But most caches are usually not designed for security, and they should not be directly exposed to external systems. To achieve security, we can add a data service on top of the cache by using the Data Service pattern and apply API security for the data service (Figure 4-22). These will add data protection and allow only authorized services to read and write data to the cache.

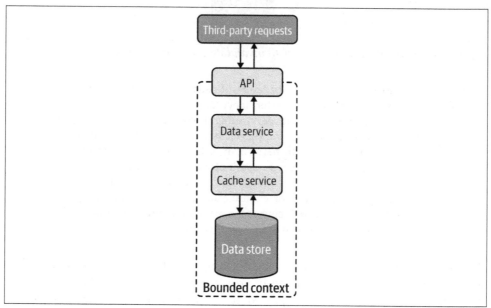

Figure 4-22. Securely exposing the cache to external services

Related patterns

The following patterns (covered in this chapter unless otherwise noted) are related to the Caching pattern:

Data Sharding pattern

Enables the cache to be scaled similarly to the way we can scale data stores. This also enables distributing data geographically so relevant data in the cache can be closer to the services that operate them.

Resilient Connectivity pattern

Provides a mechanism to serve requests from the data sources when data is not available in the cache. Chapter 3 discusses this pattern.

Data Service pattern

Along with API security, can be used to provide a service layer for distributed caches, providing more business-centric APIs for data consumers.

Vault Key pattern

Provides the capability to secure the caches by using access tokens enabling third parties to access the data directly from caches. This can be used only if the caching systems support this functionality. Otherwise, we need to fall back on using the Data Service pattern with API security.

Event Sourcing pattern

Propagates cache-invalidation requests to all local caches. This enables eventual consistency of cache data and reduces the chance of data being obsolete as data sources are updated by multiple services. Chapter 5 details this pattern.

Static Content Hosting Pattern

The *Static Content Hosting pattern* deploys static content in data stores that are closer to clients so content can be delivered directly to the client with low latency and without consuming excess computational resources.

How it works

Cloud native web services are used to create dynamic content based on clients' requests. Some clients, especially browsers, require a lot of other static content, such as static HTML pages, JavaScript and CSS files, images, and files for downloads. Rather than using microservices to cater to static content, this pattern allows us to directly serve static content from storage services such as content delivery networks (CDNs).

Figure 4-23 illustrates this pattern in the context of a web application. When the browser requests data, we can make the service respond with dynamic HTML containing embedded links to relevant static data that needs to be rendered at various locations on the page. This allows the browser to then request the static content, which will be resolved by DNS and served from the closest CDN.

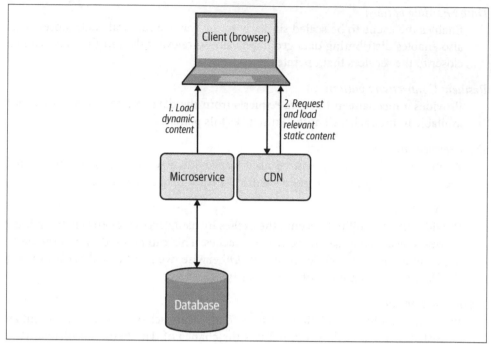

Figure 4-23. Browser loading dynamic content from a microservice while loading static content from a CDN

How it's used in practice

This pattern is used when we need to quickly deliver static content to clients with low response time, and when we need to reduce the load on rendering services.

Provide faster static content delivery.   Because static content does not change, this pattern replicates and caches data in multiple environments and geographical locations with the motivation of moving it closer to the clients. This can help serve static data with low latency.

Reduce resource utilization on rendering services.   When we need to send both static and dynamic data to clients, as discussed in the preceding web browser example, we can separate the static data and move it to a storage system such as a CDN or an S3 bucket, and let clients directly fetch that data. This reduces the resource utilization of the microservice that renders the dynamic content, as it does not need to pack all the static content in its response.

Considerations

We cannot use this pattern if the static content needs to be updated before delivering it to the clients, such as adding the current access time and location to the web response. Further, this is not a feasible solution when the amount of static data that needs to be served is small; the cost for the client to request data from multiple sources can incur more latency than is being served directly by the service. When you need to send both static and dynamic content, we recommend using this pattern only when it can provide a significant performance advantage.

When using this pattern, remember that you might need more-complex client implementations. This is because, based on the dynamic data that arrives, the client should be able to retrieve the appropriate static content and combine both types of data at the client side. If we are using this pattern for use cases other than web-page rendering in a browser, we have to also be able to build and execute complex clients to fulfill that use case.

Sometimes we might need to store static data securely. If we need to allow authorized users to access static data via this pattern, we can use the Data Service pattern along with API security or the Vault Key pattern to provide security for the data store.

Related patterns

The following patterns are related to the Static Content Hosting pattern:

Data Sharding pattern
> Can be used to shard data when you have a lot of static data.

Caching pattern
> Caches content for faster data access. The cache expiration based on time-out is not necessary, as static data will not become outdated.

Vault Key pattern
> Provides security to systems hosting static content.

Data Service pattern
> Along with API security, provides a service layer on top of the content to control data access.

Summary of Performance Optimization Patterns

This section outlined commonly used patterns of performance optimization in cloud native application development. Table 4-4 summarizes when we should and should not use these patterns and the benefits of each.

Table 4-4. Performance optimization patterns

Pattern	When to use	When not to use	Benefits
Materialized View	Part of the data is available locally, and the rest of the data needs to be fetched from external sources that incur high latency. The data that needs to be moved is small and rarely updated. Provides access to nonsensitive data that is hosted in secure systems.	Data can be retrieved from dependent services with low latency. Data in the dependent services is changing quickly. Consistency of the data is considered important for the response.	Can store the data in any database that is suitable for the application. Increases resiliency of the service by replicating the data to local stores.
Data Locality	To read data from multiple data sources and perform a join or data aggregation in memory. The data stores are huge, and the clients are geographically distributed.	Queries output most of their input. Additional execution cost incurred at the data nodes is higher than the cost of data transfer over the network.	Reduces network bandwidth utilization and data-retrieval latency. Better utilizes CPU resources and optimizes overall performance. Caches results and serves requests more efficiently.
Caching	Best for static data or data that is read more frequently than it is updated. Application has the same query that can be repeatedly called multiple times by one or more clients, especially when we do not have enough knowledge about what data will be queried next. The data store is subject to a high level of contention or cannot handle the number of concurrent requests it is receiving from multiple clients.	The data is updated frequently. As the means of storing state, as it should not be considered as the single source of truth. The data is critical, and the system cannot tolerate data inconsistencies.	Can choose which part of the data to cache to improve performance. Using a cache aside improves performance by reducing redundant computations. Can preload static data into the cache. Combined with eviction policy, the cache can hold the recent/required data.
Static Content Hosting	All or some of the data requested by the client is static. The static data needs to be available in multiple environments or geographic locations.	The static content needs to be updated before delivering to the clients, such as adding the access time and location. The amount of data that needs to be served is small. Clients cannot retrieve and combine static and dynamic content together.	Geographically partitioning and storing closer to clients provides shorter response times and faster access/download speed. Reduces resource utilization on rendering services.

Reliability Patterns

Data losses are not tolerated by any business-critical application, so the reliability of data is of utmost importance. Applying relevant reliability mechanisms when modifying data stores and when transmitting data between applications is critical. This section outlines use of the Transaction reliability pattern to ensure reliable data storage and processing.

Transaction Pattern

The *Transaction pattern* uses transactions to perform a set of operations as a single unit of work, so all operations are completed or undone as a unit. This helps maintain the integrity of the data, and error-proofs execution of services. This is critical for the successful execution of financial applications.

How it works

This pattern wraps multiple individual operations into a single large operation, providing a guarantee that either all operations or no operation will succeed. All transactions follow these steps:

1. System initiates a transaction.
2. Various data manipulation operations are executed.
3. Commit is used to indicate the end of the transaction.
4. If there are no errors, the commit will succeed, the transaction will finish successfully, and the changes will be reflected in the data stores.

   If there are errors, all the operations in the transaction will be rolled back, and the transaction will fail. No changes will be reflected in the data stores.

If we need to process user orders as a transaction, for example, we can initiate a transaction, remove the ordered product quantity from the Inventory table, add it to the User Order table, and then finally issue a transaction commit. When this happens, both data update operations will be executed as a single atomic operation. If the Inventory table is empty, the transaction will fail and the system will roll back to its initial state. But if both operations succeed, the transaction will succeed and the changes will be persisted in the data store.

The Transaction pattern adheres to the following ACID properties:

Atomic
  All operations must occur at once, or none should occur.

Consistent
  Before and after the transaction, the system will be in a valid state.

Isolation
  The results produced by concurrent transactions will be identical to such transactions being executed in sequential order.

Durable
  When the transaction is finished, the committed changes will remain committed even during system failures.

We can achieve transaction isolation at different levels. *Serializable* isolation provides the highest level. This blocks data access on selected data for parallel read and write queries during the transaction, and blocks addition and removal of data that might fall into the transaction data range. For example, if we are modifying all users under age 30 with a transaction, it will not allow us to add a new user with age 23 concurrently. *Repeatable reads* isolation provides the second-best level of isolation. This blocks data access on selected data for read and write queries during the transaction, but allows addition and removal of new data in the transaction data range. At the same time, *read committed* isolation blocks only data writes, while *read uncommitted* isolation allows reading noncommitted updates made by other transactions.

Transactions are commonly used with only a single data store, such as a relational database, but we can also coordinate operations across multiple systems, such as databases, event streams, and queuing systems. For example, when an order is made, we can make the system not only update the database but also add an entry to the delivery message queue to inform the fulfillment team about the delivery as a single transaction.

Such transactions among multiple systems are handled by consensus algorithms such as XA transactions, Paxos, and Raft. These can use two-phase and three-phase commit protocols to make sure the operations are coordinated across systems.

How it's used in practice

Transactions can be used to combine multiple operations as a single unit of work, and to coordinate the operations of multiple systems.

Combine multiple operations as a single unit of work. We can use this pattern to combine multiple steps that should all be processed completely to consider the operation valid. For example, transferring $25 from Bob to Alice's account involves two steps: deducting $25 from Bob's account and adding $25 to Alice's account. If one of these steps fails, the whole operation is considered invalid, and the system should revoke all the changes done and bring the accounts to the same state as before we started the transaction.

We can also make sure that multiple transactions do not interfere with each other. For example, both Bob and Eve will be able to transfer money to Alice's account at the same time in parallel.

Combine operations across multiple systems. This pattern can be used when we want to consume an event from an event queue, perform an update based on that to a data store, and pass that message to another event queue for further processing—all in a single transaction, as depicted in Figure 4-24. To synchronize the operations between multiple systems, we can use an XA transaction that uses a two-phase commit protocol. Most databases and event-queuing systems also natively support XA transactions, and through this we can ensure that the event will not get lost even if the processing system fails in the middle of its execution.

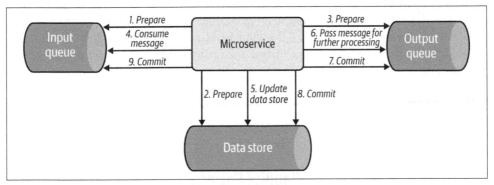

Figure 4-24. Simple message processing use case applying an XA transaction

Considerations

We do not need to use this pattern when the operation has only a single step, or when there are multiple steps but failure of some is considered acceptable.

It is important to note that the use of consensus algorithms such as XA transactions will synchronize operations and introduce latency. We recommend using this pattern only when the transaction is relatively short lived, and only if it involves few systems, as we have discussed in the order-processing example.

Whenever possible, make the operation idempotent; this will help eliminate the need for using any transactions and simplifies the system. This is because with idempotent updates, even when the same operation is performed multiple times, the results will be the same. For example, say we are always overwriting a value, such as the number of items available in the inventory. Even if we overwrite the value multiple times, it will not affect the end results. This will allow us to resend the same event multiple times to overcome system failures.

When we need to synchronize execution and have more than three systems, we recommend using the Saga pattern discussed in Chapter 3. This pattern is useful for coordinating transactions among multiple data stores, microservices, and message brokers. It enables us to execute multiple transactions in order, and to compensate previous transactions when a latter transaction fails. This can also reduce the high latency or coupling that can occur from the distributed locks used by XA transactions. But we can use Saga only when all the participating transactions can be reverted—in the event of a failure—by using a compensation transaction. This can especially become a problem when we are integrating with third-party systems and might not have a way to compensate them in the case of failure.

We recommend using XA transactions over Saga when all updates need to be done in a single data store or when all steps must be performed at the same time as an atomic operation. While Saga performs transactions in order, other systems can access data from the data stores and microservices in parallel. They can then get inconsistent results if they retrieve one part of the data from a data store that has already performed the transaction and another from a data store that has not yet processed the transaction.

Related pattern

The Transaction pattern has one related pattern, the Saga pattern. This pattern, covered in Chapter 3, reliably coordinates execution of multiple systems.

Summary of Transaction Reliability Pattern

This section outlined one commonly used pattern that provides reliability in cloud native application development. Table 4-5 summarizes when we should and should not use this pattern, as well as its benefits.

Table 4-5. Transaction reliability pattern

Pattern	When to use	When not to use	Benefits
Transaction	An operation contains multiple steps, and all the steps should be processed automatically to consider the operation valid.	The application has only a single step in the operation. The application has multiple steps, and failure of some steps is considered acceptable.	Adheres to ACID properties. Processes multiple independent transactions.

Security: Vault Key Pattern

Securing data is discussed in detail in "Security" on page 155. Here, we show how access to data stores can be controlled via the Vault Key pattern to enforce security when developing cloud native applications.

The *Vault Key pattern* provides direct access to data stores via a trusted token, commonly named the *vault key*. Some of the popular cloud data stores support this functionality.

How it works

The Vault Key pattern is based on a trusted token being presented by the client and being validated by the data store. In this pattern, the application determines who can access which part of the data.

Figure 4-25 illustrates this pattern. The client or caller service calls the application to retrieve a token to access the relevant data store. The application can be an identity provider or may contact an identity provider to validate the caller and issue a trusted vault key token for access to the relevant data store. The application can also provide a scope of operations that the caller can perform on the data store. It will also add an expiry time to the key, giving access to the service for only a defined period. The caller can then call the resource by using the given key and can perform authorized operations until the key expires.

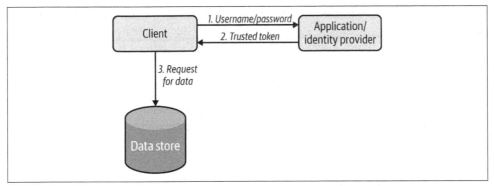

Figure 4-25. Actions performed by clients to retrieve data in the Vault Key pattern

This pattern can also support renewing the vault keys upon expiry by using a refresh token, as in API security. This facilitates smooth operation of services without getting interruptions for reauthorization.

How it's used in practice

This pattern can be used when the data store cannot reach the identity provider to authenticate and authorize the client upon data access. In this pattern, the data store will contain the certificate of the identity provider, so it will be able to decrypt the token and validate its authenticity without calling the identity provider. Because it does not need to make remote service calls for validation, it can also perform authentication operations with minimal latency.

Considerations

Once the caller service gets access to the data store, the application that governs the service usually will lose control. This pattern provides a mechanism to withhold control over the data store and enforce security. But we can apply this pattern only when the data store supports key validation. This is important to ensure that the token is issued by the identity provider and is not expired. Some advanced data stores also support access scopes; they can identify which section of the data store, such as the table or row, can be accessed by the incoming request. When the data store can't validate access based on keys, use alternative approaches such as fronting the stores with a data service and protecting with API security.

Sometimes the issued vault key can be compromised. In these cases, it is usually not possible to block the use of that token, as most data stores do not support this functionality. We can reduce the damage that can be caused by a compromised vault key by setting the expiry time to a moderate value.

Related pattern

The Vault Key pattern has one related pattern, Data Service (covered at the start of this chapter). Along with API security, the Data Service pattern provides an alternative approach for providing security when the Vault Key pattern is not feasible.

Summary of the Vault Key Pattern

This section outlined the commonly used Vault Key pattern, which provides security in cloud native application development. Table 4-6 summarizes when we should and should not use this pattern, and its benefits.

Table 4-6. Vault Key security pattern

Pattern	When to use	When not to use	Benefits
Vault Key	To securely access remote data with minimal latency. The store has a limited computing capability to perform service calls for authentication and authorization.	Need fine-grained data protection. Need to restrict what queries should be executed on the data store with high precision. The exposed data store cannot validate access based on keys.	Accesses data stores directly by using a trusted token, a vault key Has minimal operational costs compared to calling the central identity service for validation

Technologies for Implementing Data Management Patterns

As a software developer or architect, you have to select the most appropriate technologies for your use case. This includes selecting data stores as well. You have to select a data store based on factors such as what you are going to store, the amount of data (scalability), the expected write and read performance, system availability, and consistency. In this section, we discuss the types of data stores most commonly used for cloud native applications, and when you may use them.

Relational Database Management Systems

Most traditional databases fall under the category of relational database management systems (RDBMSs), which includes MySQL, Oracle, MSSQL, Postgres, H2, and more. These relational databases provide the ACID properties, and with their SQL can also have very complex data access patterns. However, if you have nonrelational data such as XML, JSON, or binary format, then an RDBMS may not be the best option, and you might need to select a distributed filesystem or NoSQL database to store data, as discussed previously in "Relational Databases" on page 102.

When building cloud native applications, instead of deploying the database yourself on the cloud infrastructure, we highly recommend using a managed version of RDBMSs provided by a cloud vendor, such as Amazon Relational Database Service (RDS), Google Cloud SQL, or Azure SQL. This will not only reduce the complexity of managing the databases, but also be better tuned for the environment.

To scale RDBMSs, we can deploy them as primary and replica databases, as discussed in the Materialized View pattern, or shard the data as in the Sharding pattern. In the worst case, if we still have issues with space, we can also periodically back up older, rarely used data to an archive such as NoSQL, and delete it from the store.

Apache Cassandra

Apache Cassandra is a distributed NoSQL database that began internally at Facebook and was released as an open source project in July 2008. Cassandra column store is well-known for its continuous availability (zero downtime), high performance, and linear scalability, which modern applications and microservices require. It also offers replication across data centers and geographies to guarantee availability across regions. Cassandra can handle petabytes of information and thousands of concurrent operations per second, enabling you to manage large amounts of data across hybrid cloud and multicloud environments. For cloud native application deployment, we recommend using managed Cassandra deployments such as Amazon Keyspaces and Asta on Google Cloud.

Cassandra's write performance is very high compared to its read performance, As discussed previously in "NoSQL Databases" on page 103, it provides eventual consistency by design. However, it also lets us change its consistency levels to achieve weak or strong consistency based on the use case.

The performance of Cassandra also depends on how we store and query data. If we will be querying data based on a set of keys, we should use its row key (partition key). If we need to query data from different keys, we can create secondary indexes. Don't overuse the secondary indexes; they can slow the data store, as each insertion has to also update the indexes. Further, Cassandra is not efficient when we want to join two column families, and we should not use it if we are to update the data more frequently.

Apache HBase

Apache HBase is a distributed, scalable, NoSQL column store that runs on top of the HDFS. HBase can host very large tables with billions of rows and millions of columns, and can also provide real-time, random read/write access to Hadoop data. It scales linearly across very large data sets and easily combines data sources with different structures and schemas.

As HBase is a column store, it supports dynamic database schema, and as it runs on top of HDFS, it can also be used in MapReduce jobs. Consequently, HBase's complex interdependent system is more difficult to configure, secure, and maintain.

Unlike Cassandra, HBase uses "master/worker" deployment, and so can suffer a single point of failure. If your application requires high availability, choose Cassandra over HBase. However, when we depend heavily on data consistency, HBase will be more suitable because it writes data to only one place and always knows where to find it (because data replication is done "externally" by HDFS). Similar to Cassandra, HBase also does not perform well for frequent data deletes or updates.

MongoDB

MongoDB is a document store that supports storing data in JSON-like documents, as discussed in "NoSQL Databases" on page 103. Documents and collections in MongoDB are comparable to records and tables in relational databases. It uses MongoDB query language to access the stored data, perform aggregation filtering and sorting based on any document fields, and insert and delete fields without restructuring documents. MongoDB Cloud provides MongoDB as a hosted solution for cloud native application usage.

Unlike Cassandra or RDBMSs, MongoDB prefers more indexes. When not indexed, its performance can suffer, as it needs to search the entire collection. MongoDB also favors consistency over availability. It achieves availability by using a single read/write primary and multiple secondary replicas. When a primary becomes unavailable, the read/write operations will be temporarily halted for about 10 to 40 seconds while MongoDB automatically elects one of its secondary replicas as the primary.

MongoDB is heavily used for mobile applications, content management, real-time analytics, and IoT applications. MongoDB is also a good choice if you have no clear schema definition with your JSON documents, and you can tolerate some data store unavailability. However, like other NoSQL databases, it is not suitable for transactional data.

Redis

Redis is an in-memory key-value data store commonly used as a cache, as discussed in the "Caching Pattern" on page 133. It supports string keys and various kinds of values such as strings, lists, sets, sorted sets, hashes, bit arrays, and much more. This makes the application less complex, as it can now store its internal data structure directly in Redis. Redis is ideal for a cache, as it supports transactions, keys with a limited time to live, LRU eviction of keys, automatic failover, and its ability to write excess data to disk. Redis also has plenty of cloud hosting options for cloud native applications to use, including AWS, Google, Redis Labs, and IBM.

Redis supports two types of persistence options: Redis Database Backup (RDB) and Append Only File (AOF). By using both options, we can achieve good write performance and a good degree of data safety upon system failures. Redis features high availability by using a single "master" and multiple "replica"s as in the CQRS pattern, and provides scalability through sharding "master" and "replica"s as discussed in the "Data Sharding Pattern" on page 118.

However, Redis is not a NoSQL replacement for relational data stores, as it does not support many standard relational data store features, such as efficient querying, and performing complex data manipulation and aggregation operations.

Amazon DynamoDB

DynamoDB is a key-value and document database that can be used to store and retrieve data with low latency and high scalability. It can handle more than 10 trillion requests per day and more than 20 million requests per second during peaks. Data in DynamoDB is stored on solid-state disks (SSDs), automatically partitioned, and replicated across multiple availability zones. It also provides fine-grained access control and uses proven secured methods to authenticate users and prevent unauthorized data access.

DynamoDB, a service provided by AWS, cannot be installed on a local server or in clouds other than AWS. Use DynamoDB only if you are using AWS as the primary cloud infrastructure for your cloud native applications. Further, DynamoDB has limited querying capability compared to relational stores and does not support relational database features such as table joins and foreign-key concepts; instead, it advocates using non-normalized data with redundancy for performance.

Apache HDFS

The *Apache Hadoop Distributed File System* (*HDFS*) is a widely used distributed file-system designed to run on cheap commodity hardware while providing high data resiliency by storing at least three copies of data in a distributed manner. HDFS is commonly used to store analytical data because the data stored in HDFS is immutable and is optimized to write and read data in a streaming manner. This also allows HDFS to be used as the data source for Hadoop MapReduce jobs for efficient processing of large data. Cloudera and major cloud vendors provide HDFS as a hosted service to use with cloud native applications.

HDFS stores data in multiple data nodes, and stores all its metadata in memory in a single-name node. When that node is not available, it can fail new reads and writes, causing unavailability. Also, based on the capacity of its name node's memory, it has an upper limit on the number of files that it can store. We recommend using HDFS to store a small number of large files instead of a large number of small files. Because it is optimized to read data sequentially, it is not the best solution when we need random reads.

Amazon S3

Amazon Simple Storage Service (*S3*) is an object storage that is part of AWS. It can be used in a data lake, as storage for cloud native applications, as a data backup or archive, and for big data analytics. It also supports the Data Locality pattern by running analytics on data nodes using standard SQL expressions of Amazon Athena. We can use S3 Select to retrieve subsets of object data instead of the entire object. This can improve data-access performance by up to four times. Amazon S3 is highly available and provides fine-grained data access control. We recommend using it when you use AWS as your primary cloud native application platform.

Azure Cosmos DB

Azure Cosmos DB is a fully managed NoSQL data store that supports key-value, document, column, and graph database semantics. It can store and retrieve data with low latency, and provides enterprise-grade security with end-to-end encryption and access control. It also provides open source APIs for MongoDB and Cassandra, enabling clients to leverage the cloud without changing their application.

Cosmos DB, a service provided by Azure, cannot be installed on a local server or in clouds other than Azure. Use Cosmos DB only if you are using Azure as the primary cloud infrastructure for your cloud native applications. Still, Cosmos DB provides some flexibility by providing migration and synchronization of data with your on-premises Cassandra cluster. Though Cosmos DB can provide transactional support, it is limited within the logical data partition.

Google Cloud Spanner

Google Cloud Spanner is a fully managed relational data store that supports unlimited scale and strong consistency. It provides the capability to run SQL queries while providing support for transactions across all the nodes in the cluster. It also linearly scales write and read transactions and provides security through data-layer encryption and access controls.

Because Cloud Spanner is a service provided by Google, it cannot be installed on a local server or in clouds other than Google. Use Spanner only if you are using Google as the primary cloud infrastructure for your cloud native applications. Though it provides SQL support, it does not fully support the American National Standards Institute (ANSI) SQL spec and so requires changes to applications before migrating from standard relational databases to Spanner.

Summary of Technologies

This section outlined some commonly used data stores that we can use in cloud native application development. Table 4-7 summarizes when we should and should not use these data stores.

Table 4-7. Data store types

Data store type	When to use	When not to use
Relational database management system (RDBMS)	Need transactions and ACID properties. Interrelationship with data is required to be maintained. Working with small to medium amounts of data.	Data needs to be highly scalable, such as IoT data. Working with XML, JSON, and binary data format. Solution cannot tolerate some level of unavailability.
Apache Cassandra	Need high availability. Need scalability. Need a decentralized solution. Need faster writes than reads. Read access can be mostly performed by partition key.	Existing data is updated frequently. Need to access data by columns that are not part of the partition key. Require relational features, such as transactions, complex joins, and ACID properties.
Apache HBase	Need consistency. Need scalability. Need a decentralized solution. Need high read performance. Need both random and real-time access to data. Need to store petabytes of data.	Solution cannot tolerate some level of unavailability. Existing data is updated very frequently. Require relational features, such as transactions, complex joins, and ACID properties.
MongoDB	Need consistency. Need a decentralized solution. Need a document store. Need data lookup based on multiple keys. Need high write performance.	Solution cannot tolerate some level of unavailability. Require relational features, such as transactions, complex joins, and ACID properties.

Data store type	When to use	When not to use
Redis	Need scalability. Need an in-memory database. Need a persistent option to restore the data. As a cache, queue, and real-time storage.	As a typical database to store and query with complex operations.
Amazon DynamoDB	Need a highly scalable solution. Need a document store. Need a key-value store. Need high write performance. Fine-grained access control.	Use in platforms other than AWS. Require relational features, such as complex joins, and foreign keys.
Apache HDFS	Need a filesystem. Store large files. Store data once and reads multiple times. Perform MapReduce operation on files. Need scalability. Need data resiliency.	Store small files. Need to update files. Need to perform random data reads.
Amazon S3	Need an object store. Perform MapReduce operations on objects. Need a highly scalable solution. Read part of the object data. Fine-grained access control.	Use in platforms other than AWS. Need to run complex queries.
Azure Cosmos DB	Need a highly scalable solution. Need a document store. Need a key-value store. Need a graph store. Need a column store. Fine-grained access control. Connectivity via MongoDB and Cassandra clients	Use in platforms other than Azure. Perform transaction across data partitions.
Google Cloud Spanner	Need a highly scalable solution. Need a relational store. Need support for SQL query processing Need transaction support across all nodes in the cluster.	Use in platforms other than Google Cloud. Support for full ANSI SQL spec.

Testing

Testing is an important step for building successful cloud native applications. As we have discussed testing microservices in Chapter 2, here we will focus on testing data services and data stores.

We can use test data stores to test data-service interactions, Though data services can have complex or simple logic, they can still cause bottlenecks in production. The following are useful recommendations for overcoming these issues:

- Tests should be performed with both clean and prepopulated data stores, as the former will test for data initialization code and the latter will test for data consistency during operation.

- Test all data store types and versions that will be used in production to eliminate any surprises. We can implement test data stores as Docker instances that will help run tests in multiple environments with quick startup and proper cleanup after the test.
- Test data mapping and make sure all fields are properly mapped when calling the data store.
- Validate whether the service is performing inserts, writes, deletion, and updates on the data stores in an expected manner by checking the state of the data store via test clients that can access the database directly.
- Validate that relational constraints, triggers, and stored procedures are producing correct results.

In addition, it is important to do a load test on the data service along with the data store in a production-like environment with multiple clients. This will help identify any database lock, data consistency, or other performance-related bottlenecks present in the cloud native application. It will also show how much load the application can handle and how that will be affected when various data scaling patterns and techniques are deployed.

When it comes to testing the cloud native microservices that depend on data services, we can simply use mock service APIs to mock the data services and omit the need for deploying data stores.

Security

Protecting data and allowing only the appropriate people and systems to access relevant data is key to the successful execution of a cloud native application, and to the success of an organization in general. The security of data should be enforced both when data is at rest and when data is on the move.

We can enforce data security at rest both physically and through software. Data servers should be guarded and accessed only by authorized persons. Data stores running in the servers should also enforce security via the Vault Key pattern and API security to control data access. When storing sensitive data, we recommend encrypting it before storing it in the data store. We also recommend encrypting the filesystem in which the data is stored as an added layer of protection.

We recommend separating sensitive data from other data so that sensitive data can be governed with additional layers of protection, along with audit trails to monitor suspicious behavior. Don't collect and store unnecessary sensitive information. When needed, mask all sensitive information such as usernames and email addresses. This can be done by replacing sensitive data with unique identifiers and storing their mapping in a protected data store. This can enable us to continuously analyze and audit user behavior while providing the capability to delete all sensitive user data by simply deleting the data mapping. This will also help enforce privacy and data regulations such as Europe's General Data Protection Regulation (GDPR).

When it comes to data in transit, we should always transmit the data via secure data transmission channels such as HTTPS. For added security, we can encrypt the messages with asymmetric keys so that the intermediary hosts will not have access to the content.

To protect sensitive information without segmenting messages, we can encrypt only the part of the message that has sensitive information. The whole message will be delivered to each client, but only the clients with the relevant key for the sensitive data can decrypt it, while others can't access that data.

Observability and Monitoring

Observability and monitoring enable us to gain deeper insights into the way cloud native applications are performing by looking at their metrics, logs, and distributed tracing results. As observability and monitoring of microservices are discussed in Chapter 2, here we focus mainly on data stores.

Observability and *monitoring* help us identify the performance of data stores and take corrective actions when they deviate because of load or changes to the application. In most applications, incoming requests interact with the data stores. Any performance or availability issues in the data store will resonate across all layers of the system, affecting the overall user experience.

Monitoring data stores is essential in order to minimize problems with performance, availability, and security. The key metrics to observe in a data store are as follows:

- Application metrics
  - *Data store uptime/health*: To identify whether each node in the data store is up and running.
  - *Query execution time*: Five types of issues can cause high query execution times:
    - *Inefficient query*: Use of nonoptimized queries including multiple complex joins, and tables not being indexed properly.
    - *Data growth in the data store*: Data stores containing more data than it can handle.
    - *Concurrency*: Concurrent operations on the same table/row, locking data stores and impacting their performance.
    - *Lack of system resources such as CPU/memory/disk space*: Data store nodes not having enough resources to efficiently serve the request.

- *Unavailability of dependent system or replica:* In distributed data stores, when its replica or other dependent systems such as a lookup service is not available, it may take more time as it needs to provision a new instance or discover and route the request to another instance.

  - *Query execution response:* Whether the query execution is successful. If the query is failing, we may need to look at the logs for more detail (depending on the failure).

  - *Audit of the query operations:* Malicious queries or user operations can result in unexpected reduction in data store performance. We can use audit logs to identify and mitigate them.

- *System metrics:* To identify a lack of system resources for efficient processing via CPU consumption, memory consumption, availability of disk space, network utilization, and disk I/O speed.

- *Data store logs*

- *Time taken and throughput when communicating with primary and replicas:* Helps to understand networking issues and bad data store nodes, so we can replace them.

When analyzing metrics, we can use percentiles to compare historical and current behaviors. This can identify anomalies and deviations, so we can quickly identify the root cause of the problem. For example, monitoring tools like SolarWinds and SQL Power Tools provide metrics such as query execution time and response time, and systems like Elastic Stack and Kibana analyze data store logs to illustrate their health and the reason for query failures. If we are using data stores managed by cloud vendors such as Google Cloud, AWS, or Azure, they too provide monitoring services to monitor system and data store metrics.

DevOps

We have discussed several data management patterns that can be applied in cloud native applications using both microservices and data stores. We already discussed the DevOps process for deploying and managing microservices in Chapter 2, so here we focus on deployment and management of data stores.

The steps and key considerations for deploying and managing data stores are as follows:

1. *Select data store types.* Select the data store type (relational, NoSQL, or filesystem) and its vendor to match our use case.

2. *Configure the deployment pattern.* This can be influenced by the patterns applied in the cloud native application and the type of data store we have selected. Based

on this selection, high availability and scalability should be determined by answering the following questions:

- Who are the clients?

- How many nodes?

- Are we going to use a data store managed by the cloud vendor or deploy our own?

- How does the replication work?

- How do we back up the data?

- How does it handle disaster recovery?

- How do we secure the data store?

- How do we monitor the data store?

- How much does the data store/management cost?

3. *Enforce security.* Data stores should be protected because they contain business-critical information. This can be enforced by applying relevant physical and software security as discussed in the preceding section. This may include enabling strict access control, data encryption, and use of audit logs.

4. *Set up observability and monitoring.* Like microservices, data stores should be configured with observability and monitoring tools to guarantee continuous operation. This can provide early insights on possible scaling problems, such as a requirement to rebalance data shards, or to apply a different design pattern altogether to improve scalability and performance of the application.

5. *Automate continuous delivery.* When it comes to data stores, automation and continuous delivery are not straightforward. Although we can easily come up with an initial data store schema, maintaining backward compatibility is difficult as the application evolves. Backward compatibility is critical; without it, we will not be able to achieve smooth application updates and rollbacks during failures. To improve productivity, we should always use proper automation tools such as scripts to automate continuous delivery. We also recommend having guardrails and using multiple deployment environments, such as development, and staging/preproduction, to reduce the impact of the changes and to validate the application before moving it to production.

By following these steps, we can safely deploy and maintain cloud native applications while allowing rapid innovation and adoption to other systems.

Summary

In this chapter, we discussed several data management patterns that can be applied to cloud native applications. We started with an overview of data architecture and then looked at various types of data such as input, configuration, and state data that can influence application behavior. We also covered forms of data, such as structured, semi-structured, and unstructured, and how we can efficiently store and manage them in various types of data stores, including relational, NoSQL, and filesystems.

We then discussed how this data can be managed and shared among cloud native applications and how to use various design patterns to achieve data composition, data scaling, performance optimization, reliability, and security. We also looked at various technologies specific to data management and how data-centric cloud native applications should be developed, tested, continuously deployed through DevOps, and observed and monitored to guarantee continuous operation. Next we will discuss patterns related to event-driven cloud native applications.

CHAPTER 5

Event-Driven Architecture Patterns

Event-driven architecture is a software architecture paradigm that promotes generation, detection, consumption, and reaction based on events. An event-driven architecture allows us to build distributed and scalable cloud native applications. In contrast to the service composition patterns, which are mostly synchronous in nature, event-driven architectures are asynchronous. They provide a clean and decoupled way of designing cloud native applications, allowing simpler scaling, and are one of the fundamental architectures for building large-scale distributed cloud native applications.

Events are used for sharing information. In most cases, the application generating the event notification does not expect any response, and it lets the consuming application decide what to do with that information. Even if the applications generating the event notification expect a response, they expect it only indirectly.

 Events can be categorized as any significant occurrence or change in a system state. Let's take an example of depositing $50 into Bob's account. Now, Bob's account balance has increased by $50; this incident is considered an event. The occurrence of this event can be sent to other systems, such as to Bob's cell phone, as a notification. The event notification is typically an asynchronous message produced and transmitted with the event occurrence information. Though events just occur and do not travel, the term *event* is also used interchangeably to denote the message that notifies the event. This is mainly because event-driven architectures are built on top of an asynchronous messaging infrastructure that uses messages to identify and communicate event occurrences.

Some events can be used to issue a command or enforce an action on other systems, such as sending an event to update Bob's current address. In this case, the application sending the event *does* expect the consuming system to perform an action, and so requires the intermediate systems to guarantee that the event is delivered. Though not required, message brokers and event buses can be used to reliably deliver such events. We'll discuss event delivery guarantees in detail in the following section.

Event-driven cloud native applications can be implemented by using microservices, as well as by using serverless computing platforms such as Amazon Lambda and Azure Functions. This is because these platforms are natively event triggered. The use of serverless is especially useful when the frequency of event occurrence is low and when we can significantly save on infrastructure cost.

This chapter focuses on patterns for building cloud native event-driven applications that process discrete events. Some use cases require processing a series of events, in order to understand behavioral and temporal characteristics. Such a series of events ordered by time is called a *stream*, and because processing a stream is quite different from processing discrete events, we have dedicated Chapter 6 to discussing stream-processing patterns.

In this chapter, we cover fundamentals of event-driven architecture, and patterns that fall into the categories of event delivery, event-based state management, and event orchestration. We will also look at technologies related to these patterns, and how to test, enforce security, achieve continuous delivery using DevOps, and operate the applications with monitoring and observability.

Event-Driven Architecture

Unlike in the synchronous communication patterns presented in Chapter 2, in event-driven architecture, we cannot always directly send messages to consumers and get an acknowledgment that they have consumed them successfully. In most cases, we need intermediate systems such as message brokers to consume, store, and deliver events to their consumers while ensuring that no events are lost across system failures. Message brokers provide different event delivery guarantees, as follows:

At-most-once delivery
 The event is delivered to the consumer only once or not at all. If the consumer is not online during a delivery attempt or if network failures occur, the consumer will not get the event. Most important, the message broker will not try to send the same event again.

At-least-once delivery
 The event is guaranteed to be delivered to the consumer. However, the consumer may consume the same event multiple times because if the message broker does not get an acknowledgment from the consumer for the event delivery, it will

assume that the consumer did not receive the event and will resend it. In this case, the consumer should be intelligent enough to handle duplicate events.

Unfortunately, we cannot achieve an *exactly once* delivery guarantee, which ensures that the event is delivered to the consumer once and only once, because of the uncertain nature of the network and systems.

Exactly Once Processing

Though the events are delivered with an at-least-once delivery guarantee, for correct execution of any business process, we need to achieve *exactly once processing*. This ensures that the event is processed once and only once. For example, we should not deposit $50 to Bob's account twice when there is an actual event occurrence of one. We can achieve this by injecting sequence numbers to the events so consumers can identify and drop duplicate events before processing them.

We can also achieve exactly once processing when events are idempotent: the outcome of receiving the same event multiple times is no different from receiving the event only once. For example, let's say the event contains an update to a user's telephone number and we have an application to update the database based on that event. In this case, processing the same event multiple times by the consumer application will not affect the final state of the user data in the database. In the end, the database will have the same updated telephone number.

For business-critical information, such as user-transaction information, we should use exactly once processing with at-least-once delivery. If the event contains information that the business can lose, such as simple notification information or a periodic update, using at-most-once delivery might be sufficient. Implementing a higher level of guarantee comes with performance considerations and increased complexity, so it is important to select the lowest required guarantee.

Message Broker Categories

Message brokers can be divided into two main categories:

Standard (store-backed) message brokers
> These are the standard message brokers that store events in a data store to enable serving to intended consumers. Most important, they purge events from their store upon delivery to consumers. Apache ActiveMQ and RabbitMQ are examples of these brokers.

Log-based message brokers
> These brokers store events in commit logs. The events persist even beyond their being consumed. Therefore, these brokers allow consumers to replay events from a previous point in time. Apache Kafka and NATS are examples of this type.

Regardless of the category, different message brokers, and at times even the same message broker, can support various delivery guarantees. We discuss message brokers in detail, categorizing them, and outlining their supported event delivery patterns in "Technologies for Event-Driven Architecture" on page 193.

CloudEvents

Like APIs and data, events should have defined schemas. This helps event producers and consumers interoperate seamlessly. When defining events for cloud native applications, we recommend using the CloudEvents specification to define the structure of the event payload.

CloudEvents is a CNCF project that provides a common standard for describing events that enable interoperability across cloud native applications. The CloudEvents specification provides a common structure for the event with required attributes such as event ID, source, spec version, and type, and optional attributes such as data content type, schema, subject, and time. It also provides software development kits in languages such as Go, JavaScript, Java, C#, Ruby, and Python so you can rapidly adopt and leverage CloudEvents-based schemas.

Event Schema

The most common event data formats are JSON and XML, but binary formats such as Avro and Protobuf are also gaining popularity in high-performance scenarios. Whatever format you choose, you should always version the schema so that changes to the format are efficiently communicated and managed. As we discussed in Chapter 2, you should also use a schema registry, where possible, to store all event schemas so that consumers can fetch schemas on demand to interpret events. Apache Kafka, for example, is a message broker that supports both Avro-based events and a schema registry.

Let's now discuss various event-delivery patterns such as Producer-Consumer, Publisher-Subscriber, Store and Forward, and Event Sourcing.

Event-Delivery Patterns

Let's start by discussing some *event-delivery patterns* that are used across event-driven architectures. These patterns build on the knowledge gained about asynchronous communication patterns in Chapter 2. Here, we discuss various delivery guarantees as well as event schema management.

Producer-Consumer Pattern

The *Producer-Consumer pattern* enables producer applications and consumer applications to communicate asynchronously by using event queues. The queue manages which consumer processes which event, and which procedures need to be followed when the consumers fail during the processing of the event.

How it works

This pattern requires an intermediate message queue that is managed by a message broker (Figure 5-1). One or more producers can send events to the queue. The message broker typically persists the queued events in a durable store, thereby guaranteeing that the events will eventually be delivered to consumers. The message broker then delivers one event at a time, mostly following FIFO order, to the consumers on request. This helps consumers process events as they have capacity and to not become overloaded.

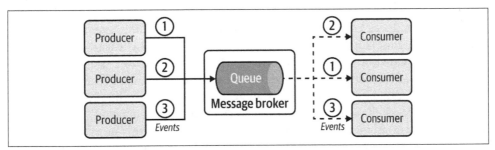

Figure 5-1. Event delivery from producers to consumers

When consumers are done processing the event, they can also send an acknowledgment to the message broker, so that the message broker can purge the event from its store.

How it's used in practice

This pattern can be used for various scenarios, such as asynchronously delivering events from one application to another, making sure only one application processes a piece of data, ensuring event delivery, sharing workload among applications, handling sudden bursts of events, and decoupling applications. Let's see how we can achieve these with some examples.

Provide asynchronous event delivery.   In asynchronous event delivery, the most common use of this pattern, we pass events to another application without blocking. For example, let's say we receive a loan application request. If the approval process takes a long time, we can simply add the request to an event queue so it can be processed by the loan processing application. At the same time, we can notify the customer that we have successfully received the request and will follow up about the outcome via email.

Process each event by a single application.   We can use the Producer-Consumer pattern when we need events to be consumed and processed by only one of the available consumers. Using event queues ensures that events are not delivered to multiple consumers. For example, in the loan processing use case, we need only one application to process the loan request so there won't be more than one credit check against the same customer.

Ensure event delivery.   Connecting producers and consumers that are not online at the same time is another key use case. For example, if we need to publish events to battery-powered wireless devices, we cannot guarantee that consumers will be online to consume the updates in real time. Devices may undergo network connectivity issues or simply run out of battery power. In this case, we can decouple the applications through queues so consumers will be guaranteed to fetch the events eventually.

Even if the producer, consumer, and message broker are online, events can get lost because of network failures. This can be overcome by using an at-least-once delivery guarantee provided by the message broker. The message broker uses acknowledgments to guarantee that the events are delivered. When the broker receives an event, it persists that durably and then sends an acknowledgment to the producer, stating that it has successfully consumed the event. The producer is updated to wait for the acknowledgment from the message broker when it publishes an event. Similarly, when the message broker delivers the message to the consumer, it expects an acknowledgment, and therefore the consumer is updated to send an acknowledgment when it receives an event. If the message broker does not receive the acknowledgment, it will try to redeliver the event, and so the consumer can get duplicate events. Messaging protocols such as AMQP support this functionality.

Handle sudden bursts of events.   We can also use this pattern to buffer event bursts over a short period. We can queue and process events without extensively scaling consumers. In the example in Figure 5-2, a data processing organization periodically pulls logs from servers for processing, resulting in a burst of logs every time we fetch a new log file. If we publish the burst of logs directly to the log processors, they will become overloaded and fail. But by buffering with a queue, we store and process the logs at the capacity of the log processors. Further, as they are using a pull-based approach, the consumers will not be overloaded as excess events are buffered at the event queue.

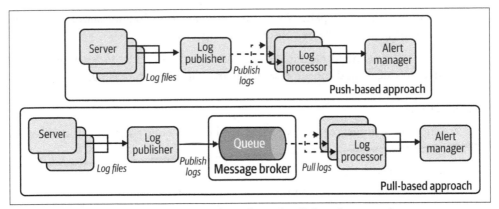

Figure 5-2. Handling bursts of logs with push- and pull-based approaches

Share workload with fairness. This pattern can be used to share the workload among multiple workers. Taking the previous example of processing log events, we have multiple log processors consuming events from the message broker in parallel and at their own speed. As the log processors are competing to pull events, we can ensure that events are processed as soon as possible. This also ensures that events are processed as long as at least one log processor is available, and no log processor will idle as long as events remain in the queue. This pattern also allows us to prioritize the oldest events by using FIFO semantics. This mimics queues in the real world: the first person in the queue will be served first. The Producer-Consumer pattern allows us to model the same event-processing semantics on cloud native applications.

Considerations

Most message brokers provide support for an at-least-once delivery guarantee. If the consumer fails to acknowledge the event delivery or times out, the broker will send that event to another consumer, making sure that the event is processed by at least one consumer.

A single message broker can host multiple event queues. We recommend that each use case and operation has its own queue; for example, events updating customer information might have their own queue, while events updating payments will have their own queue. Mixing different events in a single queue requires us to improve consumers to differentiate between events and handle them appropriately; this complicates the design, and slows performance as the number of events they receive increases.

When using queues, we have to be careful to handle bursts. While queues buffer events, there should be enough capacity to process all produced events over a certain time period. If we are constantly getting bursts of events (as in the log processing example in Figure 5-2), and if the input rate to the queue is consistently higher than the consumption rate, this pattern fails. To mitigate this risk, we should scale the number of consumers to increase consumption capacity.

This pattern helps us build decoupled systems and allows us to independently add and remove producers and consumers, scaling overall event processing.

Related patterns

The Producer-Consumer pattern is related to the following patterns (all covered in this chapter):

Publisher-Subscriber pattern
Can send the same event to multiple consumers for processing.

Fire and Forget pattern
Used when events need to be delivered to a single consumer with an at-most-once delivery guarantee without the help of a message broker.

Store and Forward pattern
Allows asynchronous at-least-once event delivery without a message broker.

Publisher-Subscriber Pattern

The *Publisher-Subscriber pattern* enables applications to communicate asynchronously by using topics. The topic delivers every event to every subscriber.

How it works

This pattern uses *topics* to propagate the events from publishers to subscribers. The topic is a message broker concept. Multiple publishers can submit events to a topic hosted in the message broker (Figure 5-3). The topic then publishes all those events to all its subscribers, and makes sure that every subscriber receives all incoming events.

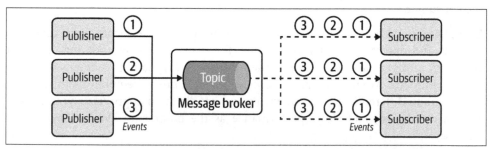

Figure 5-3. Event delivery from publishers to multiple subscribers

The standard behavior of the pattern is best effort: the events are delivered at most once. When a subscriber misses an event due to unavailability or network failure, they will never receive the event. But we overcome this problem with a *durable subscription*, which guarantees that all messages are delivered to all the consumers at least once, accounting for subscribers who are temporarily unavailable.

How it's used in practice

This pattern is used for scenarios such as broadcasting notifications in parallel to multiple recipients with both the best effort and at-least-once delivery guarantees. Let's see how we can achieve these.

Broadcast events.   This pattern is ideal for broadcasting information. For example, let's assume we are building a system like Twitter, and we can use this pattern to send a notification of all tweets published about sports with #sports (the topic) to all users who have subscribed to that hashtag. The main advantage of this pattern is that it enables us to notify all interested subscribers, instead of only a single user or application.

Deliver events with best effort.   Typically, events produced by publishers have the at-most-once delivery guarantee. For instance, subscribers do not receive events published during an outage. Though you risk losing events, this approach is still useful for scenarios such as status updates—like publishing current weather periodically to the weather topic so subscribed people can plan what to wear when they go out. Even when some updates are missed, the subscribers can appropriately take corrective decisions based on future events.

Make sure all events are delivered to all subscribers.   Event delivery with best effort is not suitable when missed events impact the function of the system. For example, someone might be tracking a topic to find out the closing date to apply for a state exam. A subscriber who misses that event will miss the deadline and miss the chance to sit for the exam. You can use durable subscriptions to ensure that subscribers receive missed events when they are online again.

Selectively deliver events to subscribers.   This pattern is useful when only specific events require delivery, in which case the most common approach is to leverage hierarchical topics. The topic name has a hierarchy such as news, news/sports, and news/politics. If the subscriber subscribes to the news topic, they will consume all events from news and all its subcategories, including news/sports and news/politics. But if they are interested in only sports news, they can subscribe to only news/sports.

An alternative approach for achieving selective delivery is to use filtering logic. A filtering condition such as news==sports is passed to the message broker upon subscribing to the topic, so that the message broker publishes only the sport news events to the subscriber.

Share workloads. This pattern can also be used to replicate and distribute events across multiple workers. In the example in Figure 5-4, we process periodically published weather data in real time. We need to publish every event to human subscribers (Alice and Bob) so they can keep track of the weather, and, in parallel, distribute events across distributed Weather Processing microservices to share and process the messages.

To achieve this, we use the client ID of the subscribers. Each subscriber has a unique client ID such as alice, bob, or P1. Since the topic keeps track of event delivery based on client IDs, it ensures that all events are delivered to both human subscribers with the client IDs alice and bob. We set the same client ID for both instances of the Weather Processing microservices to P1. By doing this, the topic publishes each event to only one of the microservice instances. This enables us to share the workload across those microservices.

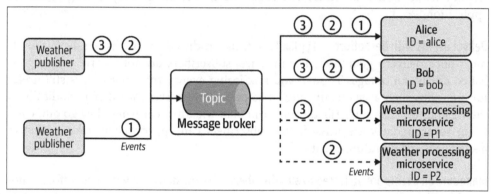

Figure 5-4. Replicating and distributing weather events across multiple microservices

Considerations

When subscribers cannot miss events published during downtime, we need a durable subscription. The message broker takes the responsibility of storing and delivering the events to subscribers as they come back online. Each durable subscription can be viewed as a dedicated event queue for each subscriber.

Alternatively, we can also use a commit log–based message broker such as Kafka or NATS to receive missed events published during subscriber downtime. These message brokers store all events to commit logs. Because they do not remove the events even after a successful or failed delivery attempt, upon request they can resend/replay previous events to subscribers. To retrieve missed events, subscribers must persist the last-processed event sequence ID, and during restart, they request the message broker to replay all the events since the last-processed sequence ID. This allows the system to achieve a higher delivery guarantee.

This pattern enables us to build decoupled systems and independently add or remove publishers and subscribers. Use the Producer-Consumer pattern when you need to share events among multiple consumers; but, as shown in Figure 5-4, you can use topics with subscriptions based on client ID to broadcast events to some subscribers while distributing the events across a subset of subscribers sharing the same client ID.

Related pattern

The Publisher-Subscriber pattern is related to the preceding Producer-Consumer pattern, which provides the capability to send an event to only one consumer for processing.

Fire and Forget Pattern

The *Fire and Forget pattern* enables clients (producers) to send events to respective consumers (services) with an at-most-once delivery guarantee without the use of a message broker. This pattern sends events by using standard APIs, discussed in Chapter 3.

How it works

Let's imagine that a weather sensor periodically sends current temperature and humidity readings to a weather-prediction service hosted in the cloud. Because of technical limitations, instead of using a message broker, as depicted in Figure 5-5, it is designed to invoke the API of the service by using protocols such as HTTP. The client is interested only in whether the server received the events, and is not interested in the final outcome. When a client publishes an event to the service, it expects only an acknowledgment of the event by a relevant HTTP status code such as 202 Accepted.

Figure 5-5. Fire and Forget event delivery from client to service

How it's used in practice

This pattern is useful when we need best-effort delivery of noncritical data, or when the receiving service does not possess the capability to subscribe or pull events from a client.

Deliver events with best effort.   As in the preceding example, the weather service tries to deliver the event only once, and upon failure discards the event. This is acceptable for this use case, as the service can continue the real-time predictions based on future events delivered by the client.

Deliver events to systems that do not support subscription. This pattern can also be used when the client is sending events to a third-party service that does not possess the capability to subscribe and pull events from a message broker. Services owned by partner organizations usually are deployed behind an API. They have the capability to consume events only via protocols such as HTTP. We also use this pattern when the client is hosted in an internal network and the service cannot initiate a connection to the client.

Considerations

This pattern is useful when processing events that have depreciating value over time, such as the current weather. These events become outdated when their processing is delayed. Instead, processing more-recent events is significantly more valuable. The Fire and Forget pattern enables us to quickly discard events and pick up the next one for processing. We should use the Producer-Consumer pattern if we do not want to discard events when they cannot be delivered.

If needed, we can design the clients to retry event delivery upon failures to improve the success rate of delivery. In the preceding example, the weather client can retry several times until it receives a 202 Accepted response from the server. But this does not provide the at-least-once event delivery guarantee, because if a service outage occurs for a sustained period of time, the client is not designed to continuously accumulate all the incoming events until the service is back.

Say we need the client to load-balance events across multiple services—for example, a single weather client sending events in a round-robin manner to five weather services. Here, we either have the weather client use an intermediary such as a network load balancer to route the events to available services, or improve the client to keep track of all the weather service endpoints and perform the load-balancing logic within itself. We do not recommend the latter approach, as it introduces additional complexity to the weather client.

Related patterns

The Fire and Forget pattern is related to the following two patterns (both covered in this chapter):

Producer-Consumer pattern
    Allows events to be delivered to a single consumer with higher delivery guarantees, as the consumer subscribes to an event queue.

Store and Forward pattern
    Delivers events to service endpoints with an at-least-once delivery guarantee.

Store and Forward Pattern

The *Store and Forward pattern* enables clients to send events to services with an at-least-once delivery guarantee. As with Fire and Forget, this pattern does not use message brokers but uses APIs to directly send events.

How it works

This pattern requires a complex client design to achieve the at-least-once event delivery guarantee. The client in this pattern first persists the events to a durable store, such as a database or queue in a message broker, before attempting to send them to the service (Figure 5-6). Upon successful event delivery, the client purges the events from the store. If delivery is unsuccessful, it retries to send the event. During this, as the client receives more events to send, it persists them to the store. Once the connection to the service is established, it will deliver all pending events, receive acknowledgment of the event consumption, and purge the events from its store.

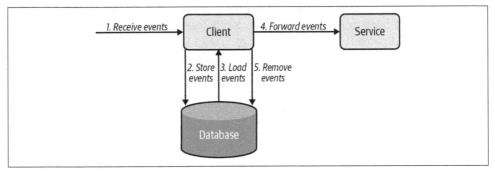

Figure 5-6. Store and Forward event delivery from client to service

How it's used in practice

This pattern is useful when delivering critical data with a message broker, or when the receiving service cannot subscribe or pull events from the client.

Deliver events to services that do not support subscription.   Let's assume we are publishing purchase order events to a partner service to fulfill the delivery. The partner services are usually hosted behind an API, and we assume they do not have the capability to subscribe and pull events from a message broker. We can use this pattern to call the service APIs via HTTP with an at-least-once delivery guarantee.

Ensure event delivery during service unavailability.   In the preceding example, our organization does not have control over the availability of the service hosted by partners and third parties. In this situation, we use this pattern to store all incoming events and then deliver those events to the services as they become available.

Considerations

We recommend this pattern when message brokers cannot be used and when we need the events to be delivered with an at-least-once delivery guarantee. This is because using message brokers and adopting the Producer-Consumer pattern greatly simplifies the architecture and reduces the operational cost.

When using this pattern, use a separate durable store (database or queue) for each client application, when possible, to greatly simplify the design. For scalability reasons, let's say we use five clients to send the order events to third-party services. But instead of using a dedicated store for each client, we recommend using a common event queue for all five clients to store the events. This allows us to distribute the events among the clients when they try to send events to the services. This also helps overcome client failures, as now other clients can fetch and publish events that are supposed to be sent by the failed client.

If you decide to use databases as the durable store, and still want to use multiple clients for event delivery, you must solve the problem of deciding which client publishes which event. We need to prevent multiple clients loading the same order event from the database and delivering it to the service. This causes duplicate events and risks overloading the service. To overcome this, we elect a single client to deliver a particular subset of events (for example, based on the hash of the event order number). Here, client selection is determined via leader election by using services such as ZooKeeper. Additionally, the same client can also deliver multiple subsets of events (for example, event order number hashes 2, 5, and 7).

Related patterns

The following patterns, covered in this chapter, are related to Store and Forward:

Fire and Forget pattern
  Publishes events to service endpoints with an at-most-once delivery guarantee.

Producer-Consumer pattern
  Allows events to be delivered to a single consumer with higher delivery guarantees when the consumer can subscribe to an event queue.

Polling Pattern

The *Polling pattern* enables clients such as web browsers to initiate a long-running job, periodically checking completion.

How it works

The frontend client or browser sends a request to initiate the process, such as insurance claim processing (Figure 5-7). Because the processing takes time, the backend service immediately sends an acknowledgment stating that it has accepted the request and initiated the asynchronous job processing. Along with the acknowledgment, it sends a job ID and, potentially, an estimated time of job completion. Based on this information, the client periodically queries the backend to check if the claim processing has completed. Upon completion, the backend returns the results as part of the response to the query, or provides a redirection to an endpoint containing the results.

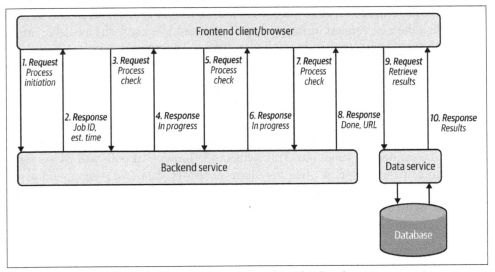

Figure 5-7. Frontend client/browser repeatedly calling backend service to retrieve asynchronous job results

How it's used in practice

This pattern is useful when we need to retrieve the result of an asynchronous job without using a subscription or callback.

Retrieve results from a long-running process that cannot notify of job completion. When we integrate frontend and backend applications, usually only the frontend can initiate the connection to the backend, and backends cannot easily call frontends. When the backends are processing an asynchronous task, they can often take more time than the connection time-out, which means clients cannot stay connected to receive the results. In this case, we use this pattern to repeatedly call the backend for results.

This mimics repeatedly calling the insurance company to check if a claim has been processed. Even though it is not ideal, we need to design the client in this way when the backend systems have no way to automatically inform the client of an update.

Deliver events to a client that cannot initiate subscription or callbacks. This pattern is used when clients cannot subscribe to a message broker or expose an endpoint to receive updates from the backend. For example, in the preceding example, the browser cannot directly subscribe to the message broker, so it periodically polls for new updates.

Considerations

When implementing this pattern, we should ensure that the life cycle of the asynchronous job is maintained in the backend, because the frontend clients may fail and get restarted. For example, when the browser window is refreshed, the user should continue to get the correct status update of the insurance claim. Therefore, when the browser initiates the connection after refresh, the backend application should be able to correlate the new request to the previously initiated job, using the available information on the request, and return the appropriate response to the client.

You should keep in mind that polling backends in a continuous manner is a waste of resources for both the client and service, and adds delay to the response, as the backend service cannot inform the client until the next poll. The amount of continuous polling can be reduced by using the long polling technique: the service does not immediately send a response but holds the connection until the response is available, or until the connection times out. This reduces the number of polls and allows services to immediately respond when they have necessary data. We recommend using the long poll if the connection time-out between the client and service is reasonably high, the network is usually stable, and the service has the capacity to hold the request until connection time-out; otherwise, fall back to periodic polling.

We do not recommend using this pattern when the application supports callbacks such as webhooks or WebSockets for communication, because those options are efficient and much less resource intensive. Callback-based event delivery is discussed in detail next.

Related patterns

The following patterns (covered in this chapter) are related to the Polling pattern:

Producer-Consumer pattern
> This is an alternative used when the participating applications publish and subscribe to a queue.

Request Callback pattern
> This is also an alternative that's used when the clients and services are capable of using WebSockets or webhooks.

Request Callback Pattern

The *Request Callback pattern* enables applications to communicate asynchronously. The application provides the callback information with the request so responses can be delivered to the given callback.

How it works

In this pattern, one application should initiate the request with the callback information so that the responding application can deliver the responses asynchronously by using the callback. This pattern builds on top of the Asynchronous Request-Reply pattern from Chapter 2, by providing two variations: using WebSockets or webhooks. Let's see how they work.

WebSockets. To use WebSockets, both client and service should have the capability to communicate via the WebSocket protocol (Figure 5-8). The client initiates the connection to the service and establishes a long-running connection. Both the client and service persist the connection and communicate by sending events. This approach is used for clients requesting information via an event and waiting on the service to respond, or for exchanging multiple events. WebSocket is an HTTP-based technology, but HTTP2 and gRPC also provide similar callback-based communication.

Figure 5-8. Client and service communicating via the WebSocket protocol

GraphQL uses WebSocket with its subscription feature, allowing clients to connect to a service and listen to real-time events according to the GraphQL query submitted when subscribing. Clients will then continuously get updates when the data in the service changes. A client can unsubscribe by sending a message to the server, or the server can unsubscribe due to errors or time-out. Refer to Chapter 2 for more details on GraphQL.

Webhooks. In this approach, the client application issues a request and has the response delivered to a callback endpoint (Figure 5-9). The client sends the request with a callback URL. If the callback URL is consistent, we configure that on the service side, so we do not have to redundantly send the URL with the request. The response, when generated, is delivered to the callback URL.

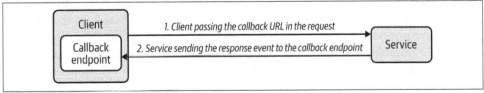

Figure 5-9. Client and server communicating via webhook

Webhooks can be implemented in multiple ways. One way is to use WebSub. This open protocol, initially designed to extend Atom and RSS protocols for data feeds, has been adopted by the World Wide Web Consortium (W3C) as a Candidate Recommendation since April 2017. WebSub uses Publisher, Hub, and Subscriber microservices and uses HTTP for communication. The publishers publish content to the hub, via HTTP calls and by using HTTP headers to denote the topic information. The subscribers discover the hubs for their interested topic and make an HTTP POST request to the hub with their topic and callback URL. They will then get served with the relevant content through the HTTP POST calls by the hub, as the hub gets new data.

How it's used in practice

We use this pattern to deliver responses asynchronously or when we need to receive continuous updates. This pattern mimics registering our telephone number as a callback so that the insurance agent can call to inform us of the status of our insurance claim. Following are some use cases in practice.

Deliver response asynchronously. This pattern is ideal when the service cannot respond within the connection time-out, such as in our insurance claim processing use case. The backend service acknowledges the request immediately, and delivers the results when the claim processing is completed. This also allows the backend to send the results instantly when the necessary data becomes available.

Deliver updates continuously. Though we can use this pattern to update the insurance claim status in the browser, this pattern is much more useful when we need real-time updates, such as monitoring stock prices. The browser establishes a WebSocket connection with the backend service to receive the latest updates and dynamically render them in the web page. This pattern can be used only when the client can receive the response from the server leveraging the WebSocket protocol, or by exposing an endpoint to be used as a callback.

Considerations

When implementing this pattern, the callback does not need to be an HTTP endpoint; it can be an email address, an event queue, or an event topic. We can also model this pattern so that when the service processing is done, instead of calling the client, the service calls another service to process the results based on the callback information provided by the client. When the result is big, the service can also store results in a durable store such as in Amazon S3, and then pass that URL to the callback so that the client can load the processed data.

The webhooks typically provide only an at-most-once delivery guarantee, as the service has to drop the response events when the callback is not available or if a network failure occurs. We can improve this to an at-least-once delivery guarantee by incorporating the Store and Forward pattern when delivering events to callbacks or by using a message broker when the participating applications have the capability to communicate via a message broker.

We recommend choosing WebSocket over webhooks when the client and server need to asynchronously communicate by sending more than one message. This is because WebSocket keeps the connection live throughout the communication, and reduces the cost of sending each new message. Subscribing to a stock symbol and receiving continuous stock price updates is a good example for this. At the same time, we recommend using webhooks over WebSocket when the client is expecting only a single response, and when the response time cannot be determined or if the response can take more than a few minutes (for example, when expecting the outcome of an insurance claim).

Related patterns

The following are related to the Request Callback pattern:

Store and Forward pattern
Complements this pattern by providing guaranteed callback event delivery (covered previously in this chapter).

Polling pattern
Provides an alternative when applications cannot establish callbacks (covered previously in this chapter).

Asynchronous Request-Reply pattern
An alternative approach to communicate asynchronously by using a message broker. This pattern is covered in Chapter 2.

Summary of Event-Delivery Patterns

This section has outlined common event-delivery patterns used by cloud native applications that are built in an event-driven architecture. Table 5-1 summarizes when we should and should not use these patterns, and their benefits.

Table 5-1. Event-delivery patterns

Pattern	When to use	When not to use	Benefits
Producer-Consumer	There is a particular event to be consumed and processed by only one of the available consumers. We cannot confirm the availability of the consumers and producers. We see burst event production over a short period. We need to ensure fairness in the processing of events.	There is continuous high traffic, and the incoming event rate is much higher than the consumed event rate. Message brokers cannot be used in the solution, and producers or consumers cannot connect to a message broker.	Delivers an event to one consumer without duplicating the events. Can tolerate availability problems in consumers and producers. Handles spikes/bursts in traffic.

Pattern	When to use	When not to use	Benefits
Publisher-Subscriber	In a notification delivery system. An at-most-once delivery guarantee is tolerated by subscribers. (It's possible to miss the events if the subscriber is not available at the time of event notification.) We need selective delivery of events to the subscribers.	You cannot tolerate any missed events by the subscriber. Message brokers cannot be used in the solution, and producers or consumers cannot connect to a message broker.	Helps build an independent and decoupled system that can publish and subscribe. Scales well with multiple subscribers interested in the same topic.
Fire and Forget	At-most-once delivery guarantee is tolerated. Dropping events is acceptable, such as when delivering non-business-critical events. The consumer cannot pull any updates from the message broker. Only a set of consumers is available to be notified.	Any issues in delivering or processing business-critical events cannot be ignored. Message brokers can be included in the system, and producers and consumers can connect to a message broker.	No need to have a message broker to transfer messages from producer to consumer. Simple to implement and no need to have additional deployment and maintenance complexities.
Store and Forward	At-least-once delivery is required when both publisher and consumer are online and reachable at any time. Message brokers cannot be used in the solution. The consumer cannot pull any updates from the message broker.	Message brokers can be included in the system, and producers and consumers can connect to a message broker.	No need to have a message broker to transfer messages from producer to consumer.
Polling	Clients do not have the capability to subscribe to a message broker or to expose an endpoint to receive updates from the backend system. The service does not have the capability to call other endpoints upon completion of a job. You have long-running jobs.	You have short jobs where success/failure can be reported immediately. The applications can support callbacks such as webhooks, or WebSocket for communication.	Executes a long-running job and gets the response without having an additional infrastructure.
Request Callback	Handling the request can take more time than the typical connection time-out of a standard request. Clients are expecting updates from the services on one or more jobs. The applications have the capability to communicate by using WebSocket, or clients have the capability to expose a callback URL and services can call that URL to send updates.	Applications do not have the capability to communicate via WebSocket, or the clients cannot provide a callback.	Executes a long-running job and gets the response without increasing the traffic to service to continuously check for updates. More scalable approach, as updates are sent when the job is completed.

State Management Patterns

In this section, we discuss how to build and maintain cloud native application state without coupling to a database, how to re-create application state at various times, and how to build applications with different domain models out of the same data. Here, we cover the Event Sourcing pattern, which is considered the foundation for building various other patterns such as the CQRS pattern introduced in Chapter 4.

Event Sourcing Pattern

The *Event Sourcing pattern* enables us to store all changes to the application state as a sequence of events. This pattern not only is used to re-create application state at various points in time, and with different domain models, but also serves as an audit history to illustrate how we ended up in the current application state.

How it works

Every time an event updates the application state, the event is also recorded in a persistence store in the order of operation. Figure 5-10 shows a banking use case, in which transactions are performed on an account. Events occur, such as Bob depositing $110, withdrawing $20, and then again depositing $50.

If we consider only the current state of the application, we know only that Bob now has a balance of $140 in his account, but we do not know the events that led up to this. Now, as each event is stored in a persistence store (or event log), in the sequence of its occurrence, we can gain an understanding of how his account balance changed over time.

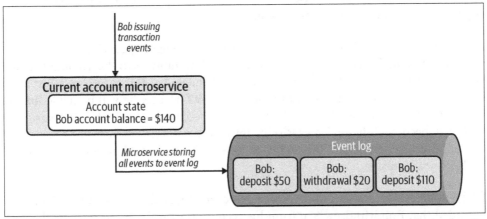

Figure 5-10. Current account microservice generating an event log while updating application state

Events are usually stored on a commit log, such as Apache Kafka, which allows us to read the events back from any point in time in a sequential manner by passing event sequence IDs. These events are read again by the application or other systems so that they can process the events that have occurred or re-create an application state with either a subset or all events.

How it's used in practice

The Event Sourcing pattern unlocks the ability to system time-travel, build different domain models based on the same sequence of events, re-create a failed application state, run temporal queries, and replay events.

Re-create application state. Let's assume the application state got corrupted during system failure. Since we have stored all the events corresponding to the state, we can simply replay all the events in order to re-create a specific application state. We also have to disable the system, prohibiting any notifications to external systems during state rebuilding. For example, while we are re-creating a state for Bob's bank account, we should not send deposit and withdrawal notifications.

Build different domain models. Let's assume Bob is enrolled in a rewards program that gives points on purchases he makes at affiliated stores. The bank uses a different domain model to calculate and keep track of the points Bob has earned. Instead of tightly coupling the rewards service with the core transaction application, with the Event Sourcing pattern the bank can asynchronously build Bob's points from the transactions stored in the commit logs. This not only allows us to build specific data views to support different access patterns to reduce load, but also helps consuming systems—such as a rewards service—to evolve and change at their own speed without interfering with the core banking system.

Run temporal queries. This pattern allows us to run temporal queries on the stored events. For example, let's say the bank charges a $5 monthly fee if the account balance falls below $100. Bob had $140 in his account at the end of the month. But just after the initial $20 withdrawal, his account had only $90. Hence, he will be liable for the $5 monthly fee. Without having the events in the commit log, achieving such use cases will become difficult. This visibility into the event log demonstrates a fully lossless architecture, unlocking the ability to time-travel and build various views based on historical data.

Replay events. This pattern also allows us to correct mistakes. Let's say the bank has recorded that Bob withdrew $50 from his account on April 15, even though he successfully canceled the withdrawal. Because of this withdrawal entry, the bank also charged the $5 monthly fee on April 30. Assume that the bank found out about this mistake on May 3. By using the Event Sourcing pattern, the bank can replay all the transactions of Bob's account starting April 15, correctly reverting the withdrawal and refunding Bob the erroneous $5 monthly fee charged on April 30.

Considerations

With this pattern, we need to decide whether the application state or the event log is going to be our single source of truth. If we are using a database to keep track of the application state, the database can be the source of truth, as it is durable. We can then use the event log only for auditing purposes and to generate other domain models. But at the same time, if we are keeping the state in memory (such as in a data structure, in-memory database, or cache), then we have to use the event log as the single source of truth, as we can always regenerate the state by replaying the events from the logs.

When using an event log as the source of truth, the recovery of system failure can take a long time; we need to re-create the application state by replaying *all* the events in the event log. To improve recovery time, we can periodically take application state snapshots, as we'll discuss in Chapter 6, and during recovery, we can load the latest snapshot and replay only the events logged after that.

Performing event playback and re-creating an application's state can be tricky, especially when the application is interacting with external services. If we need to stop the application from calling external services (such as notifying Bob again about his $50 deposit), we have to either make the service intelligent enough to know that it is performing a replay and so shouldn't send any external calls, or gate the external services with APIs and drop the service calls at the APIs. If we are replaying events on multiple services and they need to communicate with one another, we recommend adding some sort of reference point, such as date and time, to their request when calling other services. For example, rather than requesting the current account balance, we can request the account balance on 03/23 at 11:15 a.m. In this case, the responding application will be able to always respond with the correct balance at the given time, increasing the consistency of the application during event playback.

When defining the events for a commit log, they should be modeled as *change* events. In the banking use case, we should use events that reflect some kind of change, such as deposit of $50 and withdrawal of $20, and not use events such as set bank balance to $150, or set bank balance to $130. If we reverse or remove the events during event playback, we will be able to get the corrected final balance.

When designing the service, we can either store the application state as simple objects and let the application operate on them, or we can model the state within the domain model itself. We recommend building the state within the domain model, as this gives us flexibility, especially when the processing logic is complex. But we cannot use this approach if we need to reverse the events. In this case, we would need to store the state after each update, and then revert to the previous state when a reversal is necessary. This can complicate the application architecture. If event reversal is needed, we recommend storing events separate from the application logic.

When building different domain models from the same event source, we should keep in mind that those models are usually built asynchronously and so can only be eventually consistent. This is because there can be network and application processing delays to write the events to the logs, and then other services to read and populate their application state. Hence, we should not use this pattern for use cases that do not tolerate eventual consistency. We can use log-based event queries with Apache Kafka and NATS as the event logs, for example, when building this pattern as they provide the capability to store events in order, and allow us to replay past events when necessary.

While this pattern allows us to time-travel, it also enforces restrictions in the event schema. For example, we can add new attributes to the event, but we cannot remove or update existing attributes. When the system replays previous events, they will not be compatible with the running application state. If we try to handle multiple versions of the event schema in the application code, the system can soon become very complex and difficult to maintain.

 The Event Sourcing pattern is inherently complex to implement and maintain, especially with a changing event schema, and with multiple external services communicating. We recommend using this pattern only if rebuilding an application's state, or different domain models, is essential.

Related patterns

The following are related to the Event Sourcing pattern:

Periodic Snapshot State pattern
Used to generate data store snapshots so that application state can be rebuilt much faster. This pattern is discussed in Chapter 6.

CQRS pattern
Used to store commands so that multiple applications can be built to serve queries. This pattern is discussed in Chapter 4.

Materialized View pattern
Used to store data so that it can generate materialized views based on the events. This pattern is discussed in Chapter 4.

Summary of State Management Pattern

This section outlined the Event Sourcing pattern and its use in managing cloud native application state. Table 5-2 summarizes when we should and should not use this pattern, and its benefits.

Table 5-2. Event Sourcing pattern

Pattern	When to use	When not to use	Benefits
Event Sourcing	Multiple applications use the same data and need different domain models. Application state should be rebuilt. Temporal queries need to be executed in historical data. The system needs to time-travel and change past event occurrences. We need to keep track of audit information.	The data model is simple, and the consuming application can query for the intended data. The event schema changes in a continuous manner. We need all consuming applications to have data in a consistent state at all times.	Allows consumers to build application state optimized for their domain models and access patterns. Replicates the data into multiple applications, thereby increasing availability. Supports system recovery with event replay.

Orchestration Patterns

In this section, we cover various *orchestration patterns* that help build an effective event-driven architecture. These patterns resemble the service composition patterns in Chapter 3, which coordinate and orchestrate synchronous service calls. The orchestration patterns predominantly use asynchronous event-delivery patterns discussed previously to manage the movement of events across multiple applications.

Though building cloud native event-driven applications on a small scale is straightforward, the architecture can soon become complex and difficult to manage when many microservices are involved. This section covers the Mediator, Pipe and Filter, and Priority Queue patterns that can be used to streamline event flow and manage the complexity of the application. These patterns are also considered foundations of event-driven architecture.

Mediator Pattern

The *Mediator pattern* provides centralized management of event orchestration. The mediator will not only understand and route events but also orchestrate events in sequential and parallel order across applications, while also handling failures. This pattern helps keep the coordination logic in a central location, allowing us to more simply change the behavior of the system.

How it works

The key element of this pattern is the mediator microservice runtime built as part of the cloud native application. It operates by interacting with all the microservices that integrate, via event queues, topics, and APIs. It connects on various protocols and transforms events for applications accordingly. These mediator microservices are usually stateless, and might need to perform only filtering, sorting, and event transformations. But when required, they can coordinate sequential and parallel tasks.

Figure 5-11 depicts a use case of a new insurance request, which needs to perform address verification, credit verification, and referral verification in parallel. These are then followed by discount and final approval tasks. The mediator calls participating microservices by using the Asynchronous Request-Reply pattern from Chapter 2. The mediator first passes events to the verification microservice in parallel, collects their responses, combines them, and then initiates the discount and approval tasks sequentially. Finally, it publishes the result to the decision queue so downstream systems can become aware of the decision.

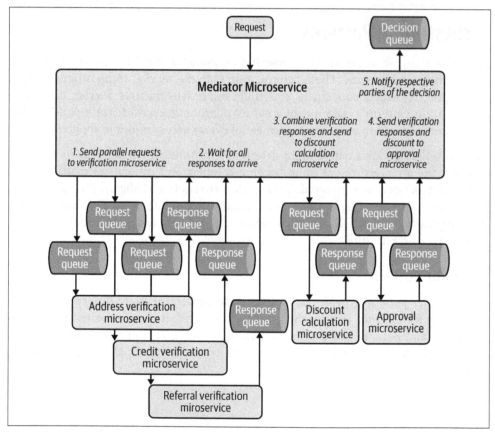

Figure 5-11. Mediator microservice orchestrating a new insurance request

Mediators sometimes need to combine events from multiple systems, and so need to be stateful. In this example, each verification microservice sends its results at different times, and the mediator needs to persist the results until it receives all three, so it can create the combined event and send that to the discount microservice.

How it's used in practice

We can use this pattern to sort and distribute events, split an event into multiple subevents, process those events in various tasks in both parallel and sequential order, and finally combine the results to generate an output.

Sort and distribute events.   This pattern is used to sort events among multiple subprocesses. For example, as we are getting orders from a single queue, the mediator sorts the orders based on region. This also helps integrate decoupled producer and consumer applications, especially when they are external. In this case, mediators format the events and perform required protocol transformations.

Split events into multiple subevents.   This pattern is also used to split one event into multiple events. For example, when we receive a new insurance application event, we need to split it into various subevents and send them to multiple systems to perform subtasks such as address and credit verification.

Ensure task execution order.   The mediator pattern is used to perform some tasks sequentially while others are executed in parallel. This enables us to combine the results of multiple parent tasks before executing a dependent task. In our insurance scenario, we process verification tasks in parallel, and then the discount and approval tasks sequentially. The discount task is executed only when all the verification tasks have been completed and their results combined.

Considerations

Use this pattern instead of Pipe and Filter when the system is undergoing rapid changes. This pattern enables us to change the integration logic and operation flow by modifying the mediator. In the Pipe and Filter pattern, we need to update multiple applications and queues to perform the change.

As the mediator contains all the coordination logic, over time it can become complex and difficult to maintain. Split coordination logic among distinct separate mediator microservices so they are more manageable. Microservice integration with this pattern can also be done via configuration-based tools such as WSO2 Micro Integrator, Apache Camel, Siddhi, and BPMN frameworks.

Do not use this pattern when central control for orchestration is not required. When this pattern is overused, it will provide all the orchestration responsibility to a single team, which can constrain the autonomy of other teams, going against the principles of cloud native application development.

Related patterns

The following patterns, covered in this chapter, are related to the Mediator pattern:

Pipe and Filter pattern
Provides a decentralized approach to orchestrate events across applications.

Event-delivery patterns
The Mediator pattern uses event-delivery patterns to communicate among applications.

Pipe and Filter Pattern

The *Pipe and Filter pattern* orchestrates events in a decentralized manner. It uses multiple event queues and topics to streamline the event flow across multiple microservices in a cloud native application.

How it works

This pattern uses event queues and topics to connect microservices. With this approach, we can build a very large graph of microservices via topics and queues to fulfill our business requirements. Figure 5-12 shows a credit card application processing flow using the Pipe and Filter pattern. Various microservices are integrated with one another via topics to asynchronously process and monitor the credit card application, and they publish the results to event queues for other microservices to consume.

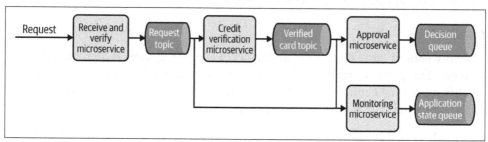

Figure 5-12. A credit card application processing flow using the Pipe and Filter pattern

How it's used in practice

Use this pattern when you need to build large-scale asynchronous systems that are managed by multiple teams.

Build large-scale decoupled systems. As the microservices are connected to each other via asynchronous protocols such as topics and queues, this pattern decouples services. We can continuously add new microservices to the topics and queues and extend the processing flow without impacting existing microservices.

In our example of the credit card application processing workflow, if we need to update users about their credit card application state, we introduce a notification microservice to consume from the application state queue and send updates to users. Similarly, we can attach a completely new workflow of printing the physical credit cards and shipping them to users by connecting it to the decision queue.

Seamlessly add and remove functionality. This pattern enables seamless addition and removal of microservices to the pipeline, and allows teams to add new business logic with minimal effect on other microservices. In the our credit card example, you can see how the status monitoring microservice is seamlessly integrated at each step without impacting the card processing event flow. If we need to add new functionality such as introducing income verification, we can simply add the income verification microservice between the Credit Verification and Approval microservices with minimal effect on the overall cloud native application.

Provide segregation of duties. As the events are distributed via multiple topics and queues, this pattern is ideal for providing a segregation of duties among teams. This allows each team to consume events, process them, and output corresponding events independently. If we are modeling a credit card application workflow, for example, then receiving and verifying the requests, performing credit checks, and taking approval decisions can be handled by various teams.

Considerations

Use this pattern instead of the Mediator pattern when building large-scale asynchronous systems with independent teams. This way, we can delegate the orchestration responsibilities to each team, as opposed to centralizing control of the event flow with the Mediator pattern. We recommend using the Mediator pattern when central control should be established across multiple services.

Because this pattern enables multiple teams to collaborate, it is vital to have well-defined event schemas. Also use a schema registry to store schemas to enable autonomous discovery and consumption of events.

At times we are interested in only specific events, such as credit card request events related to a specific region, so we can treat them differently according to the laws of that region. The microservices use filters in their subscription to consume only the events that they are interested in, or if they consume events from a topic, they can perform the filtering within the microservices.

Do not use this pattern if the flow of events changes frequently—for example, when you are rapidly experimenting or innovating on the event processing logic. More pipes and filters may need to be modified to accommodate the changes, which is more costly than performing changes via the Mediator pattern.

Related patterns

The following are related to the Pipe and Filter pattern:

Mediator pattern
> Provides a more centralized approach for orchestrating event flow in event-driven architecture. This pattern was covered previously in this chapter.

Event-delivery patterns
> The Pipe and Filter pattern uses event-delivery patterns, also covered in this chapter, to communicate among microservices.

Saga pattern
> Uses this pattern to implement data processing pipelines that can support compensation transactions. Chapter 3 describes this pattern.

Priority Queue Pattern

The *Priority Queue pattern* handles events based on their priority so that high-priority events are handled first, while low-priority events are processed as capacity allows.

How it works

This pattern combines multiple queues, as in the Producer and Consumer pattern, to enable prioritized event processing. We achieve this by building a polling client that uses multiple event queues to process events based on priority.

Figure 5-13 shows a system that handles customer requests. We need to give 60% priority to premium customer requests, 30% to gold customers, and 10% to nonmembers. We design this by making the request-handler application poll the premium queue 60% of the time, the gold queue 30% of the time, and the nonmember queue for the last 10%. You can also apply more logic to optimize what to be done with spare capacity.

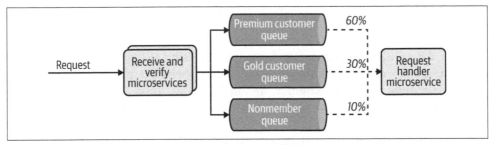

Figure 5-13. Priority-based customer-request handling

How it's used in practice

This pattern is needed when we want to preferentially handle some events over others or have insufficient capacity to process all events.

Process some events quicker than others. This pattern allows prioritization of important tasks. We presented a typical case previously: processing premium membership customer requests with higher priority over gold membership or nonmember customers.

Optimize resource utilization. Because of financial or other reasons, if we have constraints on the available processing nodes, we use this pattern to ensure that we process only the highest-value events. For example, if we are analyzing transaction fraud, we can categorize customer transactions by size and process them in that order. The application will always look to first analyze events from the largest transaction queue and then process events from the smaller queues only as capacity allows. This allows us to focus on the potentially higher-impact fraud investigations with our limited resources. Additionally, we should monitor queue depth and discard events over time that have become of little value.

Considerations

When applying this pattern, at times the client application will not have the capability to perform a polling operation. This may be because it is an external system outside our control. In this case, implement the polling client as an intermediary application that performs the prioritization and pushes events to other systems.

It is important to implement a cleaning task to discard old events based on queue depth; especially when the input event rate is higher than the processing rate, the low-priority queue can have stale events for a long time. Alternatively, you can design the application to promote events to a higher-priority queue when it has capacity and the events have stayed for a considerable time in the lower-priority queue. We recommend the prior approach when we do not have the mandate to process all events, and recommend the latter when we need to process all incoming events, and if we do not want the lower-priority events to starve when there is a steady flow of high-priority events.

You can also consider implementing this pattern by using a single topic and subscription filters, as we discussed in the "Publisher-Subscriber Pattern" on page 168. In our customer-request processing example, we can deploy six microservices that subscribe with a `membership==premium` subscription filter, three microservices with `membership==gold`, and one with `membership!=premium AND membership!=gold`. This allows us to simulate the desired behavior. But this cannot calculate queue depth for each type of request to discard events, or promote events from a lower to a higher priority.

We recommend using this alternative only if there is enough capacity to process all incoming events. In addition, do not use this pattern unless priority-based processing is necessary for your use case, as it would introduce unnecessary complexity to the architecture.

Related patterns

The following patterns, both covered in this chapter, are related to the Priority Queue pattern:

Publisher-Subscriber pattern
    With subscription filters, this can provide an alternative design to implement the Priority Queue pattern.

Producer-Consumer pattern
    Can be used when prioritization is not necessary.

Summary of Orchestration Patterns

This section has outlined common orchestration patterns for building cloud native applications using an event-driven architecture. Table 5-3 summarizes when we should and should not use these patterns, and their benefits.

Table 5-3. Orchestration patterns

Pattern	When to use	When not to use	Benefits
Mediator	To simply sort the events among multiple subprocesses. To split an event into multiple events based on the use case. Tasks need to be performed in a sequential or parallel order. The system undergoes rapid changes, and using the Pipe and Filter pattern requires more overhead during each change.	Central control for orchestration is not necessary.	Provides the central system for orchestration, so change management is relatively easy.

Pattern	When to use	When not to use	Benefits
Pipe and Filter	To provide segregation of duties among multiple teams. To add/remove business logic into multiple stages of processing without impacting other teams.	The overall flow of events is changed frequently. Central control for orchestration is necessary.	Allows seamless addition and removal of applications to the pipeline. Increases decoupling and reduces impact among multiple teams.
Priority Queue	To treat one type of an event with urgency compared to another. Resources are constrained, and we can process only a subset of events.	There is no strong need for priority-based processing.	Better utilization of resources based on priority of jobs.

Technologies for Event-Driven Architecture

Interactions among cloud native applications in event-driven architecture can be implemented using various message brokers, integration solutions such as ESB, and simple service calls.

Patterns like Fire and Forget and Polling use simple service calls to deliver events. We discussed service calls and related technologies such as REST, gRPC, and Thrift in Chapters 2 and 3.

When building orchestration patterns, we need applications that perform mediation, filtering, protocol switching, and data transformation, and that run business logic. We can implement these applications from scratch or use frameworks such as Spring Boot. When we require only standard functionalities, we can use configuration-based ESBs or integration systems such as WSO2 Micro Integrator and Apache Camel. (Refer to Chapter 3 for details on ESBs or integration systems.) Also, when these applications need stateful data processing, event sourcing, or complex event processing, we use stream-processing applications for integration, such as Siddhi and Flink. We discuss these in detail in Chapter 6.

Because event-driven architecture uses topics and queues, we also looked at commonly used technologies such as AMQP, Kafka, and NATS in Chapter 2. In this section, let's dive deep into other message broker technologies that we can use to implement these patterns.

Apache ActiveMQ

Apache ActiveMQ is the one of the oldest and most widely used open source message brokers that implements AMQP. It provides reliable messaging among the client, broker, and consumer by using queues and event acknowledgments. It also supports OpenWire, STOMP over WebSocket, and MQTT for IoT devices. ActiveMQ natively supports Java Message Service (JMS) for integrating with Java-based applications. This is an ideal system that we can use to implement the Publisher-Consumer pattern, in which we require an exactly once event-processing guarantee and only one consumer should process an event.

ActiveMQ also supports delivering events to multiple subscribers via topics and the reliable delivery of events using durable subscriptions. It supports centralized and peer-based communication to achieve clustering and uses a relational database along with a high-performance journal to provide persistence for the events stored in the broker. But because it cannot scale to high numbers of durable subscriptions, it should not be used for building highly scalable event-driven systems with multiple subscribers.

RabbitMQ

RabbitMQ is an open source message broker that supports messaging protocols such as AMQP, STOMP, and MQTT. It also supports clustering and failover. RabbitMQ uses *exchanges,* which can be compared to post offices or mailboxes.

When exchanges get events, they distribute event copies to queues by using rules called *bindings*. This provides more flexibility on modeling event distribution. It can also support both push- and pull-based approaches: the broker either delivers messages to consumers via their subscribed queues or allows consumers to pull messages on demand. RabbitMQ is a popular choice for patterns like Priority Queue.

Amazon SQS

Amazon Simple Queue Service (SQS) is a fully managed event-queuing service provided by Amazon, enabling us to decouple and scale microservices and serverless applications. SQS offers two types of event queues. *Standard queues* offer maximum throughput, with best-effort ordering and at-least-once delivery. *SQS FIFO queues* offer event processing in the exact order that events are sent, with an exactly once processing guarantee, although it comes with a throughput constraint.

SQS doesn't support standard messaging protocols like AMQP, STOMP, and MQTT. But it uses HTTPS to push and pull the events to and from the queue. Since SQS consumers need to poll the SQS queue to receive the events, they are not required to be online when the events are injected into the queue. SQS allows event processing to be retried on failure, but once the maximum number of attempts is reached, it moves the event to a dead-letter queue and removes it from the original SQS queue. This allows consumer services to not block on a corrupted message or waste resources, and enables operations to investigate messages from the dead-letter queue.

Amazon SNS

Amazon Simple Notification Service (SNS) is a fully managed messaging service that supports high-volume fan-out event delivery to all available consumers. It supports event delivery to applications such as Amazon SQS queues, AWS Lambda functions, HTTPS endpoints, and to persons via text messaging, mobile push, and email. It is often used to deliver high-volume real-time notifications following the Publisher-Subscriber pattern.

However, it doesn't support standard messaging protocols like AMQP, MQTT, and STOMP (similar to Amazon SQS), and the messages are pushed to consumers via configured notification methods such as HTTP/HTTPS, email, and text. Because it provides only at-most-once delivery, SNS is often paired with SQS so consumers have a dedicated event queue for higher-reliability processing.

Azure Event Grid

Azure Event Grid is a fully managed service that enables event-driven, reactive programming for cloud native applications. It uses a publish-subscribe model by supporting webhooks. Event Grid has built-in support for events coming from Azure services, like storage blobs and resource groups. It allows you to call serverless functions, perform ops automation, build application integration, and integrate with third-party services.

Event Grid isn't a data pipeline and doesn't deliver the actual object that was updated, but rather notifies the event occurrence. When delivering the event, it can use filters and route specific events to different endpoints, multicast to multiple endpoints, and make sure the events are delivered with an at-least-once delivery guarantee by spreading its deployment across regions and availability zones.

Azure Service Bus Queues

Microsoft *Azure Service Bus* is a fully managed service provided by the Azure messaging infrastructure that can fan out events to multiple consumers through topics as well as support event queues. It can also provide ordered event delivery with FIFO, with at-least-once and at-most-once delivery guarantees.

This can be used to integrate applications or application components that span across multiple communication protocols, data contracts, trust domains, or network environments. It allows consumers to receive events without having to poll the queue, by using a long-polling operation to wait for events to become available.

Google Cloud Pub/Sub

Google Cloud Pub/Sub is a fully managed asynchronous messaging service provided by Google. It decouples services that produce events from services that process them. Pub/Sub can be used as messaging-oriented middleware or event ingestion and delivery for streaming analytics pipelines.

It requires clients to use HTTPS to send and consume messages, and supports webhooks to push messages to consuming services. It doesn't support standard messaging protocols like AMQP, MQTT, and STOMP for event delivery. But it provides at-least-once delivery, with durable message storage and high availability. It can also provide around-the-world real-time message delivery with consistent performance at scale.

Summary of Message Broker Technologies

This section outlined commonly used message brokers for cloud native application development. Table 5-4 summarizes when we should and should not use these message brokers.

Table 5-4. Message broker technologies

Message broker type	When to use	When not to use
Apache ActiveMQ	Need queues or topics. Exactly once processing guarantee. Small- to moderate-scale deployment. Need support for standard messaging protocols.	Highly scalable deployments. High number of durable subscriptions. Replay acknowledged messages.
RabbitMQ	Need queues, topics, or to perform event routing. Exactly once processing guarantee. Small- to moderate-scale deployment. Need support for standard messaging protocols.	Highly scalable deployments. High number of durable subscriptions. Replay acknowledged messages.
Apache Kafka	Need topics. Highly scalable deployments. High number of durable subscriptions. Need replay of events. Exactly once processing guarantee. Need to acknowledge all messages up to a certain offset.	Need support for standard messaging protocols. Need to selectively acknowledge messages.
NATS	Need for topics and queues. Highly scalable deployments. High number of durable subscriptions. Need replay of events. At-least-once delivery guarantee.	Need support for standard messaging protocols.

Message broker type	When to use	When not to use
Amazon SQS	Need queues. At-least-once delivery guarantee. Highly scalable deployment. Managed infrastructure by Amazon. Need ordered delivery with FIFO.	Need support for standard messaging protocols. Replay acknowledged messages. Need to fan out the events to multiple consumers. Need a push model.
Amazon SNS	Need topics or webhooks. Highly scalable deployment. Managed infrastructure by Amazon. Need to send events to applications and people. No delivery guarantee is required. Call serverless functions.	Need support for standard messaging protocols. Guaranteed delivery. Replay acknowledged messages.
Azure Event Grid	Need topics, webhooks. At-least-once delivery guarantee. Managed infrastructure by Azure. Call serverless functions.	Need support for standard messaging protocols. Replay acknowledged messages.
Azure Service Bus queues	Need queues or topic At-least-once delivery guarantee. Managed infrastructure by Azure. Need ordered delivery with FIFO. Need to use AMQP 1.0 messaging protocol. Should store less than 80 GB of events.	Need support for MQTT or STOMP. Replay acknowledged messages.
Google Cloud Pub/Sub	Need topics, queries, or webhooks At-least-once delivery guarantee. Managed infrastructure by Google. Need consistent performance to delivery events around the world.	Need support for standard messaging protocols. Replay acknowledged messages.

Testing

In this section, we cover the most important aspects of testing in cloud native applications built on event-driven architecture. Event-driven applications need to follow conventional approaches of writing unit and integration tests. There is no difference in the way unit tests are written (such as the way business logic is isolated via well-defined interfaces and tested without need of dependent applications or network). But integration tests for cloud native event-driven applications require the following additional steps:

1. Ensure that event-transferring infrastructure is available, such as message brokers, and relevant topics or queues exist for processing.

2. Ensure that the tested application is connected with mock clients, such as test publishers to send events and mock consumers to consume the output events for validation.

3. Send input events.

4. Wait until applications finish processing the input.

5. Assert the final state, by calling the mock clients for the responses produced by the application and other systems such as databases, where the relevant updates are performed.

We recommend using a dedicated topic and queues for tests. When possible, start the message broker instance just for the test. Even when a shared messaging infrastructure is used, we recommend creating dedicated topics and queues. When running mock clients and message brokers, we recommend implementing them as containers. When possible, run the test in a namespaced environment. All these features will help isolate the cause of failures and accelerate troubleshooting. This also allows us to clean the test environment after the tests. This reduces interference between tests and other systems and increases the deterministic behavior of the test.

Though these steps seem straightforward, the complexity of integration testing comes with the asynchronous nature of the application. The tests need to wait an arbitrary amount of time for processing to finish for assertion, and during failures the system might not publish events to consumers. Hence, we need to implement the test to wait for a given time-out based on our previous experience before assuming that the test has failed. This time-out-based testing is not generally recommended because of its nondeterministic nature, as network delays and slower hardware can cause the test to fail intermittently. Unfortunately, this is something that we cannot eliminate in integration testing of event-driven applications, but we can try to reduce the impact by building the application to produce output for both success and failure cases, and by providing a way to query the application state for assertions.

In addition, because of the asynchronous nature of event processing, we cannot guarantee that the events are consumed, processed, and output in the same order that they are published by the client. For example, when we send events A, B, and C in order, the events can be outputted in B, C, A order after processing. Based on the use case we test, unless the events are commutative, writing test assertions expecting the output events to be consumed in A, B, and C order will fail the test case. In this case, use unique IDs for each event so we can uniquely identify the output and assert them.

Event-driven applications should also be tested for failure use cases, using chaos engineering. This can include simulating network failures, simulating slow producers and consumers, and bringing down consumers and message brokers for a brief period of time. This allows you to identify failures, improve the applications to have predictable behavior during failures, and enable smooth recovery.

Security

How can we enforce security for applications and systems in an event-driven architecture? Applications should enforce security by connecting to systems by using only secured protocols and encrypting data at rest and in transit.

Message brokers also support security by protecting queues and topics behind authentication and authorization mechanisms. But as the events are stored in the brokers, we need to ensure they are stored safely and not persisted longer than is necessary.

When events are transmitted through topics, we need to ensure that only authorized applications are able to consume the events. We use topic subscriptions for observability and monitoring purposes, but the same approach can also be used to eavesdrop on the events.

Not all types of message brokers and microservices used in cloud native applications can always provide the required level of security. We recommend using a bounded context that is fronted by an API or a secured message broker to consume the events from external systems and build the whole asynchronous architecture within that context. By always encrypting events before sending them to brokers, we can also make sure that the events are stored in their queues and topics encrypted, and applications eavesdropping on those events will not be able to decrypt them to access the data.

In addition to what we've discussed here, we recommend that you apply the general security best practices discussed in Chapter 2.

Observability and Monitoring

Observability and monitoring play a key role in the success of event-driven architectures. Event-driven applications with scale can soon become complex, making it difficult to even understand how an event flows through the components of the application. Without proper observability and monitoring, understanding this behavior and troubleshooting large-scale event-driven applications cannot be a reality. Furthermore, as event-driven cloud native applications can use serverless computing frameworks and process events asynchronously, clients are not usually notified of event-processing failures, so we can troubleshoot these systems only by using proper observability and monitoring tools.

Event-driven architecture forms chains of event-processing microservices that are connected via topics and queues. Failures can happen because of a bad event or a networking issue at any stage of the execution chain. This can result in the event getting dropped, and stopping it from propagating through the whole execution chain. For example, when a loan-processing request is initiated, and the event is dropped by an application error while performing a credit check, the customer or the bank cannot know the status of the request unless the organization has built proper observability around the application. This observability helps indicate that an error has occurred and where it has occurred. This helps build mechanisms to overcome the consequences of the error and recover the processing flow.

Distributed tracing applications such as Jaeger and Zipkin help us properly observe event-driven applications. First we assign a causation ID for the event; in this case, the loan request. Then as the request is processed by subsequent applications, and they produce further events, the causation ID is persisted. This causation ID propagates through the whole request flow. Having a causation ID allows us to pinpoint our current location in the flow. The distributed tracing systems enable us to visualize workflows by their causation ID, allowing us to quickly identify errors.

Tracing provides information only about where the error has happened; we need to use logging to find the root cause of the error. You should log events and errors with the causation ID at each participating microservice, and aggregate them by using log aggregation systems such as Fluentd, Logstash, Amazon CloudWatch, or Google Cloud Operations. This will help find the reasons behind those errors so you can mitigate them.

We should also continuously monitor the microservices and message brokers used in the cloud native application. This is critical to identify slow-performing microservices and to detect bottlenecks in the event-processing chain. As events are processed asynchronously, if the incoming rate of events remains higher than the consumption rate over a prolonged period, the events can excessively accumulate at the message brokers and cause the event-driven application to fail. This can be detected by observing high queue depth, and can be eliminated by scaling consumers, dropping excess events, or improving the performance of event consumers.

DevOps

In this chapter, we have discussed several event-driven architecture patterns that can be applied in cloud native applications. Because message brokers are a key component of event-driven architecture, here we focus on the DevOps process of message brokers.

The first step in deploying and managing message brokers is selecting the appropriate orchestration and delivery patterns required. This allows us to determine what type of event-delivery guarantees are needed. Based on these and the required scalability, we choose a message broker or proceed without one.

Often because of cost concerns, organizations choose a single message broker for all use cases. In such situations, we should evaluate how a delivery pattern is best implemented on the available message broker and whether that fits our requirements.

The next major step in deploying and managing message brokers is enforcing the security of the applications, protecting access to message brokers, and allowing only authorized applications to publish and consume events. See "Security" on page 199 for further details.

Because failures in asynchronous applications are difficult to troubleshoot, robust observability and monitoring is critical. As discussed earlier in this chapter, we recommend that you implement distributed tracing, logging, and monitoring. As systems encounter network failures and application errors, unprocessed events end up in dead-letter queues when available. These queues should be monitored to allow for the correcting of failed events.

Autoscaling the event-driven application is critical, as without this, message brokers can become overloaded and degrade application performance or even cause failures. When deploying applications in Kubernetes, we can use the Kubernetes-based Event Driven Autoscaler (KEDA (*https://keda.sh*)) to monitor message broker queue depth, and autoscale the consumer microservices so they can process all incoming events without increasing the backlog. KEDA supports scaling based on various message brokers and stream processors such as Kafka, NATS, RabbitMQ, Azure Event Hubs, and Amazon SQS.

To achieve continuous delivery and smooth deployments, we recommend maintaining backward compatibility of the event schema. When major changes occur in the event schema and the reuse of topics and queues is not possible, we recommend migrating the applications to new topics or queues in stages by using canary or blue-green deployment strategies. Make sure that all events in the queues and durable topics of the previous application version are successfully processed before finishing the version upgrade. Finally, we also recommend using multiple deployment environments, such as development and staging/preproduction, to reduce the impact of the changes and to validate the event-driven application before moving it to production.

By following these steps, we can safely deploy and maintain cloud native applications and the respective message brokers used in the event-driven architecture while allowing rapid innovation and adoption to other systems.

Summary

In this chapter, we looked at delivery patterns applied to cloud native applications with event-driven architectures. We explored options for achieving asynchronous communications both with and without message brokers. We reviewed message broker types and the various event-delivery guarantees.

We then discussed how to use various patterns to deliver events from one application to another, how to manage application state by using event sourcing, and how events can be orchestrated for event processing. We discussed the complexity of building scalable cloud native event-driven applications, and how they can be managed. We also reviewed robust message broker technologies and discussed how event-driven applications can be secured, tested, continuously deployed, and observed and monitored. Next, we will explore the patterns related to cloud native stream-processing applications.

CHAPTER 6

Stream-Processing Patterns

Stream-processing patterns evolved from event-driven architecture patterns. Event-driven architecture patterns revolve around event delivery and orchestration, whereas stream-processing patterns focus on how such events can be processed on the fly to extract meaningful information and take actions in real time. Without event-driven architecture patterns, we cannot implement stream-processing patterns in cloud native systems.

What Is a Stream?

A *stream* can be defined as a continuous sequence of events ordered by time. The stream consists of a name and version that uniquely identify it, such as *StockStream 1.0*. All events in a stream have a common message format and structure. For example, StockStream has a JSON format and contains *symbol*, *price*, and *volume* in its structure. Having a consistent format and structure allows events in the stream to be processed in an automated manner, using stream-processing systems. The stream version provides a way to safely modify the structure and evolve the stream over time.

What Is Stream Processing?

Stream processing is performing operations on events in motion. It can be as simple as a stateless service consuming events and transforming its event format, or as complex as storing and processing stateful data in memory with low latency and reliability.

In contrast to simple event processing, stream processing supports use cases in which events need to be handled in the order they are generated. Stream-processing patterns can also remember and use previous events when making a decision. For example, detecting if a stock price is continuously increasing over the last five minutes requires remembering previous events and processing them in order, both in real time.

 The term *real time*, in the context of stream processing, always refers to *near real time*. The system will try to provide results within milliseconds to a few seconds with best effort and always try to achieve low latency.

When building stream-processing applications, the stateless and stateful nature of the application can greatly influence the design. Therefore, we need to use a different set of patterns to preserve the state of the application. In this chapter, you will first learn how streaming data is processed to get meaningful output by using streaming data processing patterns, and then look at patterns for scaling, improving performance, and achieving reliability for both stateless and stateful stream-processing applications. Then we will discuss stream-processing technologies and how we can test, secure, monitor and observe, and continuously deploy stream-processing applications in the cloud.

Streaming Data Processing Patterns

Streaming data processing patterns focus on how we can generate useful output by processing real-time events through transformation, filtering, aggregation, and detecting meaningful sequences of events. These capabilities enable cloud native applications to process events on the fly with low latency.

A key performance consideration is avoiding heavy use of persistent data stores. In a cloud native application, the round-trip time of accessing the data store, and the potential for contention, can add significant processing latency to solutions. For some use cases, it is required, but as a general rule of thumb, it should be avoided.

The following section dives into some of the key patterns related to stream processing in cloud native applications.

Transformation Pattern

The *Transformation pattern* helps transform events from an event source and publish them to another system with a different format, structure, or protocol.

How it works

This pattern maps the data of one event to another. For example, say we are to publish weather events to a third-party system that expects the events in JSON format with a particular structure (Figure 6-1). The relevant data from the incoming event can be extracted and mapped to the new event format. We can achieve this by using

JSON and XML libraries, or by using a graphical interface or SQL-based data-mapping approaches provided by stream-processing technologies.

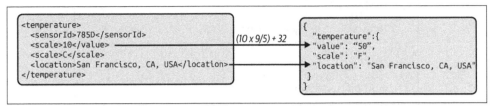

Figure 6-1. XML-to-JSON transformation

These transformations are often achieved purely with the information contained in the incoming event. But at times these transformations need other patterns, such as the Windowed Aggregation pattern, which we'll discuss shortly.

How it's used in practice

This pattern can be applied to cloud native applications in any programming language. This pattern also can be applied by systems like service buses and stream processors.

Message transformation. Messages can be transformed by using various techniques, such as via code with traditional programming languages and through specialized applications that perform data mapping. These applications include service buses and stream-processing systems that can run on the cloud, such as Apache Camel, KSQL, Amazon Kinesis, and Azure Stream Analytics.

Let's walk through an example of message transformation. Imagine that when taxis complete their journey, they publish JSON events containing relevant trip information. We need to extract pickup and drop-off locations and construct XML events for analytical applications so that they can analyze user movements and predict demand.

Figure 6-2 illustrates how we can use a standard cloud native application to consume the incoming JSON event and convert it to an XML event.

We can use JSON path expressions along with JSON libraries to extract data from the JSON event and then use that data to construct the XML messages. One of the easier ways of constructing messages is by using event templates and filling in the relevant data. Simple text templating libraries such as Mustache can be used to populate the templates and generate events. Most important, these events need to be validated for correctness by using XML libraries before sending them out. For instance, if the content of a field contains an opening XML tag such as <item>, blindly inserting them into the template will alter the final event structure and generate malformed events.

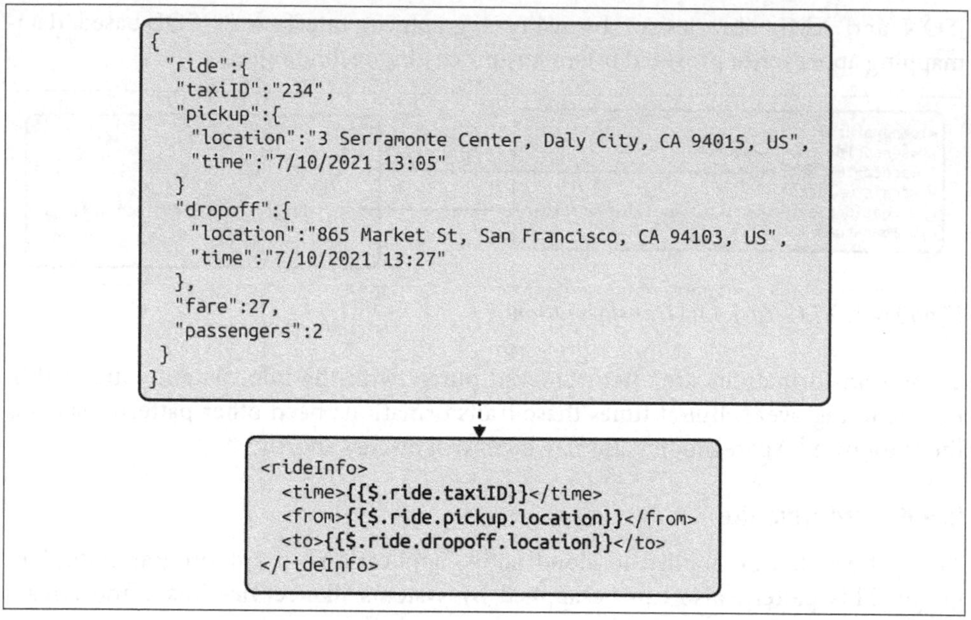

```
{
  "ride":{
    "taxiID":"234",
    "pickup":{
      "location":"3 Serramonte Center, Daly City, CA 94015, US",
      "time":"7/10/2021 13:05"
    }
    "dropoff":{
      "location":"865 Market St, San Francisco, CA 94103, US",
      "time":"7/10/2021 13:27"
    },
    "fare":27,
    "passengers":2
  }
}
```

```
<rideInfo>
  <time>{{$.ride.taxiID}}</time>
  <from>{{$.ride.pickup.location}}</from>
  <to>{{$.ride.dropoff.location}}</to>
</rideInfo>
```

Figure 6-2. Converting a JSON message to XML by using JSON path and text templating

Protocol switching. When working with partners and third-party teams, sometimes different teams will use different, noncompatible message brokers. One team might use Kafka for its message processing, while another uses Apache ActiveMQ, for instance. We cannot simply send events from one to another without some kind of conversion. Here, we use an intermediate application that consumes events from AMQP and deserializes them. Then it serializes those events as Kafka events and publishes them to Kafka.

Protocol switching alone does not require data mapping, so it can be implemented via a simple cloud native application by using the appropriate protocol libraries for both event consumption and publishing.

Considerations

This pattern is especially useful when we are working with applications that are managed by partner teams, and we need to perform transformations to allow our cloud native applications to interoperate.

For stateless transformations, the cloud native applications can be scaled horizontally without any issues. We can use serverless compute options such as Amazon Lambda or Azure Functions for these use cases.

When these transformations are stateful—for example, when we need the Windowed Aggregation pattern to calculate the average temperature over the last hour—these systems cannot be simply scaled horizontally. The Sequential Convoy pattern will show us how to partition and scale these applications.

Related patterns

The Transformation pattern can be combined with other stream data processing patterns, as data transformations can be required for incorporating results of those patterns, such as enriching events with aggregated data.

Filters and Thresholds Pattern

Sometimes we need to filter events based on given conditions, or allow only events with values that fit within a given threshold range. The *Filters and Thresholds pattern* is useful for extracting only the relevant events we need.

How it works

Users provide conditions that match against the incoming events. These conditions can include exact string matches, substring matches, regular expressions, or threshold ranges when it comes to numeric values with comparison operations such as <, <=, >, >=, and ==. Often more than a single condition is required, so those conditions are consolidated by using the AND, OR, and NOT logical operations and parentheses to generate more-complex filter conditions.

If we are processing a real-time stream of car sales and are interested in only 2010 or newer Toyota vehicles, we can define a filtering condition as shown in Figure 6-3 to emit only events that satisfy the condition.

Figure 6-3. Filtering car events based on brand and year

This pattern extracts and processes the relevant data from the input event stream by using data-mapping techniques discussed in the "Transformation Pattern" on page 204.

How it's used in practice

This pattern can be applied to cloud native applications written in any programming language, and by systems like service buses and stream processors.

Filter events by category.   Often we are interested in only certain types of events for processing. Take, for example, handling asynchronously published local and international shipment events distinctly in an ecommerce platform. In this case, when possible, use subscription filters provided by message brokers to filter only the relevant type of data for processing. But when that is not possible, we recommend implementing an intermediate microservice or serverless function to filter and publish only the relevant events. This also improves security and eliminates potential misuse of data, especially when the data is published to third parties.

Scenario: Apply a threshold for alerting.   Sometimes we're not interested in certain events, and processing everything at all times is not computationally feasible. In this case, it is essential to filter only the most critical data based on a threshold. For example, in a banking use case with hundreds of transactions performed every minute, performing human verification on all events to detect fraud is not possible.

Banks filter only high-value transactions for human verification. The filtering condition may contain not only the value of the transaction, but also the location of the transaction and whether it took place online or in a store. Example 6-1 shows a sample query used to determine if a transaction is high risk. Such transactions are then sent for human verification so that they cross-check with the card holder if the given transaction is legitimate.

Example 6-1. Request for human interaction only for online transactions of more than $1,000 in the United States and for all non-US transactions greater than $500

```
(amount > 1000 AND place == "USA" AND isOnline == true)
OR (amount > 500 AND place != "USA")
```

Considerations

This pattern not only allows cloud native applications to extract relevant events for processing but also reduces their load by dropping events that are irrelevant or lower priority.

It is important to note that modern message brokers such as Kafka now natively support this functionality, allowing cloud native applications to subscribe to their topics with a filter condition. This also avoids running additional containers just for filtering. This option is not always available, especially when publishing events to third-party systems.

Filters can be implemented as stateless microservices and deployed in front of any other cloud native application to filter and pass only the events that are relevant. We can also readily leverage serverless compute options such as Amazon Lambda and Azure Functions to implement this pattern.

Related patterns

The Filtering and Thresholds pattern can be applied with all the other stream data processing patterns, as we often need to filter events for those patterns (for example, to aggregate only a particular type of event).

Windowed Aggregation Pattern

The *Windowed Aggregation pattern* enables us to analyze a collection of events based on a condition. Here, aggregation analysis can include operations like summation, minimum, maximum, average, standard deviation, and count, and the window defines the collection of events used for aggregation.

These windows can be based on the time or event count, such as the last five minutes or the last 100 events. These windows may also have behaviors such as sliding or batching, defining when events are added and removed from the window.

This pattern enables us to aggregate data on the fly and make time-critical business decisions within milliseconds.

How it works

Understanding how windows operate is fundamental to understanding the behavior of this pattern. Let's look at some of the most common windows—such as length sliding, length batch, time sliding, and time batch—that are supported by most stream-processing systems. The aggregation operations are performed on top of these windows, as windows limit the number of events that need to be considered for aggregation, and the aggregation output is emitted as a stream for further processing.

Let's explore how these windows operate. For example, a time sliding window of one minute, considers only the events that occurred during that last minute. Events are added and removed from the window as time progresses. This window emits aggregations of all the events within it upon every addition or removal of an event from the window. For implementation optimizations, instead of adding events as soon as they arrive, some stream-processing systems require us to provide a sliding interval, defining how often the window will slide—in other words, how often the events will be added and removed from the window. For example, a one-minute sliding window that has a sliding interval of one second will slide by one second at a time. During that slide, the window will add all the new events that arrived in the preceding second and remove all the events that were from the oldest second. In this case, the aggregations are emitted every second as events are added and removed.

As an example, let's say we're continuously monitoring a purchase stream, to count the total number of units ordered over the preceding minute, using a one-minute sliding window with a one-second sliding interval, as shown in Table 6-1.

Table 6-1. Summation of units ordered over a one-minute time window that slides each second

Time in milliseconds	Input: number of units ordered in each purchase event	Output: number of units ordered over the preceding one minute
5:30:20 000 (start of first 1 minute)	-	-
5:30:20 007	5	-
5:30:20 115	6	-
5:30:20 545	11	-
5:30:21 000 (start of second 1 minute)	-	$0 + (5 + 6 + 11) = 22$
5:30:21 100	2	-
5:30:21 393	14	-
5:30:22 000 (start of third 1 minute)	4	$22 + (2 + 14 + 4) = 42$
5:30:47 560	7	-
5:30:48 000	-	$42 + 7 = 49$
5:30:23 000 (start of fourth 1 minute)	-	-
5:30:24 000 (start of fifth 1 minute)	-	-
...	...	...
5:31:19 000 (start of 60th 1 minute)	-	-
5:31:20 000 (end of first and start of 61st 1 minute)	-	-
5:31:20 345	8	-
5:31:21 000 (end of second and start of 62nd 1 minute)	-	$49 + 8 - (5 + 6 + 11) = 35$
5:31:21 500	15	-
5:31:22 000 (end of third and start of 63rd 1 minute)	13	$35 + (28) - (20) = 43$

In contrast, a length batch window of size 4 will process and emit aggregations after every fourth event arrives. Continuing with the previous example of monitoring a purchase stream, as shown in Table 6-2, the new purchase events are added to the window as they arrive, but the aggregated unit count is emitted only when the fourth event is added to the window. At that time, the window all events stored in the window will also expire.

Table 6-2. Summation of units ordered over a length batch window of size 4

Time in milliseconds	Input: number of units ordered in each purchase event	Output: number of units ordered during the last four purchases
5:30:20 007	2	-
5:30:20 115	6	-
5:30:20 545	4	-
5:30:21 000 (end of first batch)	3	$(2 + 6 + 4 + 3) = 15$

Time in milliseconds	Input: number of units ordered in each purchase event	Output: number of units ordered during the last four purchases
5:30:21 100	2	-
5:30:21 393	14	-
5:30:22 000	7	-
5:30:47 560 (end of second batch)	5	$(2 + 14 + 7 + 5) = 28$
5:30:48 000	4	-
5:31:20 345	7	-
5:37:26 353	3	-
5:38:21 500 (end of third batch)	1	15
...	...	...

The aggregation operations can be applied to any of these windows, and the point where the aggregation emits results depends on the type of window chosen. For example, a length batch window of size 10 produces aggregated results for every 10 events, and a time sliding window of five minutes with a one-second sliding interval will emit output every second.

The aggregation functionality can also be combined with group by, having, order by, and limit operations (similarly to SQL), to group the aggregations by a field, filter, sort, and limit the output as per our needs.

Finally, it is important for this pattern to use the Transformation pattern to map the aggregated results into the output.

How it's used in practice

The Windowed Aggregation pattern is stateful, meaning it stores data related to the events in memory. Therefore, when designing noncritical use cases such as monitoring that tolerates data loss, we can implement this pattern on any cloud native application. But when the use case requires reliable event processing, we need to combine this pattern with the reliability patterns, which we discuss later in the chapter.

Aggregate events over time. Some use cases require us to aggregate multiple events over a period of time. For example, let's consider a fraud detection use case: instead of analyzing individual transactions, we want to learn the top 10 users by finding the total amount that they have transacted during the last 10 minutes. This detects whether someone is splitting a large sum of money and transferring it by using lots of small transactions.

We can use a 10-minute time sliding window with a 1-second slide interval, a sum aggregator to sum the transactions, a group by aggregator to group the aggregations by the user, and finally the sort and limit to extract only the top 10 users out of that. Example 6-2 shows this.

Example 6-2. Aggregating events by transaction value over the last 10 minutes and outputting the top 10 users with their total amount transacted

```
select userName, sum(transactionValue) as totalTransaction
from InputStream
window time (10 min, 1 sec)
group by userName
order by totalTransaction desc
limit 10
```

In this example, system downtime may cause business impact. Therefore, we have to apply reliability patterns such as the Two-Node Failover pattern, covered later in this chapter, to make sure that accurate aggregation calculations are continuously emitted for decision making.

Aggregate events over length.   Sometimes the number of events is an important aspect of the aggregation, and those cannot be modeled with time. Say we want to receive an alert when the server rejects three consecutive requests. We can use a length sliding window to identify whether it has rejected the last three events it has received. See Example 6-3.

Example 6-3. Determining whether the last three consecutive requests were rejected

```
select serverId, sum(isRequestRejected) as totalRejectedRequests
from InputStream
window length (3)
having totalRejectedRequests == 3
```

In this case, `isRequestRejected` will contain 1 when the server rejects a request and 0 when it has served the request successfully.

We assume that all the events processed by the query are produced by a single server. Otherwise, we need to combine this pattern with the Sequential Convoy pattern (discussed later in this chapter) to partition the query to process events arriving from multiple servers.

If the service is not critical for the business, system downtime may not cause business impact. Therefore, we don't need to worry about preserving the window state, and so there is no need to use reliability patterns.

Considerations

The most important aspect of this pattern is that it is stateful. Windows rely on multiple events, and a system failure or restart can cause those events to get lost, causing the aggregations to emit inconsistent results. When aggregations are not used for mission-critical use cases, it may be acceptable to lose those events during system failures or restarts. In this case, some aggregation outputs will not be published or will be inaccurate. But when the aggregation outputs are critical, we can apply reliability patterns (discussed later in this chapter) to make sure that we are appropriately rebuilding or recovering the state after a failure or restart.

It is also important to consider that we cannot implement all types of aggregations with high accuracy and efficiency. For example, we can use windows to model the mean (average), but not the median. The mean needs only the sum and the count of events in the window, and techniques can be used to progressively alter these values as events are added and removed from the window. This enables us to rapidly compute the average (sum/count) by not iterating through all the events in that window. But on the other hand, to calculate the median, we need to iterate through all the events in the window. This will not only add latency to the calculation, but persisting all events requires more space, which becomes more problematic as windows get larger.

This now brings us to scaling of these operators. It is vital that we design the system to withstand high load and scale on demand. Because windows are collections of events, the most effective way of scaling them is by sharding. Figure 6-4 illustrates splitting the incoming events into different windows, aggregating the events in isolation, and then using the Stream Join pattern (which we detail next) to build bigger aggregations. We discuss scaling based on sharding in the "Sequential Convoy Pattern" on page 225.

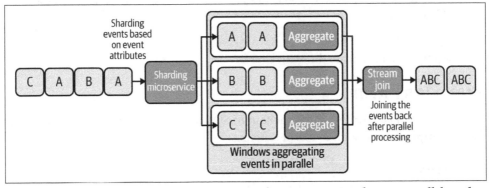

Figure 6-4. Sharding events based on event attributes, processing them in parallel, and joining the results

It is also possible to perform aggregations without a window. Consider that the window spans from the service startup to the current time. Aggregations would reflect all the events that occurred during that period. But it is important that we implement these window aggregations to operate with constant space complexity (consumption of memory not depending on the number of events processed); otherwise, the system could run out of memory.

Implementing the Windowed Aggregation pattern from scratch can be time-consuming and error prone. We recommend that you use cloud native stream processors or stream-processing libraries such as Esper or Siddhi when possible to fulfill these use cases.

Related patterns

The following are related to the Windowed Aggregation pattern (all are covered in this chapter unless otherwise noted):

Transformation pattern
Appropriately maps the aggregation to the output.

Reliability patterns
Help make the window and aggregation state survive system failures.

Sequential Convoy pattern
Allows aggregations to be performed in parallel based on shard keys. This not only helps scale aggregation processing, but also allows us to aggregate different types of events in isolation and produce aggregations per event type.

Service Orchestration pattern
Splits the events by different shard keys for processing. This pattern is described in Chapter 3.

Stream Join pattern
Aggregates results from different shards.

Stream Join Pattern

The *Stream Join pattern* resembles the join of SQL tables and enables us to join events from multiple streams with different schemas.

How it works

This pattern works by defining a condition to identify the joining events. This condition will pick attributes from each joining event stream and define the condition under which they should be joined. This can be a simple equal condition, like joining events from all event streams having the same ID, or it can be more complex.

The join should also define a buffer that determines how long events should wait for corresponding events to arrive from other event streams. This buffer period can be common across all streams or can vary among streams. Most stream-processing systems define this buffer period via windows that you learned about in the previous section. In Figure 6-5, we see the buffer defined as a one-minute window.

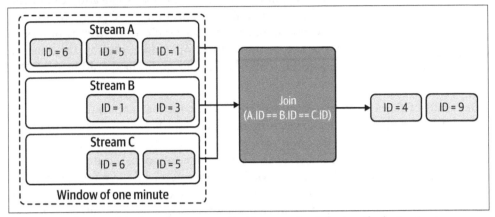

Figure 6-5. Stream Join based on events that have arrived during the last minute

In this example, we assume that events with IDs 4 and 9 arrived in all streams (A, B, and C) during the last minute; those events are joined and emitted. Events with IDs 6, 5, 1, and 3 are still waiting in the window for their corresponding events with the same event ID to arrive in all streams so that the join condition can be satisfied.

Finally, as in the Windowed Aggregation pattern, it is important for this pattern to use the Transformation pattern to map the joining events and their attributes to the output.

How it's used in practice

The Stream Join pattern is stateful, as it buffers events for the join. Like the Windowed Aggregation pattern, this one can be implemented in any cloud native application as long as the use case is not business critical and can tolerate event loss. But when event loss is not acceptable, this pattern should be applied along with reliability patterns, so the application can withstand system failures and restarts without event loss.

Scatter and gather. In *scatter and gather*, we process the same event in parallel, performing different operations, and finally combine the results so all event outputs can be emitted as a single event. This is one of the most common scenarios for using this pattern.

For example, let's consider a loan application process. The loan application can be initiated by an event that contains a unique loan application ID. Operations for this event—credit check, address verification, and identity verification—can be processed in parallel. But at the end, the outputs of all three operations need to be joined in order for the bank to make a decision on whether the applicant should be granted a loan.

The results of all the parallel operations contain the same loan application ID, and we can implement a microservice to perform join operations based on that ID. To generate an output, the join operation will wait for all three corresponding events to arrive. It is critical that all the parallel processors send a response event, whether the response is a success or failure, as this will help perform the join in a more deterministic way. When processors do not send events because of errors or network failures, we should have a defined strategy for handling that scenario. The buffer period we define can help identify missing events and still emit the joint event with missing results, so that when possible, a decision can be made from the partial results (for example, if the partial results have a failure, the loan is rejected, or if we cannot determine a decision, a reprocessing of the data is initiated).

Join various types of events. The Stream Join pattern can also be used to join various types of events based on a defined condition and a window, as discussed in the "Windowed Aggregation Pattern" on page 209. Let's take an example of identifying stock prices at times when certain tweets are published.

As depicted in Figure 6-6, we use a window to store all the latest stock prices from the Stock stream, and when we identify a new tweet containing, say, a company name such as Apple, we join that event against the stock events in the window. According to the join condition, the tweet will match the stock event having the same company name (in this case, the event with symbol AAPL), and the joined event is emitted as an output with the latest stock price.

This kind of join can be an inner, a full-outer, a left-outer, or a right-outer join, as in SQL queries. During outer joins, we can replace event attributes with null when we cannot identify matching events in the window.

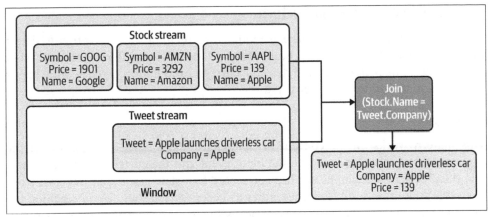

Figure 6-6. Joining stock prices with tweets based on company name

Considerations

Join is a stateful operation; it needs to wait for all matching events to arrive before it makes a valid join. When event loss cannot be tolerated, we use reliability patterns to ensure that events are preserved across system failures and restarts.

But for simple scenarios such as scatter and gather, we can directly read events from message brokers and defer acknowledgment until those events are successfully joined. With this approach, we do not lose those events upon a system failure or restart, as the message broker will republish those. More details about this approach are discussed in "Replay Pattern" on page 240.

Joining many events during a long time period can be challenging, as systems may suffer from increased space requirements and increased processing times. In this case, we recommend the Sequential Convoy pattern discussed later in this chapter to shard events based on the joining attributes. This will parallelize joining and ensure that related events fall into the same shard so they can be joined successfully.

Related patterns

These patterns (covered in this chapter) are related to the Stream Join pattern:

Transformation pattern
   Appropriately maps joining event attributes to build the output.

Reliability patterns
   Helps the joint state survive system failures.

Sequential Convoy pattern
   Scales joins by performing them in parallel by allowing relevant joining events to fall into the same shard.

Temporal Event Ordering Pattern

The *Temporal Event Ordering pattern* is unique for stream processing. It tries to detect various interesting complex event occurrences by identifying patterns based on event arrival order. The pattern can also detect occurrence and nonoccurrence of incidents based on events emitted by various systems.

How it works

This pattern works on the concept of nondeterministic finite-state machines: the application state changes based on the input event and the current application state. The possible state transitions can be represented as a state graph that traverses from one state to another until it reaches either a success or fail state. Upon reaching the success state, the user is notified, as it means the expected events have occurred in order.

Figure 6-7 shows an example of the Temporal Event Ordering pattern. We detect a continuous stock price increase followed by a single drop, and the user will be notified as soon as the first drop is detected.

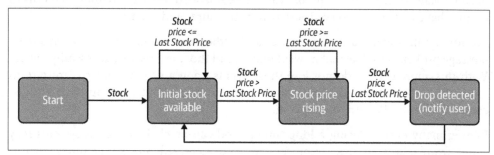

Figure 6-7. Using the Temporal Event Ordering pattern to detect a continuous stock price increase followed by a single drop

This pattern can also be used to identify sequences of events that are immediately followed by one another or scattered randomly among other events. We can also use this to detect the nonoccurrence of events by combining state transitions with time-outs.

Use cases such as stock monitoring most often require the event sequence to be detected repeatedly. To achieve this, a new state machine instance should be initiated upon each event arrival that triggers the initial state of the state machine. In the preceding example, the event that triggered the final state can be used as the initial event for a new instance of the state machine.

How it's used in practice

Like the Windowed Aggregation and Stream Join patterns, this pattern should also be combined with reliability patterns to preserve data loss during system failures and restarts. Furthermore, as event arrival order is critical for the success of this pattern, we recommend using patterns like Buffered Event Ordering (discussed later in this chapter) to guarantee ordering of events before processing them.

Detect sequence of event occurrence. The most common use of this pattern is for identifying an incident by having a sequence of events happen in a prescribed order. Let's consider an example of detecting fraudulent credit card transactions. A fraudster can copy and use credit cards without the card holder being aware. But this kind of fraud can be detected by using predefined rules, such as a transaction happening in the US followed by another transaction happening on the same credit card outside the US within three hours. Figure 6-8 depicts using a state machine for the detection.

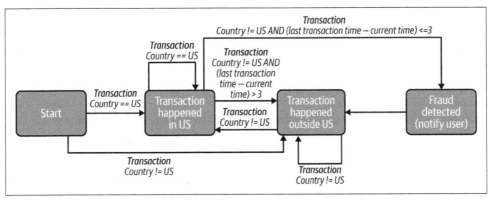

Figure 6-8. State machine for detecting transaction fraud

In this example, a new state machine instance should be created for each credit card, which can then keep track of the previous transaction to determine whether the next transaction is occurring outside the US within three hours.

Detect nonoccurrence of event. Now, let's say we want to identify an incident by an expected event *not* occurring. These are commonly used for detecting erroneous situations, such as notifying a homeowner that their garage door has been left open.

The user needs to receive a notification if the garage door is left open for one minute after the car drives out. This pattern expects the door-close action to take place within one minute of the car leaving and notifies the user if the door does not close within that time frame (the nonoccurrence of the event). Figure 6-9 depicts how this detection can be designed.

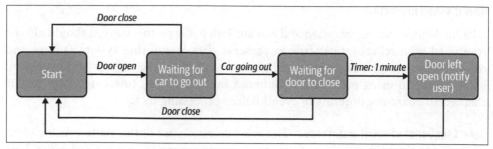

Figure 6-9. Detecting the garage door left open for more than 1 minute after the car leaves the garage

This requires a timer task to be initiated to keep track of the time, and that timer should be cancelled as soon as the door is closed, to prevent an erroneous notification from being sent.

Considerations

As state machines are inherently stateful, this requires applications to rely on reliability patterns (discussed later in this chapter) to persist their states across system failure and restarts. Also, we should ensure that each cloud native application has enough in-memory space to maintain the state machines. In addition, we should apply the Sequential Convoy pattern to distribute events to various nodes so that the sequence matching can be scaled and parallelized, while making sure all relevant events for a successful match are still routed to the same node.

One of the other important aspects of this pattern is that it requires events to be processed in the order they are generated. Though it is not possible to always determine relative ordering of events, correlating and ordering events based on event-generation time can still help overcome out-of-order events that happened during transmission. We recommend you use the Buffered Event Ordering pattern to guarantee ordering of events if they can become out of order during transmission.

As with earlier patterns discussed in this chapter, implementing this pattern can be time-consuming and error prone. Therefore, we recommend you use cloud native stream processors to fulfill these use cases. Stream processing systems like Azure Streaming Analytics, Apache Spark, Apache Flink, Esper, and Siddhi are some that can provide this functionality by default. We recommend building this pattern from scratch only when such systems are not available in your environment.

Related patterns

The following are related to the Temporal Event Ordering pattern; all are covered in this chapter:

Transformation pattern
Appropriately maps the matched events in the sequence to generate a meaningful output.

Reliability patterns
Helps state machines survive system failures.

Sequential Convoy pattern
Scales sequence matching by performing it in parallel by allowing relevant events to fall into the same shard.

Buffered Event Ordering pattern
Orders events based on event-generation time to facilitate correct behavior of this pattern.

Machine Learner Pattern

We can use machine learning models in real time to generate predictions and automate decision making. Machine learning models can be prebuilt to produce predictions without updating themselves based on new input events. Online machine learning models can produce predictions while continuously learning, based on new incoming events, whether or not they're pre-generated, making our cloud native application much more intelligent.

How it works

We can generate predictions in cloud native applications in two ways: by executing prebuilt machine learning models and by using online machine learning models. We discuss these approaches in detail next.

Prebuilt machine learning models.   These models can be generated by a data scientist using data processing tools and machine learning frameworks such as Apache Spark, TensorFlow, or even Python. Some of these models can be imported into running applications via technologies such as Predictive Model Markup Language (PMML), and we can query them on the fly to generate predictions. We can also run them as separate cloud native applications and call them via APIs. Because these models are prebuilt and cannot adapt based on new incoming events, we need to update them periodically to maintain and improve their prediction accuracy.

Online machine learning models.   These are models that tune themselves based on the information they receive as they produce predictions. In some cases, the models require a feedback loop with the results from their previous predictions so that they dynamically train themselves. These models can be embedded into applications or run as separate microservices. Figure 6-10 shows a microservice with an online machine learning model that also continuously updates itself based on past results.

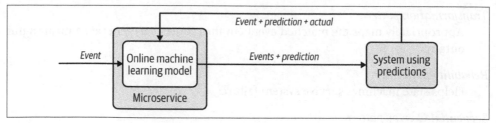

Figure 6-10. Microservice with an online machine learning model using a feedback loop to continuously learn

How it's used in practice

Machine learning has now become an integral part of many applications, and cloud native applications should also be well equipped to incorporate them. One common way of integrating machine learning models is to deploy them as individual microservices and make service calls. This is no different from calling other services, as covered in Chapter 3. Alternatively, machine learning models can be embedded into the applications, which can continuously produce predictions based on incoming events. Some scenarios using this pattern are described next.

Predict based on prebuilt machine learning models.   Using a prebuilt machine learning model is ideal when we have abundant historical data, and when the prediction pattern does not change with new events. Let's consider an example of automating detection of defective parts in a production line. Detecting defects early in a production line can reduce cost.

A microservice can be deployed with a prebuilt linear regression model to examine the parameters of parts and detect any defects, and to allow the parts that do not have defects to progress along the pipeline (Figure 6-11). If the manufacturing happens in a controlled environment with the same input materials, temperature, and machinery, the prediction will be accurate for a longer period, and we don't need to update the prebuilt models as often.

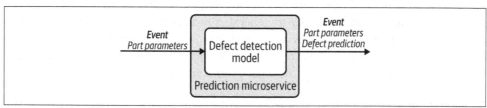

Figure 6-11. Running a prebuilt machine learning model to detect defects

Continuous learning with data. We recommend using continuously learning online machine learning models if we expect them to learn new behaviors (as we receive new data) in the future. To give you an example of this type of scenario, let's say we want to predict the expected wait time for an airport security scan, and display that wait time on screens throughout the airport.

We can use a machine learning model to make predictions based on the number of people waiting in line, available security check counters, and the time taken for them to finish the check. But because of ever-changing environmental effects, such as insider information about potential security threats, using a prebuilt machine learning model with historical data will not produce accurate predictions.

But using an online machine learning model is beneficial, as it learns from its feedback and adjusts its predictions in real time (Figure 6-12). For this model to work successfully, we need an application that provides input, continuously feeding in the number of passengers waiting in the line, the available counters, as well as the actual time taken. This will enable the model to continuously emit more-accurate predictions on the screens.

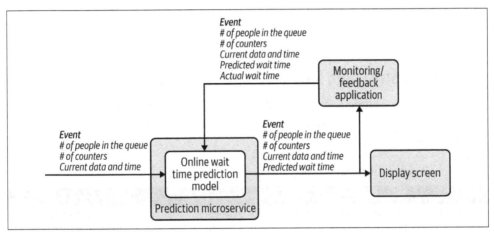

Figure 6-12. Emitting accurate wait-time predictions through feedback

Considerations

Prebuilt machine learning models are much simpler to implement and generally have high accuracy when we have enough data. At the same time, they cannot adapt to new trends. For these cases, online machine learning algorithms perform much better. But these algorithms can fluctuate in accuracy, because most are constrained by the amount of data they can store in memory and therefore have limitations on how much data they can learn. This compromises their ability to produce data with high accuracy. Therefore, we recommend combining prebuilt and online machine learning algorithms where possible, so you can override the predictions of the prebuilt models when you have higher accuracy from the online machine learning models.

When using prebuilt machine learning models, it is important to update them periodically. Over time, the model accuracy can degrade because of changes in circumstances. In cloud native applications, these models can be embedded, so updating the application version along with a newer model provides an easy deployment path.

Online machine learning models store what they've learned in memory. We recommend using reliability patterns on those cloud native applications so they recover state across system failures and restarts.

Related patterns

The following patterns, covered in this chapter, are related to the Machine Learner pattern:

Transformation pattern
Appropriately maps the predictions of the machine learning model to generate a meaningful output.

Reliability patterns
Store and restore online machine learning algorithm state.

Summary of Streaming Data Processing Patterns

This section has outlined streaming data processing patterns used by cloud native applications. Table 6-3 summarizes when we should and should not use these patterns, and their benefits.

Table 6-3. Streaming data processing patterns

Pattern	When to use	When not to use	Benefits
Transformation	To transform the event format, structure, or protocol. To add or remove partial data to or from the event. Third-party systems do not support the current event.	The consuming system has the ability to understand the event.	Allows incompatible systems to communicate with one another. Reduces event size by containing only relevant information.
Filters and Thresholds	Only a subset of events is relevant for processing.	All events are needed for decision making.	Reduces the load on the system by selecting only events that can produce the most value to the use case.

Pattern	When to use	When not to use	Benefits
Windowed Aggregation	To aggregate events over time or length. To perform operations such as summation, minimum, maximum, average, standard deviation, and count on the events.	For operations that cannot be performed with fixed memory such as detecting the median of the events. High accuracy is needed without the use of reliability patterns.	Reduces the load on the system by aggregating events. Provides data summary to better understand the behavior as a whole.
Stream Join	To join events from two or more event streams. To collect events that were previously split to parallelize processing.	Joining events do not arrive in relatively close proximity. High accuracy is needed without the use of reliability patterns.	Allows events to be correlated. Enables synchronous processing of events.
Temporal Event Ordering	To detect the sequence of event occurrences. To detect the nonoccurrence of events.	Event sequencing cannot be defined as a finite-state machine. High accuracy is needed without the use of reliability patterns. Incoming events arrive out-of-order.	Allows detecting complex conditions based on event arrival order.
Machine Learner	To perform predictions in real time. To perform classification, clustering, or regression analysis on the events.	We cannot use a model to accurately predict the values. Historical data is not available for building machine learning models.	Automates decision making. Provides reasonable estimates.

Scaling and Performance Optimization Patterns

Cloud native applications that perform stream processing have unique scalability and performance requirements. For instance, these applications require event ordering to be maintained while processing events. Furthermore, as most of these applications have in-memory state, they also need a strategy to scale so they can process more events without compromising their accuracy.

In this section, we discuss key patterns used to scale streaming cloud native applications. We also look at patterns commonly used to order events and to improve performance.

Sequential Convoy Pattern

The *Sequential Convoy pattern* scales cloud native stream-processing applications by separating events into various categories and processing them in parallel. It also works to persist event ordering so events can be combined at a later time, while preserving the original order of the events.

How it works

As the name suggests, this pattern sees events as items moving along a conveyor belt. It groups the events into categories based on their characteristics and processes them in parallel. One example is an ecommerce application that provides different product delivery time guarantees based on type of customer and order size (Figure 6-13). This application can categorize purchase events by the type of customer (such as premium, gold, or not a member) and can categorize gold member purchases by their order size (such as $50 or less as small, $50 to $500 as medium, and more than $500 as high). This allows events to be partitioned and processed in parallel to provide various types of delivery guarantees, such as the same day, in two days, and in one week.

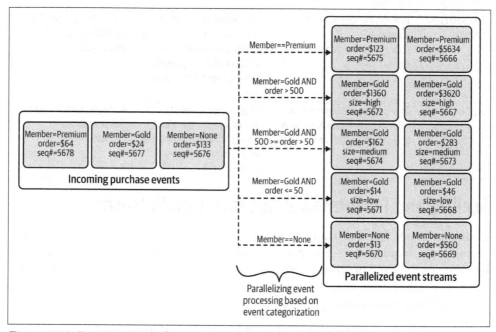

Figure 6-13. Partitioning and processing order events in parallel

Each event also can be labeled with a sequence number before separation. This allows each substream to maintain the event order during processing by applications that require guaranteed ordering, such as when using patterns like Windowed Aggregations or Temporal Event Ordering.

This sequencing can also be used to join the parallel streams together at a later time, based on the original event order. We use a merge sort by selecting the smallest sequence number among all the substreams, as shown in Figure 6-14. This enables us to group the events back in their original order and emit them for more processing.

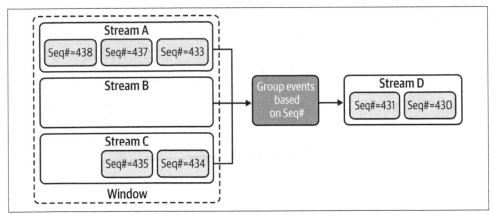

Figure 6-14. Grouping events based on event sequence number

Some events are still stuck in the windows, as the event with Seq#432 has not yet arrived. Once that arrives, it will be emitted next, and the event with Seq#433 will follow. Likewise, other events will also be emitted in the sequence number order until the next missing sequence number is detected.

Message brokers and event queues, discussed in Chapter 5, play a vital role in realizing this pattern. They allow us to split and transfer events to substreams and to buffer events for grouping back into a single stream.

How it's used in practice

This pattern is used for scaling event processing so we can process more events with cloud native applications that have limited memory capacity, and for partitioning events so that each substream is processed differently. Let's look at how this pattern can be used in various scenarios.

Scale stream-processing applications. The Sequential Convoy pattern helps overcome cloud native stream-processing application limitations such as CPU, memory, and bandwidth, and allows us to process events with high throughput and low latency. For example, say we're processing an event stream that transfers large amounts of confidential data. The events are encrypted and compressed to transfer the data much faster. Performing CPU-intensive operations such as uncompressing, decrypting, and transforming the data in real time is time-consuming, and performing such complex operations not only slows events, but also adds latency for the following events in the stream. This can lead to backlog buildup in the queues and cause bottlenecks for the whole system.

By simply partitioning the events into multiple substreams and parallelizing their processing, we can eliminate the latency addition and the event buildup in queues

(Figure 6-15). We can use a simple round-robin strategy to distribute events to multiple substreams, which will process events much faster.

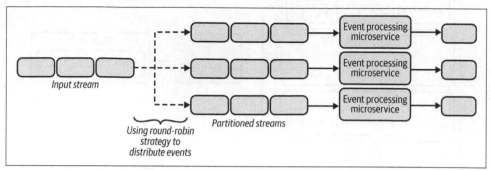

Figure 6-15. Using a simple round-robin strategy to partition events

Let's say the event-processing microservice also needs to enrich the event based on customer ID from a data store lookup. Retrieving data from data stores can be time-consuming and can potentially introduce latency to the overall processing time. One way to improve the performance is by caching the data in the microservice, as discussed in Chapter 4. But we cannot cache all the data because of the limited storage capacity of the microservice, and cache misses will still add latency.

We can use the Sequential Convoy pattern to separate events into different substreams based on hash values of customer IDs. This will process all events belonging to the same customer ID on the same node, improving the chance of cache hits. By reducing the number of customer IDs processed by a single microservice, we further increase cache hits, thereby meeting our performance goals.

Partition the stream processing.   The Sequential Convoy pattern enables us to execute different use cases against the same event stream by partitioning different event types into parallel streams. For example, imagine an ecommerce platform providing extra discounts to premium customers. It can use customer data to categorize customers at different levels, such as premium and standard, and provide extra discounts for premium customers. By using the Sequential Convoy pattern, it can split the events into multiple substreams based on customer attributes, and then use different types of microservices to process those substreams through two pipelines to provide relevant discounts (Figure 6-16).

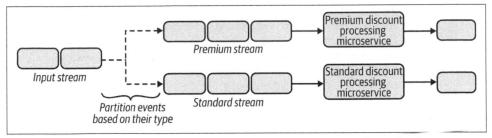

Figure 6-16. Generating different pipelines to process premium and standard events

Considerations

The ability to categorize events based on event attributes is crucial for meaningful stream processing. Sometimes events can be categorized based on a single attribute such as customer ID or product ID, but in other cases we might need to combine various attributes such as order value or place of order to better process related events together and in parallel.

When events are separated in multiple substreams, they can go through various cloud native applications, and during this process some events get filtered and dropped. This can make the sequence numbers noncontiguous. Therefore, we have to be mindful when events are regrouped as we might not find all of them. We can assume events have been dropped based on the next emitted events. But when we cannot reliably determine missing events, we employ a time-out to determine that the events were dropped.

A better approach to regrouping events is an *end-of-sequence message*. This can be emitted by the processing applications with the last process message ID in a periodic time interval. This tells us that all IDs before the given end-of-sequence ID have been processed by the upstream applications and that the missing IDs smaller than the last ID are dropped messages. This unblocks the processing of later events.

When grouping based on sequence numbers is not possible, we can simply collect events and publish them to a single topic, and then use the Buffered Event Ordering pattern (discussed later in this chapter), to buffer and sort events based on sequence numbers or event timestamps.

It is also important to plan for scaling the number of streams when we detect that the stream-processing microservice is becoming a bottleneck. One approach is to reshard by altering the relevant categories to divide the saturated substream into multiple other substreams for processing events. We also need to migrate the application state across all substreams. Therefore, it is important to store the application state in such a way that we can separate those streams when we need to scale. We discuss in detail how to store state in "Periodic Snapshot State Persistence Pattern" on page 243.

It is important to evaluate the throughput when using this pattern, and whether it meets expectations. For use cases that require extremely high throughput and low latency, adding sequence numbers to events and rejoining events based on those numbers can create a bottleneck, and in these cases we need to reevaluate whether ordering is really essential.

Related patterns

The following are related to the Sequential Convoy pattern:

Producer-Consumer and Publisher-Subscriber patterns
Can be used as the base for building the Sequential Convoy pattern. These patterns are covered in Chapter 5.

Buffered Event Ordering pattern
Provides an alternative way to order events while joining events from multiple event streams together. This pattern is covered next.

Periodic Snapshot State Persistence pattern
Stores substream application states and supports scalability. This pattern is covered later in this chapter.

Buffered Event Ordering Pattern

Network delays and connection retries can cause events to get out of order. The *Buffered Event Ordering pattern* allows us to reorder events before processing them downstream. We can order events based on time or on the order they are generated.

How it works

For events to be ordered, they must have an incremental value by which to order them. This value can be a sequence number or a timestamp, for example. Sequence numbers will continuously increase, and we can guarantee that each event in a stream will have a unique number. But with a timestamp, we cannot guarantee that all events will have unique values, because multiple events can be generated in the same millisecond.

Figure 6-17 illustrates the use of sequence numbers. If we have most recently received an event with sequence number 7, and now we receive an event with sequence number 8, we can immediately send it for processing because we know that 8 follows 7. But if after 8 we get 10, we know that we are missing an event and so cannot send 10 for processing. Instead, we need to use a time-out (of 30 seconds, for instance) to wait for the missing event. Then, if the missing event 9 arrives in time, we send it as well as event number 10. But if it does not arrive in time, we have to send the event with sequence number 10 before 9.

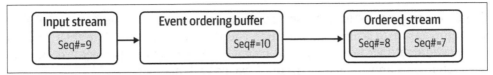

Figure 6-17. Ordering events based on sequence number

The event with sequence number 9 could be dropped upstream for many reasons. Rather than waiting for the time-out, the previous processor can send an empty event with sequence number 9. We could also annotate the next event, number 10, stating that it has processed all events before that. This can help the ordering application make a faster decision on whether an event has been dropped, without adding latency.

When ordering events by timestamp, we cannot perform this type of optimization, as we are working with duplicate and missing timestamp values. We need to rely on the last-seen timestamp and wait for time-outs to order the events.

When we detect an out-of-order of event, through either timestamps or sequence numbers, we need to modify the wait time-out so that this issue is less likely to occur. For example, if we receive an event with a timestamp of 700 seconds and then receive an event with a timestamp of 650 seconds, we need to increase the wait time-out by the event time gap—50 seconds. For more details on implementing this behavior, refer to algorithms such as K-slack and AQ-K slack.

How it's used in practice

This pattern can be deployed in front of any use case that needs ordered events, as long as the events have attributes that can be used for ordering.

Order events generated on distributed event sources. Events generated by distributed sources usually become out of order because of data transmission latency added by network and intermediate systems. Consider an example of distributed surveillance sensors emitting events. These events can reach the processing system at various times because of transmission latency, so they will be out of order when we combine all of them into a single stream for processing.

As the sensors are distributed, the only way to order the events is through timestamps. The out-of-order events can be sent to a single topic in a message broker, and by using a microservice, those events can be fetched, reordered through the Buffered Event Ordering pattern, and sent downstream for further processing. We can use this pattern only when the sensors have their times synced and the ordering based on the timestamps is reasonably accurate for processing.

Reorder events generated from the same event sources.   Often we need to parallelize event processing to achieve performance, and then reorder events into their original sequence for further processing. For example, say we want to parallel-process user interaction on a browser and merge those events back in order.

Because all the events needed to track user behavior are generated from the same browser, we recommend adding sequence numbers to those events along with the timestamp. This will not only allow us to process the events in parallel, to improve efficiency, but also group them back together, as we discussed in the Sequential Convoy pattern. We can feed the processed events to a topic in a message broker, and use a cloud native application to fetch and order the events based on their sequence numbers.

Considerations

This pattern is useful when we need to aggregate events over time or when a sequence of actions needs to be detected. In all other cases, we do not recommend using this pattern, as it can add latency or introduce a bottleneck to the system.

Events can be reordered with high accuracy, but only when those events are generated from a single source. We can't ensure that ordering by event timestamps will produce true ordering, as the distributed sources that generate events will not have their timestamps synchronized to the millisecond.

When events are generated from a single source, always try to add sequence numbers to the events along with the timestamp, because ordering events based on sequence number is much more efficient. It also does not add the same amount of latency as ordering events by timestamp.

When we have detected a late-arriving event, we have to decide whether to send the out-of-order event forward for processing or drop it. This decision depends on the use case. For example, if the events are reporting a current status (like temperature of the furnace in an industrial setup), dropping an old event will not cause issues because we have more-recent data for processing. But if the events are credit card transactions that we track to monitor fraud, dropping events can cause issues. This can lead to detecting invalid sequences if the processing application is using patterns such as Temporal Event Ordering.

The microservice implementing the Buffered Event Ordering pattern needs to store some events in the buffer while it is waiting for older events to arrive; this means that the microservice has state. It is important to employ reliability patterns like Periodic Snapshot State Persistence or Replay so the service can recover its state across failures and restarts.

Related patterns

The following patterns, covered in this chapter, are related to the Buffered Event Ordering pattern:

Temporal Event Ordering and Windowed Aggregation patterns
> These patterns can benefit from the Buffered Event Ordering pattern, as they require events to be ordered to produce more-accurate results.

Reliability patterns
> For storing and retrieving events that are waiting in the buffer for ordering, during system failure and restart.

Course Correction Pattern

The *Course Correction pattern* attempts to report its analysis of events as soon as possible, and then later correct its analysis and report again, as soon as it retrieves missing (or late) events. This produces early analysis with low latency rather than sending an accurate analysis with higher latency.

How it works

This pattern should be combined with patterns like Windowed Aggregation or Temporal Event Ordering. Rather than waiting for all events to arrive, we send aggregation and event sequence detection as soon as we have a result. The results of the aggregation and sequence detection are an early estimate and may not be accurate. Later, when we receive missing events, we send updated results.

For this pattern to work, downstream applications should be able to know that these events can be partial updates and to adapt based on more-accurate updates that will arrive later.

How it's used in practice

This pattern should be used only when we need events in order, have a requirement for low latency, and can cope with inaccurate early estimates. Let's consider some example scenarios to understand this in more detail.

Update results with new information. This pattern is commonly used when users are eager to obtain aggregated results quickly. This can especially be useful when we are displaying results in real time on a screen. In these cases, we simply need to hold the events for more time, and alter the decision based on late event arrivals.

For example, let's say we want our application to calculate the sum of orders arrived per minute, and report the number of orders on a per-minute basis. As shown in

Figure 6-18, we simply need to create buckets for each time period, such as 2021.05.03-07:30 and 2021.05.03-07:31, denoting the time periods in minutes, and then keep a counter within the bucket to continuously count the values arriving during that period. We will be able to emit the events when the time period ends, as well as send an update if events arrive later, such as sending an update for 2021.05.03-07:30 along with the output of 2021.05.03-07:31.

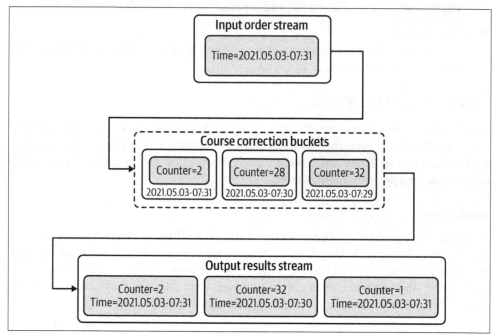

Figure 6-18. Aggregate events over multiple buckets to course-correct previous results

Be careful about when to purge the buckets, as having multiple buckets can use large amounts of memory. Purging them early can cause calculation errors, as events arriving late won't have their respective bucket with previous aggregations.

Correct previous decisions. Sometimes we need to make an early decision, and when the situation changes, we send compensation events so that corrective actions can be taken. Let's say we want to dispatch a taxi as soon as a user requests one.

When a user requests a taxi, we broadcast that message to all taxis in the region, and when we know a taxi has accepted the ride, we send another broadcast message to all taxis to inform them that the ride is accepted. During the initial request, there is a chance of multiple taxis accepting it, but we discover that only later because of network delays. Because we could mistakenly dispatch more than one taxi for the ride, we send a correction event to cancel the other taxi assignments.

Considerations

This pattern can be used only when early estimates are useful and the use case allows for compensation or course correction based on an update. For use cases that do not support course correction, we have to delay the decision making by using patterns like Buffered Event Ordering.

In most cases, events will be stored in memory while we are waiting for late event arrivals. This can cause high memory usage, so we need to find a balance between how long the system can wait for late events without running out of memory.

Since course correction also needs to remember previous values or previously emitted results, we need to apply reliability patterns to ensure that their state is preserved across system failures and restarts.

Related patterns

The following patterns, covered in this chapter, are related to the Course Correction pattern:

Reliability patterns
  For storing application state holding previous events and previously emitted outputs.

Buffered Event Ordering pattern
  Can be used instead of this pattern when the use case does not support course correction.

Temporal Event Ordering and Windowed Aggregation patterns
  These patterns can benefit from the Course Correction pattern as they can use course correction to correct their early estimates.

Watermark Pattern

The *Watermark pattern* is useful for periodically aligning stream processing across multiple microservices within a cloud native application that are connected in a mesh-like structure via event streams. This alignment will help determine whether all microservices have processed all arrived events before a given event, which is commonly referred to as the *watermark event*. We can use this pattern to sync multiple microservices without using system times.

How it works

For watermarks to work, a watermark generator should generate a watermark event periodically and send it through all the external inputs of the cloud native application. This event should be considered special, and microservices should pass it through to their dependent systems. We also need to be sure that each intermediate microservice that consumes this event can resend it in the same position among the sequence of events it has received and processed, and not before or after other events.

When the input systems are time synchronized, we can make those systems independently generate the watermark events at given intervals, such as once every minute or every five minutes, as shown in Figure 6-19.

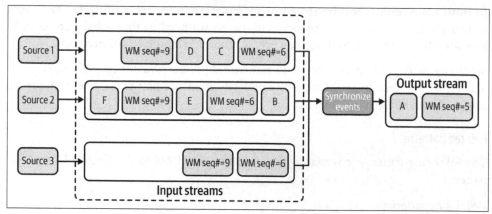

Figure 6-19. Generating watermark events and synchronizing events based on them

When the microservice receives a watermark event in a stream (such as the watermark event with sequence number 6 in this example), it should not continue processing any more events from that stream, and process only events from other streams (such as Event B of the second stream), that have not yet received the corresponding watermark event. When we receive all corresponding watermark events on all streams, we can pass that watermark event to all its dependents and continue processing other events from all the input streams until we receive the next watermark event in a stream. This process is repeated, and this approach ensures that event processing is synchronized at each watermark event.

When the preceding options are not possible, we can also make the input sources poll a global counter to fetch the next watermark event sequence number and emit it periodically along with the events. In this case, we should make sure that watermark events arriving in multiple streams are processed in a sequential manner. If we find a sequence number out of sync, we should halt the execution of events from that stream until we receive a watermark event with a lower sequence number on another stream.

How it's used in practice

This pattern can be used when multiple source systems are not synchronized on time, or when network latency or processing time can affect event arrival time. In this case, events in one stream can arrive earlier, while events from other streams can arrive later, and this can cause issues when analyzing events across multiple streams. This pattern is ideal for synchronizing the event processing periodically to reduce errors.

Synchronize events generated from event sources that are time synchronized. Watermarks can be used to generate synchronized event groups that can produce accurate aggregation results. Consider aggregate readings from multiple servers in a server farm that are in sync and emit events. We simply need to emit the watermark events at given time intervals to the input streams generated by those servers. This helps us collect the events between those watermarks and perform aggregation operations, as shown in Figure 6-20. This also ensures that the given aggregation is accurate and not affected by any network delays or other external factors.

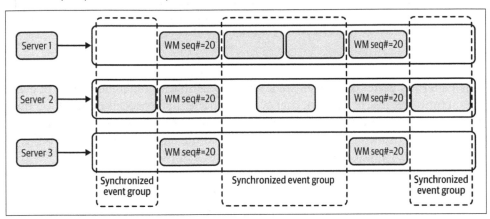

Figure 6-20. Aggregating events based on synchronized event groups generated between watermark events

In this case, we are not using event timestamps for synchronization because some streams may not publish events for a long period of time.

Synchronize events generated from nonsynchronized sources. Let's say we want to detect interesting incidents by using Temporal Event Ordering from multiple surveillance sensors deployed across the neighborhood. As events are emitted from distributed sensors, some sensors can be emitting them with a delay, or their events may arrive later because of network latency. To enforce synchronization, each sensor client can periodically fetch a sequence number from the global counter deployed on a central server and inject it along with the sensor reading. Figure 6-21 shows that we can synchronize the events based on the sequence number of the watermark events, and use the timestamps of those watermark events to determine the relative time of events, thereby determining the true order of the events and detecting event occurrence patterns.

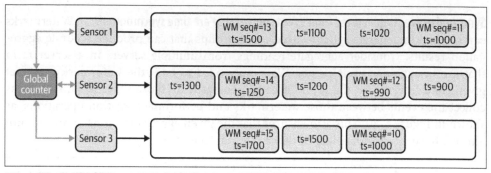

Figure 6-21. Ordering events based on continuous watermark events

Considerations

This pattern is useful only when we know that significant differences exist in event arrival times because of network latency or when the input systems do not have their times in sync. In other cases, this pattern does not bring us many advantages. For example, when systems are already synchronized on time, we can use the Buffered Event Ordering pattern to sort events by their timestamps.

 This pattern can only *reduce* the time synchronization issues among streams; we cannot guarantee that it can produce accurate results for all use cases. Even with periodic time syncs, we can have issues resolving which event of one stream arrived before an event from another stream.

We also do not recommend using this pattern unless you have a strong reason to process events on the actual time they are generated and need relative ordering of those events. Avoid using this pattern when it is not truly necessary because of the architectural and technological complexity it adds to the whole infrastructure.

Where possible, we also recommend using stream-processing systems like Apache Flink, which has the watermarking feature available by default. Using a stream-processing system is beneficial when your use case depends heavily on the order of events, such as fraud detection or surveillance.

Related patterns

The following are related to the Watermark pattern; all are covered in this chapter:

Buffered Event Ordering and Course Correction patterns
Can be used instead of this pattern when event arrival times are not affected by network latency or other processing delays by the systems.

Temporal Event Ordering and Windowed Aggregation patterns
These patterns can benefit from the Watermark pattern as they require events to be ordered to produce correct results.

Periodic Snapshot State Persistence pattern
The Watermark pattern can be a prerequisite for Periodic Snapshot State Persistence to perform state snapshots in a synchronized manner among multiple streams.

Summary of Scaling and Performance Optimization Patterns

In this section, we outlined scaling and performance optimization patterns often used by cloud native stream-processing applications. Table 6-4 summarizes when we should and should not use these patterns and their benefits.

Table 6-4. Scaling and performance optimization patterns

Pattern	When to use	When not to use	Benefits
Sequential Convoy	To scale stream-processing applications. To partition streams so each stream can be used for various use cases. To allow processing events in parallel and regroup them based on the original order.	Streaming applications have enough capacity to process the events.	Supports scalability of stream processing Preserves event ordering when events are processed in parallel.
Buffered Event Ordering	To order events based on timestamp or sequence number. To order events that are already out of order and published via a single event stream.	To group events from multiple ordered event streams. We need true ordering of events that are generated from distributed sources. Reliability patterns cannot be applied to the application.	Can be applied in front of any application that needs events in order.
Course Correction	To correct previously produced results. To produce early aggregation estimates. To guess the event-sequence order and correct the decision later.	The dependent downstream applications cannot handle continuous event updates.	Allows us to produce early estimates and correct them as we have more data.
Watermark	To perform aggregation operations on event streams that are out of sync. Try to order events that are generated by distributed systems.	We cannot inject watermark events closer to the event sources. Intermediate systems cannot bypass watermark events. Network bandwidth is a concern.	Periodically synchronizes events across multiple streams. Helps overcome network and processing latency added by intermediate systems.

Reliability Patterns

Most cloud native stream-processing applications store their state in memory so they can process events with low latency and high throughput. For this reason, reliability is key for stream processing applications. As we've mentioned throughout the chapter, *reliability patterns* guarantee that the state of our applications can be preserved across failures and restarts.

Reliability patterns also help us achieve at-least-once event delivery—sending an event one or multiple times—and allow exactly once event processing—processing events once and only once, even during system failures. This section dives deep into various reliability patterns that are used to preserve cloud native application state during critical situations.

Replay Pattern

By using the *Replay pattern*, the state of a microservice can be restored by replaying the events it has processed in the past, especially when its state depends only on recent events.

How it works

This pattern works by resending events when the system is down. The number of old events it needs to send depends on the use case. For example, if the microservice is aggregating events over the past three minutes, then during failures, resending the events arrived during the last three minutes is sufficient.

When the stateful microservice can store its state periodically, we will be able to identify the last successfully processed event from the latest snapshot, and we should be able to replay all events arrived after that.

To re-create the state of a system, the source of the data should contain the events even after they are retrieved by the microservice. We cannot use standard message brokers with their automatic event acknowledgment feature, because the events will be deleted from the message broker as we read them, unless we use queues or durable subscriptions and differ the acknowledgment of consumed events. As shown in Figure 6-22, we can delay sending acknowledgments to the queues until the microservice is done processing and cleaning out its state, or until it persists its state in durable storage.

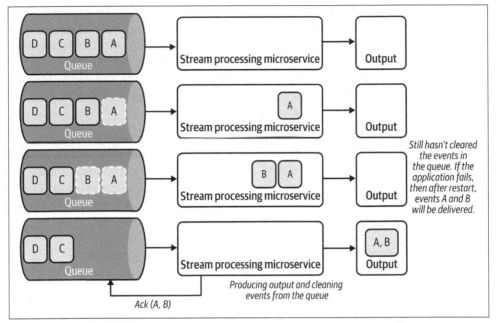

Figure 6-22. Deferring acknowledgment until after outputs are generated

We can use this pattern with microservices that consume events from log-based message brokers, such as Kafka and NATS, because these brokers will not delete the events when they are delivered to the microservice, and the microservices can request events to be played back from the last sequence number they have successfully processed. We can also use this pattern when events are read from persistent data stores like RDBMS databases, NoSQL stores, or filesystems.

How it's used in practice

This pattern can be used to restore an application's state by replaying the lost events due to system failure or restart. Let's look at how this pattern could be used in a few scenarios.

Replay events when system state is not persisted. What if we want to generate one-minute aggregations of purchase orders? We are processing data in one-minute batches, and at the end of each minute, the microservice generates the aggregation and clears its state. If we are retrieving events from a durable topic subscription, we can defer the acknowledgment for the retrieved events until the end of the minute; this will ensure that we are deleting the events from the message broker only when we have successfully processed them and produced the output.

Let's consider another example—analyzing log files for errors—and let's assume that the event processing is stateless. We can model the microservice in such a way that it will move the log file from one folder to another when it is done processing that file. Then, if the application fails during the processing, and when it is restarted or when a new instance of the service is spawned, it can reprocess the last file as it has not yet been moved to the done folder. This ensures that all events are processed.

Replay events when the system persists its state. What if we want to aggregate the average temperature over the last hour? Let's assume the processing microservice consumes events from Kafka and sends updates every minute to its dependents. By storing its aggregation state to a data store every minute when sending the updates, during failure, it can retrieve the last state from the data store, and replay all events from that point.

Considerations

Though the Replay pattern helps re-create the application state, it can produce duplicate events as a result of the replay. In this case, the dependent systems should be idempotent. We should not use this pattern when duplicate events can cause confusion on the part of dependent systems.

Sometimes events get lost even with the Replay pattern. For example, say we buffer events at the source for an extra two minutes so we can republish on demand. If the processing application encounters a failure, and it takes more than two minutes to start up, the source might have dropped events to accommodate new events. Therefore, we recommend using this pattern when consuming from event sources that can store events for a longer time period. We also recommend using this pattern in conjunction with the Periodic Snapshot State Persistence pattern, which we discuss next, especially when the processing application needs to persist state.

Related patterns

The following are related to the Replay pattern:

Publisher-Subscriber pattern
> Can be used to establish durable subscriptions with event sources so they can be replayed during failure. This pattern is covered in Chapter 5.

Periodic Snapshot State Persistence pattern
> This can be used in conjunction with the Replay pattern to restore application state and reduce the time to bring the application back alive. This pattern is covered next.

Periodic Snapshot State Persistence Pattern

Persisting the application state upon processing each incoming event is not feasible, as this introduces extremely high latency to cloud native applications due to the round-trip time of accessing state. The *Periodic Snapshot State Persistence pattern* allows us to persist the application state in a periodic manner so that we can restore the state reliably after system restarts or failures.

How it works

This pattern periodically makes a copy of its current state and persists that to a durable store between processing events. For this to work, we should ensure that the microservices can read and write state to a persistent storage (for example, Amazon S3).

To ensure that events are not lost during failures and to guarantee at-least-once event delivery, we must use message brokers to retrieve events. When using a log-based message broker like Kafka, we should store the event sequence number with the snapshot (Figure 6-23). With this approach, upon a restart, we reload the last stored snapshot and request the message broker to deliver events from the stored event sequence number.

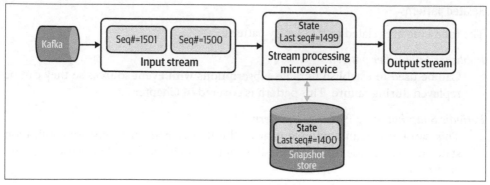

Figure 6-23. Storing periodic state snapshots with Kafka event sequence numbers

When using standard message brokers like ActiveMQ, we should acknowledge the processed messages only when storing the snapshot. This way, we can ensure that when the microservice is restarted the message broker sends all unacknowledged events.

By using these approaches, we can ensure at-least-once delivery. In this case, the events arrived after the last snapshot, and the failure will be sent again. Therefore, those events will be processed again and sent to the downstream systems a second time, causing duplicate event delivery.

Figure 6-24 shows an example of consuming events from Kafka and processing an aggregation operation The microservice performs a snapshot after processing an event with sequence number 1499 and when the running sum is at 50. Then it processes two events with sequence numbers 1500 and 1501, producing output events with sums 56 and 59, respectively, before failing. After restart, the microservice restores its state from the last snapshot, requesting Kafka to publish events that arrived after event 1499. This leads Kafka to send the events with sequence numbers 1500 and 1501 again, causing the microservice to reprocess and output events with sums 56 and 59, respectively, and duplicate event delivery to downstream systems.

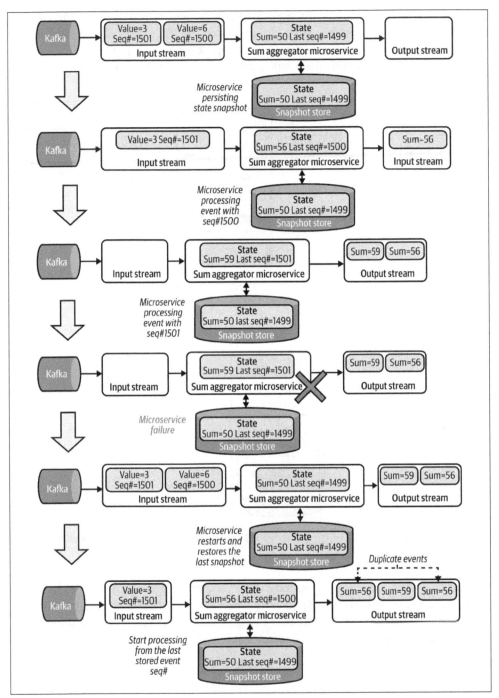

Figure 6-24. Performing an aggregation operation with snapshot state persistence and restoring state after system failure

If the dependent systems do not support duplicate events, we can also introduce a new output sequence number from the microservice (Figure 6-25). The dependent systems can detect that the same sequence is repeating and drop the duplicate events without reprocessing them. This will achieve exactly once event processing even across system failures.

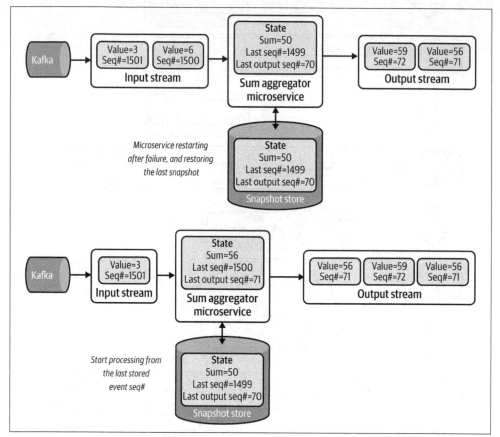

Figure 6-25. Microservice emitting the output sequence number for the dependent system to detect duplicate events

Instead of taking snapshots at periodic intervals, this pattern can also leverage the Watermark pattern to take snapshots only when event synchronizations are based on watermark events. This will ensure that all events before the given watermark are processed and persisted.

How it's used in practice

This pattern can be used to store state when microservices process data in memory, and when their state cannot be persisted after every event.

Let's say we want our application to detect if a stock price has continuously risen over the last 10 minutes. We need to keep track of only the last time we saw a dip in the stock price, and continuously check if that time is now older than 10 minutes. If so, we will alert the user.

If we are retrieving the events from a Kafka topic, we also need to remember the last-processed event's sequence number along with the current stock price, and the last time we saw the stock price dip. These three represent the *state* of the microservice. To recover the microservice from failure, we need to persist all three values to a database or similar storage, in a periodic manner. During the recovery process, the microservice can restore the last stored snapshot and replay the Kafka events from the last stored event sequence number to ensure that the system state is preserved across system failures.

Considerations

We should use this pattern only when we are processing critical data that cannot be lost on system failure, because the pattern introduces significant operational overhead that is not worthwhile if data loss is acceptable. For example, if our processing window is small (say, one minute), system failure impacts for only as long as the system is down. To restore state, we can use the Replay pattern to reprocess the events during the lost period. But if our application state contains data from the previous day, we need to replay events from the previous day to re-create the state, which may not be feasible because of the processing time for the quantity of events. In such cases, we advise using the Periodic Snapshot State Persistence pattern.

In some situations, the state itself is quite large and requires significant time to store and retrieve. To mitigate this, use incremental snapshots, store only the delta between the current state and the last snapshot, and then replay incremental snapshots to re-create system state. For example, when using a time window of five minutes with one-minute time shifts for aggregation, store snapshots every minute with only the changes that happened during the last minute. When there is a failure, we load the last five snapshots to re-create the state of the five-minute window.

When performing snapshots and persisting them in a data store, we recommend using threads, or something similar, so persisting state doesn't block the processing of more events.

We do not recommend making the snapshot interval overly short, as this introduces overhead without significant benefit. But don't set the snapshot overly long either, as this leads to not only writing and reading bigger snapshots (which takes longer), but also replaying more events on application restoration (which can increase the time for applications to become live again).

Related patterns

The following patterns, covered in this chapter, are related to the Periodic Snapshot State Persistence pattern:

Temporal Event Ordering and Windowed Aggregation patterns
> These patterns can benefit from the Periodic Snapshot State Persistence pattern, as they require state to be stored to achieve reliability.

Replay pattern
> This is used to re-create states from the missing events based on the last snapshot loaded during application recovery.

Watermark pattern
> This can be used to synchronize state snapshots across multiple microservices.

Two-Node Failover Pattern

Low-latency microservices do not have the luxury of taking a couple of minutes after failure to restart and restore their states. For these microservices, it is operationally superior to run a redundant microservice to allow failover. We can run such a microservice by using the *Two-Node Failover pattern*.

How it works

This pattern focuses on running a parallel backup microservice. When microservices are deployed, they perform a leader election; we can use systems such as ZooKeeper or native cloud services to designate one microservice as primary and the other as secondary.

These two microservices, shown in Figure 6-26, will process all the incoming events. Both microservices consuming the same event are achieved by subscribing to a common topic, as discussed in the Publisher-Subscriber pattern in Chapter 5. As both microservices process the same events, they have consistent state. Only the primary will be emitting the output to its dependencies, and it also sends the output to the secondary. The secondary matches its output against the primary's and drops all events that have been processed by the primary (Event B).

At this point, if the primary fails, the secondary will be promoted to become the primary, and, while continuing to process events, it will also start publishing to the dependencies. Because it knows the last event published by the previous primary (Event B), it will be able to determine which events have not yet been sent and send those events (Event C) first before publishing new events (Event D).

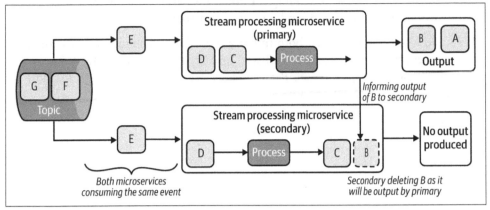

Figure 6-26. Running microservices as primary and secondary to enable failover

If the failed microservice is restarted in a later state, it is demoted to operating as the secondary, where it will consume events, process them, and drop them based on the outputs generated by the current primary.

Over time, the secondary's state will become equal to its primary and will become eligible to be a failover target. If the microservices leverage Periodic Snapshot State Persistence, they can recover quickly by restoring state faster and improving the availability of the system.

How it's used in practice

This pattern can be used when degradation of latency and system downtime cannot be tolerated. Say we retrieve stock order events from NATS, process the number of stock bids and asks in real time, and publish them to stockbrokers so they can instantly identify changes in market trends. Using the Two-Node Failover pattern, we cannot only switch to the secondary node instantly upon detecting that the primary has failed, but also ensure that no events are dropped. This is because the secondary publishes only data that the primary has not.

Considerations

Use this pattern only when low latency is the main requirement. Otherwise, use other patterns such as Periodic Snapshot State Persistence. This pattern is complex to implement, and the architectural complexity is not worthwhile if we can tolerate downtime during system failure.

This pattern requires both microservices to have robust connectivity, as the primary needs to publish its output to the secondary. Furthermore, a risk of network partitioning between the primary and secondary exists. In this case, we require a third system to function as the leadership elector; otherwise, both microservices could become primary in parallel and send outputs downstream.

We should also be mindful that both microservices can fail simultaneously; then the system would become unavailable and we'd lose their state. As a mitigation, we can adopt the Periodic Snapshot State Persistence pattern or Replay pattern to allow for state restoration in such a scenario.

> Though we are using two nodes, we will not be able to process more data with this pattern, as the second microservice is used only as a failover. If scalability is needed, we must use the Sequential Convoy pattern and replace each microservice in that pattern with primary and secondary pairs.

Related patterns

The following are related to the Two-Node Failover pattern:

Periodic Snapshot State Persistence and Replay patterns
These patterns, covered in this chapter, can be used with the Two-Node Failover pattern to restore the state of the microservice when they restart it as a secondary after failure.

Sequential Convoy pattern
Used if we need to scale the stream-processing application. This pattern is covered in this chapter.

Publisher-Subscriber pattern
To allow both primary and secondary microservices to consume the same events. Chapter 5 details this pattern.

Summary of Reliability Patterns

In this section, we outlined some reliability patterns commonly used by cloud native stream-processing applications. Table 6-5 summarizes when we should and should not use these patterns, and their benefits.

Table 6-5. Reliability patterns

Pattern	When to use	When not to use	Benefits
Replay	The system state contains only recent events. To restore state only when there is access to the previously processed events. To process data from persistence stores, filesystems, and log-based message brokers.	We cannot guarantee that previously processed data cannot be accessed again. Dependent systems cannot process duplicate events. Systems cannot take time to re-create their state. The system state needs to contain events that span over a long period.	Allows re-creating state without storing large snapshots.
Periodic Snapshot State Persistence	The system state needs to contain events that span over a long period. To restore state only when there is access to the previously processed events. To process data from persistence stores, filesystems, and log-based message brokers.	The system state contains only recent events. We cannot guarantee that previously processed events can be accessed again. Systems cannot take time to re-create their state.	Allows re-creating state faster. Supports larger and long-running system states. Supports dependent applications that cannot process duplicate events.
Two-Node Failover	We cannot take time to restore the application after failure. The system state needs to contain events that span over a long period. To restore state only when there is access to the previously processed events.	We cannot guarantee that previously processed events can be accessed again. Systems can take time to re-create their state.	Supports low-latency and highly available stream processing. Supports dependent applications that cannot process duplicate events.

Technologies

Stream processing can be designed as part of a microservice, or deployed entirely by using a stream-processing system. When it comes to simple patterns such as Transformation, and Filters and Threshold, we can implement the logic within our microservice. But for more-complex patterns, using a stream-processing technology will provide better outcomes.

In this section, we briefly discuss various stream-processing technologies with the goal of showing how and where we can use them in the design of our cloud native applications.

Esper

Esper is a complex event-processing library released under the GPL v2 license. It can be used to implement stream-processing logic in Java and .NET-based microservice applications. It supports stream-processing constructs including transformations, filtering, thresholds, windowed aggregations, joins, and temporal event ordering.

Esper can be used to reduce the complexity of an application, as we can offload most of the processing logic to it. We can model events as Java or .NET objects and pass them to Esper for processing, and then subscribe to it to receive outputs. It also supports a query language to configure the stream-processing logic. We recommend using Esper for implementing stream-processing logic within our microservices or serverless functions.

Siddhi

Siddhi is a Java-based stream-processing library and a microservice released under Apache License v2. As a library, Siddhi (like Esper) can be embedded into microservices to process stream-processing logic. It allows stream-processing logic to be defined via Siddhi Query Language and supports stream-processing constructs including transformations, filtering, thresholds, windowed aggregations, joins, temporal event ordering, and machine learning. We recommend using Siddhi for implementing stream-processing logic within microservices or serverless functions.

We also recommend using Siddhi if you want to run stream processing as a stand-alone microservice supporting all the reliability patterns, including Periodic Snapshot State Persistence and Two-Node Failover. Users can use Siddhi Query Language to configure the sources from which Siddhi should consume events, its processing logic, and where it should publish its output and deploy that to Kubernetes.

ksqlDB

ksqlDB is a stream-processing and a database system that is part of Kafka. It works only in environments where Kafka is used as the broker for distributing events. We can define rules in ksqlDB to retrieve events from a Kafka stream, and then process and publish them. It supports stream-processing constructs such as transformations, filtering, thresholds, windowed aggregations, and joins. It also provides a feature to build materialized views from the input events, which can be queried on demand by cloud native applications. Its ability to pull data on demand is useful, as it can be modeled as a relational database. We recommend using ksqlDB when Kafka is used as the message broker for the cloud native application, and when you need to query event logs via materialized views.

Apache Spark

Spark is a big-data and stream-processing platform released under Apache License v2. It can run on Apache Mesos, Hadoop YARN, and Kubernetes. Though it is strong in batch processing, it can also support stream-processing constructs such as transformations, filtering, thresholds, windowed aggregations, joins, and machine learning.

It uses both queries and a structured programming approach, allowing users to program using Java, Scala, or Python to support both stream and batch processing. It achieves reliable processing by periodically checkpointing data into durable storage. It is an ideal choice when use cases are mainly oriented toward batch processing while having some streaming requirements.

Apache Flink

Flink is a fully fledged stream-processing platform released under Apache License v2. It can run on platforms like Kubernetes, Knative, and AWS Lambda. It supports stream-processing constructs such as transformations, filtering, thresholds, windowed aggregations, joins, and temporal event ordering, along with graph processing. It also supports exactly once semantics, and supports reliable data processing using watermarks, and snapshots by storing them in storage such as S3, GCS, and HDFS.

Flink supports simple query language for defining stream-processing logic, the Table API for declarative data processing, and data stream and stream-processing APIs in Java for more-granular level configurations. We recommend using this for large-scale stream-processing use cases that have high scalability and availability requirements.

Amazon Kinesis

Kinesis is a fully managed scalable stream-processing offering from AWS. It supports SQL-based and Flink-based data processing in the cloud and allows users to build their own cloud native applications and run them in Amazon Lambda or EC2. With its SQL mode, it can support transformations, filtering, thresholds, windowed aggregations, and joins.

With Flink, it supports all standard stream-processing constructs. In addition to streaming events, it can also stream video content. We recommend using Kinesis if AWS is the hosting environment for your cloud native application.

Azure Stream Analytics

Azure Stream Analytics is a fully managed scalable streaming analytics platform offered by Microsoft. It supports defining stream-processing logic by using SQL queries and a graphical user interface. It supports stream-processing constructs such as transformations, filtering, thresholds, windowed aggregations, joins, temporal event ordering, and machine learning.

It also supports hybrid architectures for running stream-processing queries in the cloud and on the edge node. We recommend using Azure Stream Analytics if Azure is your hosting environment.

Google Dataflow

Google Dataflow is a fully managed scalable stream-processing platform offered by Google. It supports defining stream-processing logic using Apache Beam SDK, SQL queries, and via GUI. It supports stream-processing constructs such as transformations, filtering, thresholds, windowed aggregations, joins, temporal event ordering, and machine learning.

With its Apache Beam SDK, it allows developers to deploy stream-processing logic into on-premises stream-processing systems such as Apache Flink. We recommend using Dataflow if Google Cloud is your hosting environment.

Summary of Stream-Processing Technologies

This section outlined commonly used stream-processing systems for cloud native application development. Table 6-6 summarizes when we should and should not use these technologies.

Table 6-6. Stream-processing technologies

Stream-processing technology	When to use	When not to use
Esper	To embed into cloud native applications. To support transformations, filtering and thresholds, windowed aggregations, joins, and temporal event ordering.	To run as a standalone application. To run machine learning models. Built-in reliability is required.
Siddhi	To embed into cloud native applications. To run as a standalone cloud native application. To support transformations, filtering and thresholds, windowed aggregations, joins, temporal event ordering, and machine learning.	High scalability is needed.
ksqlDB	Kafka is used in the infrastructure. To support transformations, filtering and thresholds, windowed aggregations, and joins. To build materialized views from the input events.	Kafka is not used in the infrastructure. Temporal event ordering and machine learning is needed.
Apache Spark	Support for both stream and batch processing is needed. To support transformations, filtering and thresholds, windowed aggregations, joins, and machine learning.	A lightweight system is needed for stream processing. Temporal event ordering is needed. To embed into cloud native applications.
Apache Flink	To support transformations, filtering and thresholds, windowed aggregations, joins, and temporal event ordering, along with graph processing. For high scalability and availability requirements.	A lightweight system is needed for stream processing. To embed into cloud native applications.

Stream-processing technology	When to use	When not to use
Amazon Kinesis	To support Flink in AWS. To support transformations, filtering and thresholds, windowed aggregations, joins and temporal event ordering, along with graph processing.	Other cloud providers are selected. To embed into cloud native applications.
Azure Stream Analytics	To support transformations, filtering and thresholds, windowed aggregations, joins, temporal event ordering, and machine learning. To support stream-processing queries to run in the cloud and on the edge node.	Other cloud providers are selected. To embed into cloud native applications.
Google Dataflow	To support transformations, filtering and thresholds, windowed aggregations, joins, temporal event ordering, and machine learning. To support portable stream-processing logic that can also run on on-premises stream-processing systems.	Other cloud providers are selected. To embed into cloud native applications.

Testing

In this section, we cover the most important aspects of testing stream-processing cloud native applications. When testing stream-processing applications, we need to follow conventional approaches of writing unit and integration tests. Because stream-processing applications are asynchronous, we recommend you follow all testing suggestions provided for event-driven architecture in "Testing" on page 197, along with the suggestions provided here.

One of the key aspects that we need to test in stream-processing applications is their ability to handle state. When we use reliability patterns, we should run chaos testing to test whether the application is continuously producing correct results despite system failures. To assert the application state deterministically, we can use the Watermark pattern to publish watermark events at the end of each test for the application to persist its state and to ensure that it has completed event processing.

When testing time-bounded patterns such as Windowed Aggregations or Temporal Event Ordering patterns, the application could produce different results for each test cycle, due to fluctuations of network and application latency. Instead of asserting the results with a margin of error, we recommend updating the stream-processing applications to process events based on event timestamps generated at the source. With this approach, we can eliminate the network and intermediate application latency and generate reproducible results.

Security

How can we enforce security for cloud native stream-processing applications? As discussed in Chapter 5, stream-processing applications can enforce security by connecting to message brokers and other systems via secured protocols, and using data and encrypting data in transit and at rest.

If enforcing security at the application level is not possible, we recommend using a bounded context, fronted by an API or a secured message broker to consume the events, and build the whole stream-processing system within that context. We also recommend you apply all the general security best practices discussed in Chapters 2 and 5.

Observability and Monitoring

Observability and monitoring are key for successfully operating stream-processing applications. Because of the asynchronous and stateful nature of the applications, without proper monitoring, we will not be able to detect issues until system failure.

Because stream-processing applications contain state, monitoring their memory consumption is critical. Say a system is running a time-bounded query, such as aggregating values over a five-minute window. If an event spike occurs as the system is storing events in memory, the system could run out of memory, resulting in a failure. Having monitoring and load-shedding mechanisms can help mitigate the risk of abnormal conditions. But if the spike is consistent, we should consider partitioning or remodeling the stream-processing pipeline to cater to higher loads.

Stateful stream-processing systems can utilize the Periodic Snapshot State Persistence pattern to recover their state after failure. Monitoring that these snapshots are properly saved and garbage-collected once outdated is critical. Furthermore, if the application state is large (for example, 500 MB or more), writing the snapshot takes a long time and negatively impacts the available network bandwidth for new events. Therefore, monitoring the size of the snapshots and the time taken to write them, as well as monitoring the network bandwidth, CPU, and memory of the applications when storing the snapshots, will help you properly architect the application to reliably store and restore its state.

The complexity of the stream-processing logic, and network latency, can make events in one stream arrive later than events in other streams. This can cause errors in the final output. Therefore, monitoring what event timestamp is being processed at each streaming application can help identify such discrepancies. We can apply the Buffered Event Ordering, Course Correction, or Watermark pattern to synchronize the applications and mitigate the error.

It is also critical to log and track events by using causation IDs to identify and handle failure situations in production. Refer to Chapter 5 for details on applying them, and for other recommendations on monitoring and observing asynchronous stream-processing applications.

DevOps

In this section, we focus on how DevOps applies to stateful applications such as stream-processing applications. The first DevOps step is selecting the appropriate reliability pattern for achieving reliable stream processing. This should be influenced by the system's availability and scalability requirements.

When a pattern is identified, an appropriate persistence store should be selected to enable the rapid persistence and restoration of state, and store the state durably. We also need to empirically determine the optimal snapshot size and frequency. This should minimize the latency introduced by snapshotting. As part of the DevOps process, we should also monitor and garbage-collect redundant snapshots. Encrypting the snapshots so the sensitive data remains secure is also important.

As discussed in Chapter 5, we recommend encrypting events when we are dealing with sensitive data, and purging events and snapshots as soon as they are no longer needed for processing. We also recommend using a bounded context when possible, so we can protect all the applications, via API or a topic in the message broker, from external threats.

Because failures in asynchronous applications are difficult to troubleshoot, we also recommend setting up observability and monitoring by using distributed tracing, logging, and monitoring systems. In addition, continuous delivery is crucial for modern DevOps. For smooth deployments, we recommend maintaining backward compatibility of event schema and snapshots at all times. When major changes occur, we recommend running both versions of the applications in parallel until the new system rebuilds its state. Finally, we recommend using multiple deployment environments, such as development and staging/preproduction, to reduce the impact of changes to the application, and to validate the application before moving it to production.

By following these steps, we can safely deploy and maintain cloud native stream-processing applications and systems.

Summary

In this chapter, we discussed several stream-processing patterns that can be applied to cloud native applications. We explored options for processing continuous streams of events by using patterns like Transformation, and Filters and Thresholds; using time- and length-based aggregations; joining multiple event streams; detecting interesting incidents based on event occurrence order; and using machine learning to perform real-time predictions.

We covered how to parallelize and scale stream-processing applications, order out-of-order events, synchronize stream-processing operations, and, finally, how to achieve reliable stream processing. We also discussed stream-processing technologies that we can use when applying these patterns, and briefly reviewed how stream-processing applications can be secured, tested, continuously deployed through DevOps, and observed and monitored to guarantee continuous operation. In the next chapter, we will explore the patterns related to API management.

CHAPTER 7

API Management and Consumption Patterns

When we are building cloud native applications, we can build the business capabilities by using a wide array of design patterns covered throughout the book. Once you have the business capabilities implemented as microservices, you then need to present those services to external or internal consumers as managed APIs by using *API management patterns*.

In this chapter, we explore some of the most commonly used patterns in API management. We also cover a few API consumption patterns, which are essential in building frontend applications such as a web, mobile, or desktop applications on top of the managed APIs. Let's begin our discussion with API management patterns.

API Management Patterns

Any cloud native application must have a given set of business capabilities that are exposed to its external consumers (customers, partners, and so forth) as well as internal consumers (other teams or departments in the same organization). These business capabilities are exposed to consumers through APIs. *API management* is the process of creating, managing, securing, analyzing, and scaling APIs on top of existing microservices.

API management enables consumers of your cloud native application to do the following:

- Have better engagement with the APIs you expose
- Integrate your application with other services and build new capabilities
- Monetize the consumption of your APIs

- Generate business analytics and insights
- Expose business capabilities as managed, secure, and resilient

Before diving into API management patterns, let's first understand some key concepts related to API management.

An *API* or an *API proxy* represents a business capability of your cloud native application that is exposed to consumers in a managed way. An API may be backed by one or more backend microservices and is usually hosted in a separate API gateway runtime. The logic of the business capability that we expose should reside with the backend microservices, while the API provides only capabilities such as security, throttling, versioning, and so on. We should try to avoid putting business logic in the API layer, as the underlying service is responsible for supporting the required business logic. A given API can offer more than one backend microservice (for example, an order API can be backed by an order management capability hosted at *<host>:<port>/order/management* services and an order status capability hosted in a different context (*order/status*). But we do not recommend creating compositions such as service orchestrations at the API layer. APIs are usually exposed via REST/ OpenAPI or GraphQL.

An *API product* is a concept occasionally used when it comes to presenting an API to developers via the API developer portal. The API product has one or more APIs and is usually mapped to a high-level business capability. For example, in cloud storage services, Storage Services can be the API product, while we can have multiple APIs such as the File API, Blobs API, and Disk API under that one API product.

In the following sections, we'll explore commonly used patterns in the API management of cloud native applications. Let's start the discussion with the API Gateway pattern.

API Gateway Pattern

The *API Gateway pattern* is the most common way of exposing the business capabilities of your cloud native application to the consumer. With this pattern, you put a separate layer in front of the capabilities that are designed as microservices and that you wish to expose to consumers. With this approach, an API gateway acts as the front door to your cloud native applications.

How it works

An API gateway layer is often built on top of existing microservices. Any microservices or composite services that you develop can be exposed as managed APIs through the API gateway. The API gateway operates alongside the API control plane and developer portal. Before we dive into each of these components, let's first understand the roles that you may encounter in a typical API management process:

API creator/API developer

A person in a technical role who understands the technical aspects of the API (including interfaces, documentation, and versions) and uses the API publisher to provision APIs into the API store. The creator or developer uses the API store to consult ratings and feedback provided by API users. Creators and developers can add APIs to the store but cannot manage their life cycle.

API publisher

Manages a set of APIs across the enterprise or business unit and controls the API life cycle, subscriptions, and monetization aspects. The publisher is also interested in usage patterns for APIs and has access to all API statistics. (In certain cases, the API creator and publisher roles may be combined into a single role.)

Application developer

Uses the API store to discover APIs, read the documentation and forums, rate/ comment on the APIs, subscribe to APIs, obtain access tokens, and invoke the APIs.

API control plane admin

Hosts and manages the API management solution. This person is responsible for creating user roles in the system, managing databases, and ensuring security.

If we look at a typical life cycle of an API and how these roles come into the picture at different stages, we can identify the key steps of API life-cycle management as follows:

1. We identify the business capabilities that we are going to expose as managed APIs.

2. The API creator (this can also be a person who develops services) creates a managed API (or API proxy) on top of the corresponding microservices of the business capability. The downstream services can be individual microservices or service compositions. The API is created at the API gateway.

3. API publishers can publish the APIs that are created so that they are available in the developer portal to be discovered by the application developers.

4. Application developers subscribe to APIs that they wish to consume through the API developer portal and learn more about the API so that they can consume applications on top of those APIs.

5. The applications that consume those APIs (such as mobile, web, or desktop applications) send requests via the API gateway to consume the business capabilities.

6. API publishers and creators control, observe, and manage the API exposed to the consumer.

Figure 7-1 shows how each role maps to the key components of the API Gateway pattern.

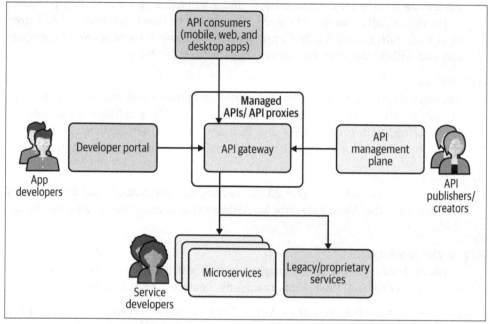

Figure 7-1. API management using API Gateway and associated roles

Let's discuss each component and their interactions in detail.

API gateway. The *API gateway* is the front door to your APIs. The APIs that you create in front of the downstream microservices are hosted inside the API gateway runtime. None of the roles that we've discussed directly interacts with the API gateway, but the API consumers do (for example, the consumers of the mobile and web applications that are built on top of the managed APIs)

The API gateway is responsible for accepting the API calls and applying security validations such as tokens, certificates, and other credential validations. It also applies various quality-of-service attributes to the API calls, such as throttling (quotas, rate limiting), caching, and versioning. In certain scenarios, you may also implement lightweight transformation logic (such as JSON to XML, or minor changes to the payload), but again we should not try to expose any logic related to the business capability of the API that we offer. An API gateway is also responsible for collecting all the data related to observability and API analytics.

API management plane. The *API management plane* is the main interface that the API creators and publishers use to control and administer the behavior of the APIs hosted through the API gateway and developer portal. Using the control plane, we can define and create APIs (and API products), change the life-cycle state of the APIs, and manage API access policies such as throttling, caching, security, and versioning. Management of users, schemas, and API visibility are also done at the control plane.

API developer portal. The *developer portal* is where you present your APIs to the application developers so they can discover and learn about your APIs, try them out, subscribe to them (or to API products), rate them, and provide feedback. (This is similar to the concept of an app store that you usually find with mobile devices such as iPhone or Android). The developer portal also allows developers to generate required security keys and tokens and use them when building applications that consume those APIs. Developers may also use the developer portal to obtain analytics on their own usage.

The API gateway is a mandatory component for implementing the API Gateway pattern, and the rest are optional. Based on your use case, you can choose whether you need a management plane or a developer portal. The roles of API creator and API publisher may be merged into one in most cases, as the microservices developers themselves can expose selected services as managed APIs by using the API Gateway pattern.

How it's used in practice

The API Gateway pattern is usually used as a facade on top of existing microservices. Not all your microservices need to be exposed as APIs. When you want to expose a certain capability as an API, you first create a microservice that caters to that capability and then you can create an API by using that microservice as the backend.

Figure 7-2 shows the Order API exposing the business functionalities related to order management in an online application. This requires multiple services to interact, and we may use the Service Orchestration or Service Choreography patterns to implement the service composition. Once we have the composite service (Order service, in this case), API creators/publishers can create an Order API by using the API management plane, and then publish it. Once you publish the API, it becomes available in the developer portal for the app developers. They can then build apps that consume the Order API.

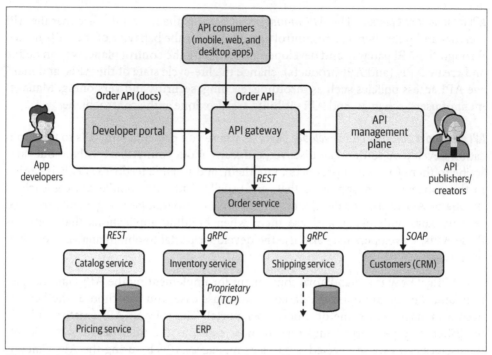

Figure 7-2. Implementation of remote procedure calls

The applications that are built to consume the Order API send requests to the API gateway, where security, throttling, caching, versioning, and other policies are enforced. Since we start from microservices and then expose APIs later, this approach is known as a *bottom-up API management* technique.

The API Gateway pattern can also be used in a *top-down* approach, in which we start with the API design. Depending on the use case, this approach requires us to first design the API and then delve into the implementation, where we develop one or more microservices and their interactions.

Top-down API management is usually suitable when you have API management requirements at the time you start building a cloud native application. If you are adopting API management later into the development of your cloud native application, the bottom-up approach works better.

Considerations

Here are some of the main considerations to keep in mind when applying the API Gateway pattern:

- The API gateway layer should not have business logic–related capabilities. To have better separation of concerns, the underlying service should take care of the business capabilities.

- We can have multiple API management layers to expose APIs to internal and external consumers.

- At the initial stages, you may require only an API gateway, while the API control plane and developer portal are not mandatory. API publishing, and obtaining the information on published APIs, can be supported via dedicated interfaces of the API gateway (for example, the REST API).

- As your API management requirements become more advanced, you will need dedicated API control plane and developer portal components. Depending on the requirements, you also can adopt new components to handle API monetization, traffic management, and so on.

- The API gateway layer is often used as a monolithic runtime. If the gateway layer does any heavy lifting related to security, policy enforcement, and so forth, you may have to split it into multiple runtimes. The API Microgateway pattern that we discuss next can be used in such scenarios.

Related patterns

API management patterns can be used along with any of the service composition patterns that we discussed previously. We can use different variations of the API Gateway architecture to cater to specific requirements of cloud native applications. These variations are discussed in "API Microgateway Pattern" on page 265 and in "Service Mesh Sidecar as an API Gateway Pattern" on page 268.

API Microgateway Pattern

The *API Microgateway pattern* is a simple variation of the API Gateway pattern. The key idea is to make the API gateway a distributed component so that each API deployed in the API gateway has an independent runtime. So, the API gateway is no longer a monolithic component in this pattern.

How it works

In the API Gateway pattern, the API gateway component hosts the runtime for all APIs that we expose through our API management layer. However, when the number of APIs that we expose grows, this monolithic API gateway layer can become really bulky and will start giving us all the problems of a conventional monolithic application. And a monolithic API gateway layer goes against some of the core principles of microservices in a cloud native application.

The APIs that we expose from an API management layer represent business capabilities that are designed, developed, deployed, and managed independently. Therefore, a true cloud native application shouldn't have a monolithic or central API gateway layer. Instead, each API should have its own runtime—called a *microgateway*—and we should be able to manage all these runtimes together by using a central API management plane that is exposed via a central API developer portal. Figure 7-3 illustrates how to segregate an API gateway into multiple runtimes so that each API has its own runtime.

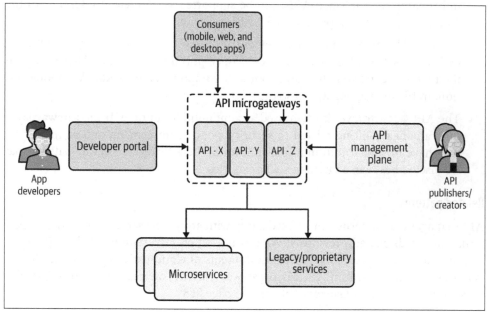

Figure 7-3. API management with microgateways

How it's used in practice

The API Microgateway pattern is similar to the microservices concepts presented in Chapter 1. A microgateway is usually implemented using a lightweight gateway runtime deployed as a container. Therefore, we can leverage containers and container orchestration systems to run microgateways. The rest of the components of API management work exactly the same as in the API Gateway pattern. Figure 7-4 illustrates a typical use case of an online retail application, in which different APIs are exposed to consumers by using microgateways.

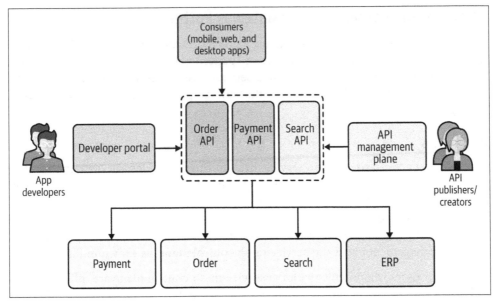

Figure 7-4. API microgateways in action

As you can see, each API is an independent entity that doesn't share the API gateway runtime with other components. For example, if the Search API gets more traffic than the Order API, the Search API can be independently scaled.

Considerations

The API Microgateway pattern requires support from the underlying API management platform to have such a decentralized deployment of the gateway. Since we are using one gateway for each API, the gateway runtime must be extremely lightweight. When it comes to managing and scaling such a decentralized system, we need a container orchestration system such as Kubernetes to handle the operational overhead. In most API management solutions offered as cloud services, the existence of the microgateway is transparent, and the cloud service takes care of handling it seamlessly.

Related patterns

The API Microgateway pattern uses the same terminology as the API Gateway pattern. All the concepts that we discussed for the API Gateway pattern are equally applicable to the Microgateway pattern. The Service Mesh Sidecar as an API Gateway pattern is an application of the Microgateway pattern in the context of service mesh, which we discuss next.

Service Mesh Sidecar as an API Gateway Pattern

We covered the Service Mesh and Sidecar patterns in Chapter 3. The key idea behind the Service Mesh Sidecar as an API Gateway pattern is that, in an environment where we use service mesh, rather than using a separate API gateway runtime, we can off-load the tasks of the API gateway to the sidecar proxies running alongside each microservice.

How it works

Suppose you are already using a service mesh to run your microservices and want to include API management in the same deployment. For the microservices that you want to expose as APIs, you can leverage a sidecar proxy to function as the API gateway in addition to supporting the normal service mesh capabilities. Each service mesh sidecar proxy that is colocated with the microservices can also be controlled via the API management plane and service mesh control plane, as shown in Figure 7-5.

The type of users who interact with the service mesh control plane are different from those who interact with the API management plane. Service developers or DevOps primarily control the service mesh behavior, while API creators and publishers manage the API life cycle.

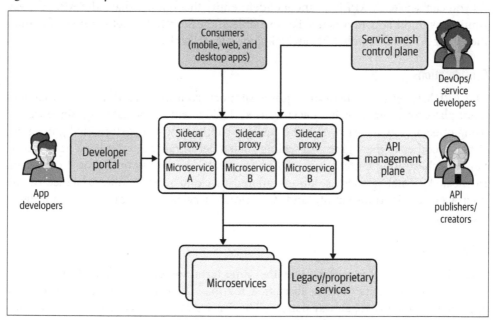

Figure 7-5. API management through service mesh sidecars

One of the main reasons for using a sidecar proxy as an API gateway for each microservice is that the requirements of a service mesh sidecar proxy and an API gateway are similar. Both intend to work as *proxies* and are controlled by a separate control plane. So, when we need to expose a capability as a managed service, we select the capability that is often implemented as a separate microservice (if no such service exists, we have to build it). Through the API management control plane, you can convert it to an API that is published to the developer, stored, and served via the same sidecar proxy runtime.

How it's used in practice

The implementation of this pattern is taken care of by the API management solution that you use for most parts, and most of the underlying details are transparent to the users who use the API management solution. The API control plane can directly manage sidecar proxies or can use the service mesh control plane APIs to manage them. In a cloud environment that provides API management as a cloud service, the implementation details of the API gateway may become irrelevant. This pattern is used when you are already using a service mesh and want to include API management capabilities on top of it.

Considerations

This pattern has some of the most complex distributed architecture comprising multiple distributed components. Its operational complexity is even greater than that of the Service Mesh pattern. If you are adopting this pattern, you should be ready to handle this complexity or leverage a cloud service that is already doing it for you.

Related patterns

The application of this pattern requires a solid understanding of the Service Mesh pattern (covered in Chapter 3), as well as the API Gateway and API Microgateway patterns (covered in this chapter).

Technologies for Implementing API Management Patterns

The current API management technology space is a crowded market. The on-premises offerings include Kong (*https://konghq.com*), MuleSoft (*https://oreil.ly/eD5Yi*), Red Hat 3scale API Management (*https://oreil.ly/1rPne*), and WSO2 API Manager (*https://oreil.ly/qrAOU*).

All the leading cloud providers have a significant footprint in cloud offerings for API management such as Google's Apigee (*https://oreil.ly/5mSRW*), Azure API Management (*https://oreil.ly/NYAye*), Amazon API Gateway (*https://oreil.ly/3BnPg*), and MuleSoft Anypoint Platform (*https://oreil.ly/Gtzb9*).

Summary of API Management Patterns

Table 7-1 lists the API management patterns, and details when and when not to use them.

Table 7-1. API management patterns

Pattern	When to use	When not to use
API Gateway	Essential in all the API management use cases. API management plane and developer portal are optional for small-scale use cases but require those components if you plan to do end-to-end API life cycle management.	(Not applicable.)
API Microgateway	Only when the API gateway layer requires scaling and isolation per each API.	If your cloud native application exposes a handful of managed APIs that don't do any heavy lifting, using this pattern will incur a redundant complexity.
Service Mesh Sidecar as API Gateway	Only when you are using a service mesh in production and want to include API management without using a separate layer.	If you don't have a service mesh or plan to use it at the production level, using this pattern is overkill. Even if you use a service mesh, you can still use API management as a separate component.

API Consumption Patterns

Most of the connectivity patterns that we discussed so far are applicable to backend services and systems. In this section, we will explore some of the commonly used patterns to connect frontend and backend applications when building cloud native applications.

In a typical cloud native application, we have a collection of microservices, a messaging infrastructure, data stores, and frontend applications that expose capabilities directly to consumers. So, frontend and backend connectivity patterns are built around the ways that you can integrate frontend applications (such as web, mobile, and desktop applications) with the backend microservices and systems.

Direct Frontend-to-Microservices Communication Pattern

When you build a cloud native application's backend by building a series of microservices that expose business capabilities, the frontend applications can directly consume those microservices.

How it works

To facilitate the direct consumption of microservices by the frontend application, you need to expose all the microservices required for your frontend applications as public-facing services. Figure 7-6 shows what this looks like. The frontend applications access these services via a load balancer, and extra care needs to be taken to secure these microservices as they are directly exposed to the public.

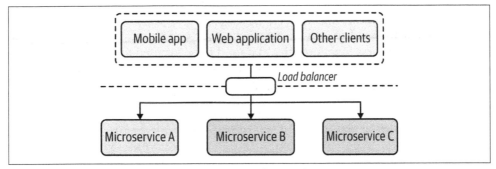

Figure 7-6. Directly exposing microservices to frontends

Each application is directly coupled to the service interface of these microservices; client applications need to change when the service gets changed. All the cross-cutting capabilities such as authentication, authorization, and observability need to be implemented at the level of each microservice.

How it's used in practice

This pattern is suitable if you are building a simple cloud native application with a few services and systems. This pattern is often used in small-scale microservices deployments that can't afford to have a dedicated API management layer to expose microservices as managed APIs, which we'll discuss in the next section. Later, when the system needs to scale for more consumers and more microservices, we can bring in the API Gateway pattern.

Considerations

As discussed, this pattern has inherent limitations, including tight coupling between the frontend and backend services, security risks of directly exposing microservices to the public, and no central place to apply cross-cutting capabilities across multiple microservices.

Related patterns

This pattern often gets extended to use an API gateway instead of directly consuming the microservices.

Frontends Consuming Services Through API Gateway Pattern

When you have to expose the business capabilities of your cloud native application, rather than exposing microservices directly to consumers, you can use an API management layer. Instead of accessing the microservices directly, frontends access microservices via the API management layer.

How it works

We implement frontend to API management layer communication by exposing all the services or business functionalities that need to be exposed to the external parties via an API management layer (Figure 7-7). This layer comprises an API gateway, API management plane, and a developer portal.

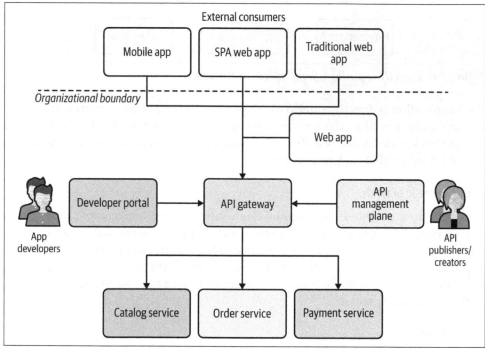

Figure 7-7. Frontends are consuming business capabilities via an API management layer

To expose a given microservice as an API, you need to define an interface (via an API contract) that is provided to the consumers who access your API. The API gateway adheres to that contract. The API contract that you expose from the API gateway may or may not be the same as the API of the backend microservice. The API management layer acts as the facade, and the internal implementation details of the microservices can be changed without breaking the consumer frontends. Frontends completely rely on the APIs exposed via the API gateway, and have to adhere to all the cross-cutting requirements enforced by the API management layer such as security, throttling, service access policies, and so on.

How it's used in practice

Most organizations increasingly adopt this API management pattern and are moving all their frontend developments to rely on the organization's exposed APIs. When you are not using an API management layer to build your frontend applications, you should consider gradually introducing API management into the architecture and rebuild the frontends so that they use exposed APIs rather than invoking microservices directly.

Considerations

When building a frontend application using APIs, one of the limitations you face is that your frontend application has to depend on a general-purpose API rather than something specifically serving the needs of the frontend application (for example, the requirements of a mobile application versus desktop application may be drastically different). Proper design of the APIs hosted at the API management layer is critical, as well as being able to customize APIs for your frontends, which may also be required in certain use cases. This is discussed in the next section.

Related patterns

This pattern is built on top of API management patterns that we discussed in the previous sections. You may also further extend this pattern with the Backend for Frontends pattern, which creates a dedicated API for each frontend component.

Backend for Frontends Pattern

With frontend applications, we expose the capabilities of our cloud native application via different frontend application types such as mobile, desktop, or web applications. When we use a general-purpose API and build all these frontend applications on top of it, we often hit roadblocks because the required functionality is not directly available in these common APIs. The *Backend for Frontends pattern* solves this problem by introducing APIs that are tailor-made for specific frontend applications.

How it works

The requirements of a frontend application can significantly vary from one application type to another. The frontend of a mobile application may be drastically different from that of a web application, for instance. In such scenarios, if we want to expose a general-purpose API of the business capability to consumers via the frontend application, we may face quite a lot of constraints and roadblocks. To build the best user experience for each frontend application type, we will need to use an API that is tailor-made for the requirements of the specific frontend application that we develop. These APIs are known as *backends for frontend applications* (*BFFs*).

Rather than depending on a single general-purpose API, we can build different backend APIs for each frontend application type (Figure 7-8). These APIs may directly interact with the backend microservices (in this case, the Order microservice) or can rely on a general-purpose API that exposes the core business functionality.

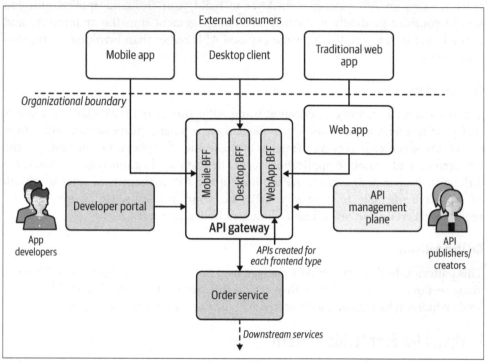

Figure 7-8. The Backend for Frontends pattern in action: each frontend application has a corresponding backend for frontend API/service at the API gateway

The APIs that are specific to a particular frontend type are usually managed by the same team that develops the frontend application. This pattern also allows each BFF the freedom to have its own life cycle so that changes in one API won't impact the other APIs.

How it's used in practice

The Backend for Frontends pattern is commonly used when we want to enable a different experience for consumers through different frontend applications. The frontend application requirements can drastically vary. Mobile applications want certain data formats, lightweight and free messages, and different security protocols compared to desktop applications, for instance. Therefore, when designing BFFs, you have the freedom of choosing the most suitable technology for building the best consumer experience for the business capability that you offer.

Considerations

While BFF reduces the complexity of having a general-purpose API, it also adds operational overhead, as the same capability is now being offered via multiple APIs. It's usually a good practice to use a generic downstream service or API to build a BFF, as it can be used to track the consumption of the API and to generate analytics for the API usage. This pattern has inherent drawbacks due to the proliferation of APIs when the number of APIs that we expose increases as well as the type of frontends that we support increases. You should be using BFF only when it significantly improves the user experience for your cloud native application.

Related patterns

BFF is commonly used along with the API Gateway and API Microgateway patterns covered earlier in this chapter. With this pattern, we can also leverage service composition patterns such as Service Orchestration and Service Choreography (covered in Chapter 3).

Summary of API Consumption Patterns

Table 7-2 lists the API Consumption patterns and when and when not to use them.

Table 7-2. API consumption patterns

Pattern	When to use	When not to use
Direct Frontend-to-Microservices Communication	API management is not a critical requirement.	Often you need to bring managed APIs into the picture at some point. So this approach is suitable only when getting started.
Frontends Consuming Services Through API Gateway	The consumers are homogeneous and don't have disparate requirements to fulfill at the frontend level. The API exposed to consumers works for all the disparate sets of consumers.	The API needs frequent changes due to frontend requirements. The successful consumption of an API largely depends on the frontend application.
Backend for Frontends (BFF)	We want to have a unique experience for each frontend application.	You have a single type of frontend application or its requirements are homogeneous.

Summary

In this chapter, we explored how the business capabilities are presented to your consumers as managed APIs, which allow us to control, secure, monetize, and govern the consumption of the business capabilities of our cloud native applications. We also connected the dots between the frontend applications, API layer, and backend microservices by looking at the patterns related to frontend and backend connectivity.

In the next chapter, we'll apply some of the cloud native patterns discussed throughout this book to a complete use case.

CHAPTER 8

Cloud Native Patterns in Practice

In this book, we've explored a lot of patterns related to building cloud native applications. Now it's time to see how to apply some of those patterns in a real-world use case. This final chapter will show you how to apply cloud native patterns when building various aspects of cloud native applications—connecting services, managing decentralized data, event processing, stream processing, exposing managed APIs, connecting frontend applications, and performing dynamic management of the applications. Let's begin by looking at the details of the use case that we are trying to implement.

Building an Online Retail System

As our real-world use case, we chose a simple online retail application that we can use to search for goods, purchase them, and ship them to our preferred locations. While an actual retail application can be overwhelmingly complex, we have selected a simplified yet diverse set of business capabilities and requirements to better demonstrate the application of cloud native patterns. We can categorize the key requirements and capabilities of this system as follows: product catalog, order management, order tracking and prediction, product recommendations, and customer and partner management. Let's look at each of these business capabilities and requirements in more detail.

Product Catalog

We need to build a product catalog that allows customers of the online retail application to search for products and obtain essential product details to make a purchase decision.

The key functionality of the product catalog includes the following:

- Search for products.
- Obtain the product details to make a purchase decision.
- Enable product administrators and sellers to add, remove, and update products.

Order Management

Once the customer decides to purchase a given product, they select it and the required quantity and add it to the shopping cart. Then the customer should be able to place an order for those items. The key functionality of the order management subsystem includes the following:

Place an order
    After a customer decides to purchase a given product with the required quantity, they should be able to place an order.

Payment
    When placing an order, the customer should be able to pay for that order by using a payment method of their choice.

Order Tracking and Prediction

Once an order is placed, the customer should be able to obtain or receive order and shipment updates and notifications. They key functionalities of the order tracking and prediction subsystem include the following:

- Track the status of the shipment.
- Get notification on the changes to order status, delivery estimates, and other important changes.
- Provide a delivery prediction: the system should be able to predict the delivery time based on the past order, real-time data from warehouses, and shipping services.

Product Recommendations

A customer should get recommendations of various products based on their search queries, past purchases, and currently available deals.

Customer and Partner Management

A customer should be able to manage their accounts and profile information. The customer may be using various types of applications (such as mobile or web) to access the system. Certain business capabilities may be exposed to multiple parties such as customers and partners via different frontend applications (customer mobile app, partner mobile app, and so on).

Also, as nonfunctional requirements, we can assume that the entire application needs to be highly available, scalable, secure, observable, and dynamically manageable across an on-premises data center and a public cloud platform.

Based on these business requirements and capabilities, we can build the solution as a cloud native application by applying certain patterns that we explored in previous chapters. Let's start by building the high-level architecture of the system.

Building the High-Level Architecture

The high-level architecture of the online retail application is shown in Figure 8-1. As we have clearly identified the requirements and use cases, we can map those into the business capabilities (such as product search, order placing, payments, order tracking, and so forth) that the application needs to expose to its consumers. As you learned in Chapter 7, these capabilities can be consumed by frontend applications directly or through managed APIs. To give more controlled and managed access to the capabilities, we will expose them as managed APIs.

The architecture comprises the frontend layer, then the API management layer that connects with the rest of the system. All web applications and mobile applications of the retail system are built on top of that API layer. These APIs are backed by the microservices that implement the business logic for each capability.

The interservice communication among these services may be implemented using communication patterns such as Service Connectivity, composition patterns, or event-driven patterns. These microservices can connect to external and internal systems (e.g., a legacy ERP application) that are not implemented as cloud native applications. The entire system should support cross-cutting concerns such as scalability, high availability, security, and observability through a control plane.

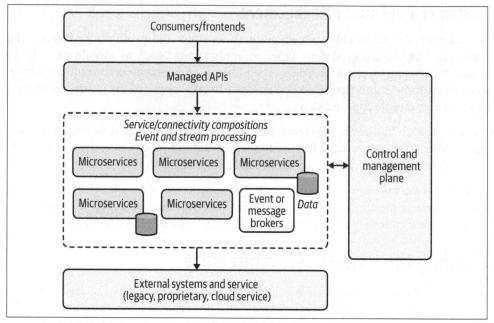

Figure 8-1. High-level architecture of the online retail cloud native application

Now, let's dive into each aspect of this cloud native application and discuss the details of the implementation.

Building External APIs

Since our focus is on realizing a set of business capabilities, it makes sense to start from the business capabilities that we want to expose to the consumer of the retail application. These business capabilities are essentially the APIs that we would expose from our retail application. These APIs can be used by the frontend application of the organization or by any external applications such as partner applications. Therefore, let's start building this cloud native application by looking at how to model the front-end applications around those APIs (we are following the top-down approach of API management covered in Chapter 7).

We identify the key business capabilities that we want to expose: product catalog, order management, payments, recommendations, tracking, and delivery prediction (Figure 8-2). We then model these capabilities as managed APIs and expose them to the external parties, such as consumers and partners, via an API management plane. The microservices that back those APIs implement the required business logic by integrating with other microservices, external systems, databases, and other resources. In this use case, we apply API management patterns such as API Gateway (discussed in Chapter 7) to expose these services as managed APIs.

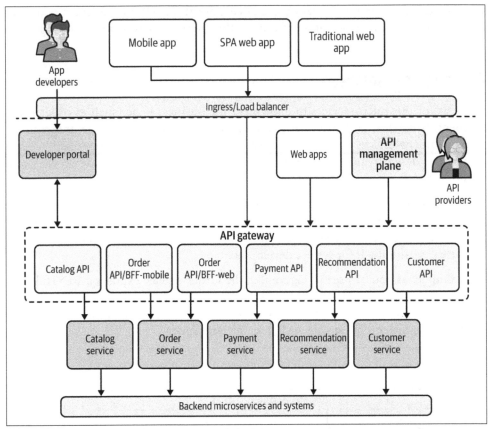

Figure 8-2. Designing APIs and frontend applications

These APIs are accessible to external client applications, such as mobile and web applications, through a load-balancer layer. The frontend application development can leverage patterns such as Backend for Frontends to implement certain features. For example, the order API may have different BFF-style APIs for mobile and web applications. As we discussed in Chapter 7, most of the API traffic can be exposed as RESTful or GraphQL services through the API gateway. The cross-cutting capabilities such as security, throttling, caching, and policy enforcement are applied at the API gateway layer. The API runtimes that we implement at the gateway layer may use patterns such as API Microgateway to enable independent runtimes for each API.

The ownership of these APIs can be assigned to the team that owns the underlying microservice backing a given API. For example, if the Catalog service is owned by Team A, the same team can own the catalog API as well. The key idea here is to segregate the API management layer based on ownership so that we can change, scale, and manage APIs independently. Therefore, you may opt to use patterns such as API Microgateway to decentralize the gateway layer further.

Once we decide on the APIs that we need to expose at the API management plane, we can dive into the implementation of each of the microservices that are backing those APIs.

Connecting Services

In order for our microservices to implement the business logic (such as order management, payments, and customer management), we need to integrate and connect multiple microservices and systems. Based on the APIs that we've identified, we can design the downstream microservices such as Order service, Catalog service, and Customer service.

These services invoke other services, such as Inventory and Payment, while also communicating with systems such as ERPs, message brokers, and databases. Therefore, we should pick the most suitable communication protocol to implement a given business use case and use it for service development.

For example, as you can see in Figure 8-3, the Order service exposes a RESTful API, while the Customer service uses GraphQL. Also, the Order service accepts messages through a synchronous protocol such as REST/HTTP, while it asynchronously enqueues the order request with AMQP using RabbitMQ.

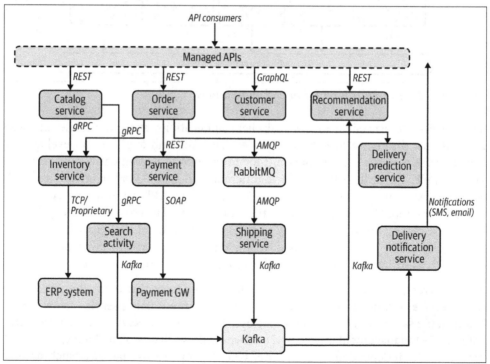

Figure 8-3. Connecting services and systems in our online retail application

The internal services can communicate by using high-performance synchronous messaging techniques such as gRPC.

Most of the connectivity patterns that you learned in Chapter 3 need to be applied when connecting these services. For example, resilient connectivity techniques such as time-outs, retries, and circuit breakers need to be applied when invoking services. If the deployment runs on top of a service mesh, most of the interservice communication can be managed and observed via the service mesh control plane. When it comes to creating compositions, we have used a hybrid of the Service Orchestration and Service Choreography patterns. For example, the Order service is orchestrating the composition across multiple other services, while the Shipping service operates in a reactive way (based on messages or events).

Now, let's dive into some of the details of data management in this use case.

Performing Data Management

As we explored in Chapter 4, one of the key aspects of cloud native data management is to manage data decentrally at the microservice level. This approach removes most of the coupling between microservices and gives the microservice owners the freedom to choose the most suitable data management technique. In our retail application, we can use these principles to manage data to implement the requirements that we discussed earlier. Rather than focusing on how data management happens across the entire application, let's look at specific use cases of data management.

Let's focus on how data management is done at the Catalog and Inventory services (Figure 8-4). The Inventory service has a dedicated relational database for building the inventory capabilities, while some services such as Catalog that do high-intensive data writes use a NoSQL database. We can apply patterns such as CQRS to split the capabilities of the Catalog service into multiple independent services, which allows us to have command and query components. The command part can be implemented using an RDBMS, while the query part leverages a NoSQL database underneath.

The eventual consistent data synchronization between these two service components is achieved via *eventing*, in which we use an event broker such as NATS or Kafka. With this approach, the command and query parts of the Catalog service are completely decoupled, and we can scale them independently based on our business needs (for instance, the Catalog query service may get much higher load compared to the Catalog command service).

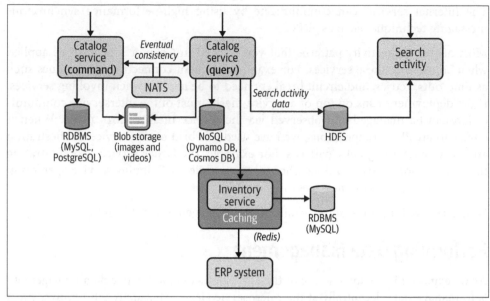

Figure 8-4. Decentralized data management with private databases, CQRS, caching, and heterogeneous databases

Based on the type of data that we have to store, we may opt to use dedicated data stores. For example, suppose we have to store images and videos of the products; then we can use a dedicated and optimized binary data store such as a blob store and include references from the product database. We can also apply patterns related to caching for the inventory service, where we use a caching layer between the inventory and the legacy ERP system.

Using Event-Driven Architecture

Order status management is one of the key business capabilities; we need to keep track of all state-changing events related to orders and allow the consumers (such as Shipping and Tracking services) to process those events independently. This requires the application of event-driven patterns that we explored in Chapter 5. Let's look at how we can use those patterns when realizing order status management across online retail applications.

The Order service uses an event-driven approach to propagate the order status across multiple microservices (Figure 8-5). A given order can have multiple states that are managed by various microservices during the order life cycle. When an order is created, the Order service enqueues the order message, which creates a *command* to the consumers of that queue to process the order request.

The Shipping service consumes the message from the *orders* queue. When the Order service enqueues the message, the order status update event is published to a distributed event log via an event broker. So, we use the Event Sourcing pattern to record all the life-cycle state-changing events of the order processing. This distributed event log can reside on an event broker such as Kafka, Amazon SNS, or Azure Event Grid.

Because the events related to orders come from multiple sources, we can use a common event representation convention such as CloudEvents. With CloudEvents-based events, we use common metadata across all the event types that we use for event sourcing.

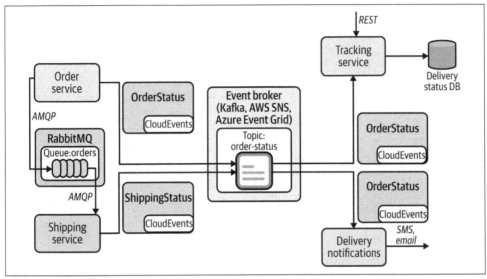

Figure 8-5. Event-driven communication with event sourcing and CloudEvents

The subscribers of the order status events can consume the event notification through the event broker component. Because we use CloudEvents, the original event's metadata is preserved in a standard format that can be used across multiple services and systems. For example, the Tracking service can consume those events and store the required information in a data store to serve the consumers of the Tracking service, while the Delivery Notifications service uses the event log to notify customers of order and shipment changes via text messages or email. Since we record all order-related events in a distributed log, if there are future business requirements related to order processing, we can simply extend the support for those use cases by adding a new event consumer at the event-broker level that can independently process the event log.

Using Stream Processing

The delivery-prediction capability of our online retail application can use the stream-processing patterns from Chapter 6. The main business capability here is to build a service that predicts the delivery time of an order based on multiple input data sources such as real-time warehouse data, data from past orders, and real-time information from shipping companies.

We can design a microservice that can process events originating from multiple sources such as IoT devices or sensors. These events can then be ingested by a distributed event broker or data store. Our Delivery Prediction microservice uses a disparate set of event stream sources (Kafka, Azure Event Hubs, Amazon Kinesis), as shown in Figure 8-6.

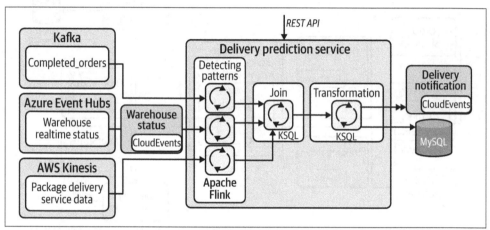

Figure 8-6. Processing multiple streams of data and predicting the delivery time

The business logic of the service consists of identifying delivery patterns by processing a continuous stream of delivery-related events in real time (using patterns such as Filters and Thresholds and Windowed Aggregation), and then joining (via the Stream Join pattern) and transforming (via the Stream Transformation pattern) them before we send the notification to the event-sink service or systems.

The stream-processing logic can be built using multiple stream-processing technologies based on your use case. Here we have used Apache Flink and KSQL. The results can also be stored in a data store such as an RDBMS to serve the consumers of the Delivery Prediction service. Therefore, this service can serve any request regarding a specific delivery as well as send a notification to interested parties on updates to delivery times, and so on. (This is a place where you can apply artificial intelligence and machine learning patterns to predict delivery time as well. However, we don't go into the details of these patterns as they're beyond the scope of this book.)

Implementing Dynamic Management in a Cloud Environment

So far, we have discussed the implementation of various business capabilities and requirements for our online retail application using cloud native design patterns. However, as we discussed in Chapter 1, we also need to deploy, run, manage, and govern our application. Often this can be achieved using existing cloud services. You could also build these capabilities from scratch with your own data center.

Let's suppose we are using a cloud provider such as AWS, Azure, or GCP to build this application. We can use the cloud platform to implement the following nonfunctional requirements of our online retail application:

Technology
> The microservices of the online retail application can be developed using any technology of your choice. For instance, some of these microservices can be implemented using a technology stack such as Spring Boot or .NET, or you can use serverless functions offered from the cloud service.

Automation of development, release, and deployment
> We can simply use the provided development and CI/CD service of the cloud platform to achieve this.

Run on a dynamic runtime environment
> Since the retail application needs to scale and be highly available, we can use the container and container orchestration service (e.g., Kubernetes service) of the cloud provider.

Use supporting backing services
> We need quite a few backing services such as event brokers, databases, and caching components to realize our business capabilities. When you are using a cloud platform, you get all these services as managed services with all the nonfunctional capabilities including high availability, security, autoscaling, and resilience.

Service connectivity
> When you deploy and run a service on a cloud platform, you often get the service-connection-related features such as service discovery, service resiliency, routing, and even a full-fledged managed service mesh as a cloud service.

Security
> The application that you deploy on such a cloud platform can be secured using transport-level security or application-level security protocols such as OAuth2 or OpenID Connect.

Observability
When the application is running, you should be able to get metrics, logs, and other operation data through the observability layer of the cloud service.

Single control plane for hybrid and multicloud deployments
It is not mandatory to stick to a single cloud platform. If you have workloads in multiple clouds or even in your own data center, you can use a control from one cloud platform to manage the other workloads. For example, you can use offerings such as Azure Arc or Google Anthos for this purpose.

Summary

In this chapter, we applied certain patterns presented earlier in the book to build the key components of an online cloud native retail application. Our primarily focus was on exposing business capabilities as managed APIs, establishing service connectivity and creating compositions, building event-driven capabilities using EDA, using stream processing to handle specific data-stream-processing capabilities, and finally running the entire application on top of a dynamically managed cloud native application using a cloud platform.

While the focus of the book has been on *designing and building* cloud native applications, we encourage you to seek out additional resources to gain an understanding of other aspects of cloud native applications, such as security, deployment, and DevOps.

Index

reconciliation loops, 12
Service abstraction in, 9, 16, 63-64
service discovery in, 67
Sidecar pattern with, 74
as universal runtime abstraction, 18
Kubernetes Event Driven Autoscaler (see
KEDA)

L
legacy data stores, abstract, 113
length batch window, 210
length sliding window, 212
Linkerd service mesh implementation, 79
load balancing
in Data Sharding pattern, 122
Service Abstraction pattern, 63
service registry, 65
local cache, 133, 136
log aggregation systems, 200
log processing, Producer-Consumer pattern,
166
log-based message brokers, 163, 241
Logic Apps, 97
long polling technique, 176
lookup-based data sharding, 120
LRU (least recently used) execution policy, 133

M
Machine Learner pattern, 221-224
managed API, 17
(see also API management plane)
Materialized View pattern, 128-130, 142
mediator microservices, 186-188
Mediator pattern, 185-188, 192
Memcached, 104
message brokers, 27, 34
(see also EDA)
categories, 163, 241
DevOps, 200-201
event-delivery guarantees, 162, 169
in Service Choreography pattern, 89-90
in Single-Receiver pattern, 35
technologies of, 193-196
message transformation, 205
messages, 28
metadata repository, 43-44
Micronaut, 96
microservices
cloud native architecture as, 2-5

coupling between microservices, reducing,
113
mediator, 186-188
monolithic versus distributed applications,
2-3
reactive, 89
service-led interactions, 16
testing of, 15
Microservices for the Enterprise (Indrasiri and
Siriwardena), 54
MongoDB, 104, 150, 153
MongoDB Cloud, 150
monitoring (see observability and monitoring)
monolithic versus distributed microservices
applications, 2-3, 22
MRU (most recently used) execution policy,
134
MuleSoft, 97, 269
MuleSoft Anypoint Platform, 97, 269
Multiple-Receiver pattern, 36-38, 40, 52

N
NATS, 52, 196
Neo4j, 105
Netflix Conductor, 97
Newman, Sam
Building Microservices (O'Reilly), 4
nondeterministic finite-state machines, 218
nonoccurrence of event, Temporal Event
Ordering pattern, 219
NoSQL databases, 103-106, 149-151, 152, 153
Nygard, Michael
Release It! (Pragmatic Bookshelf), 68

O
object-relational mapping (see ORM)
observability and monitoring, 19
communication patterns, 54
data management, 156-157
event-driven architecture, 199
patterns in practice, 288
and Saga pattern, 96
stream-processing systems, 256
online machine learning models, 221, 223, 224
online retail system, 4-5, 277-279
OpenAPI service definition specification, 42
orchestration patterns, 185-192
API microgateways, 266
Mediator pattern, 185-188, 192

About the Authors

Kasun Indrasiri is an author, a product manager, and a software architect with extensive experience in microservices and cloud native architecture and building messaging and integration platforms. He's the author of *gRPC: Up and Running* (O'Reilly, 2020), *Microservices for Enterprise* (Apress, 2018), and *Beginning WSO2 ESB* (Apress, 2017). He was a speaker at several conferences including, KubeCon + CloudNative-Con North America 2020, O'Reilly Software Architecture Conference 2019 in San Jose, GOTO Con 2019 in Chicago, API Specification Conference 2020, APIDays Interface 2020, and GOTOpia Europe 2020. He is also a committer and a PMC member at Apache Software Foundation.

Sriskandarajah (Suho) Suhothayan is a software architect with over nine years of experience in architecting and developing data processing platforms and event driven systems. He was the founder of Siddhi, a cloud native stream processor that can perform scalable data processing using microservices and the Kubernetes ecosystem. As a visiting lecturer Suho has conducted postgraduate courses on big data, distributed systems, and data science. He has presented at several conferences, including O'Reilly's Strata Data Conference 2017 London, Structure Data Conference 2016 San Francisco, BigData Days 2019 Moscow, and at many WSO2 User Conferences in San Francisco, London, Barcelona, and Colombo.

Colophon

The animal on the cover of *Design Patterns for Cloud Native Applications* is the Malayan peacock-pheasant (*Polyplectron malacense*), a small pheasant native to the lowland country of central Malaysia. Their name in Malay is *burung merak pongsu*.

Adults weigh 1-2 pounds and measure 16-20 inches in total length. They are generally light brown all over, with small black spots. Males also have iridescent blue-green eyespots on the feathers of their back and tail and a dark blue-green crest.

These birds live in rainforests, eating fruit and small insects. Males crouch and fan their spotted tails and wing feathers in displaying to females during courtship. After gestation, females lay one egg in a scrape on the ground.

The IUCN lists this species as Vulnerable; with dramatic habitat loss from its already limited range being compounded by its slow reproductive rate. Many of the animals on O'Reilly covers are endangered; all of them are important to the world.

The cover illustration is by Karen Montgomery, based on a black and white engraving from *Riverside Natural History* (1888). The cover fonts are Gilroy Semibold and Guardian Sans. The text font is Adobe Minion Pro; the heading font is Adobe Myriad Condensed; and the code font is Dalton Maag's Ubuntu Mono.